AN INNOCENT ON EVEREST

AN INNOCENT ON *EVERREST*

RALPH IZZARD

NEW YORK
E. P. DUTTON & CO., INC.
1954

PRINTED IN THE U.S.A.

FIRST EDITION

Library of Congress Catalog Card Number: 54-8120

ACKNOWLEDGMENTS

I wish to express my gratitude to Mr. Guy Schofield, editor of *The Daily Mail,* for permission to reprint news stories and articles written for *The Daily Mail* while I was in Nepal and India during the period of operations of the British Mount Everest Expedition, 1953. It is my hope that by reproducing some of my own writing verbatim, I shall preserve topicality and not be accused of being too wise after the event.

I should like to make it quite clear that where I have ventured an opinion on controversial matters my views must in no way necessarily bc taken to represent those of *The Daily Mail.*

RALPH IZZARD

CONTENTS

AN INNOCENT ON EVEREST

CHAPTER I

THAT MOUNTAIN

I AM no mountaineer, although I might modestly make a claim to be regarded as a "mountain traveler"; my only excuse for opening this book in formal fashion with a brief account of what led up to the final ascent of Everest is that in studying the history of the mountain, a few points occur to me as a layman, which I feel may be of interest to laymen. The first questions which appeal to me as worth answering are: when, why, and how did the climbers' history of Everest begin?

According to the late Sir Francis Younghusband it all began at a meeting of the Royal Geographic Society, in London, in 1919. In 1852 the height of "Peak XV" had been computed by the Geographical Survey of India as 29,002 feet, making it the highest known mountain in the world, and it was promptly renamed "Everest" after Sir George Everest, a former Surveyor General. The officers of the survey were unaware at the time that the Tibetans already had a name for it: Chomolungma, which can be translated as "Mother Goddess of the Winds," "Goddess mother of the world," and possibly more correctly as: "The Bird Country of the South." Now that the mountain has at last been climbed, agitation is afoot in the East to rename it "Tenzing Peak," while one Indian Newspaper, in an ecstasy that Sherpa Tenzing finally opted for, and adopted, Indian nationality, has advanced the slightly absurd and certainly anachronistic suggestion that the mountain be known henceforth as "Mount Government of India."

We can be thankful that Sir George was blessed with a surname which has an appropriate touch of sublimity about it which is worth preserving. Had he borne any of a score of humdrum, undistinguished or even equivocal names which all of us could think of, the rest of the world might have just cause for complaint.

In the closing years of last century, and in the opening years of this, a number of adventurous men had harbored thoughts of climbing Everest, but few, for fear of being laughed at, had had the temerity to voice their thoughts. To the mountaineers of those days there were at least three factors which seemed to make the mountain for ever unattainable.

Firstly: magnitude. No man had ever presumed to pit his strength against such a sheer mass of rock, ice and snow before.

Secondly: altitude. It had long been thought that, owing to oxygen lack, a man might be expected to drop dead in his tracks at 20,000 feet. (It is true that this figure was speedily disproved by a number of high altitude climbs culminating, in 1909, in a height of 24,600 feet being reached by the Duke of Abruzzi's expedition when attacking K2 (Mount Godwin Austen). But even after this success it was still felt that the utmost limit of human endurance could not be higher than 26,000 feet.)

Thirdly: inaccessibility. Everest lies on the border of Nepal and Tibet and from time immemorial the authorities of both countries had followed a rigid policy of exclusion of Westerners. In this respect the Nepalese had been even more adamant than the Tibetans. Prior to the Great War, Lord Curzon, when Viceroy of India, had attempted to obtain permission for a small party to visit Everest. His request had been promptly and firmly turned down.

Following the 1914-1918 war a spirit of restlessness, not to say recklessness was abroad which was soon to culminate in the record-breaking craze of the twenties. Something of this spirit seems to have affected that august body, the Royal Geographic Society, for by all accounts the meeting (in 1919) at which the first decisive thought regarding the ascent of Everest was spoken was rather a heady one.

Sir Francis Younghusband, in *Everest: the Challenge* (Nelson), states it was the President of the Alpine Club who took the plunge:

> Captain J. B. Noel was delivering a lecture on a surreptitious reconnaissance towards Everest which he had made before the war. In it he made no reference to anything more than approaching the mountain: he made no mention of attempting to reach its summit. But in the discussion which followed delivery of the lecture, Captain Farrar, who was then President of the Alpine Club, made the decisive leap forward. He spoke of the summit itself. He said that the Alpine Club naturally viewed with the keenest interest the proposal to attempt the ascent of Mount Everest. Moreover, it seemed to him that the attempt now commanded chances of success not previously available. The Alpine Club was prepared not only to lend such financial aid as was in its power, but also to recommend two or three young mountaineers quite capable of dealing with any purely mountaineering difficulties that were likely to be met with.

Sir Francis continues:

> This was the spark which set flame to the train. I was sitting by Farrar as he spoke. When he finished, I asked the President

of the Geographical Society to let me say a few words, though the evening was already late. I said it was now twenty-six years since Captain Bruce had made the proposition to me that we should "go up Mount Everest." Our own Society was interested in the project. We had heard the President of the Alpine Club say they had magnificent young mountaineers ready to undertake it. And it must be done, I said, though there might be one or two attempts before we were successful.

Sir Francis, himself, shortly succeeded to the Presidency of the Royal Geographic Society and he tells how he was determined to make the Everest venture the main feature of his three years' tenure of office. It was thus, during his presidency, that the Mount Everest Committee, composed of representatives of the Society and the Alpine Club came to be born, and the Thirty Years War between man and the mountain begun. Throughout this period the committee has acted as General Staff Headquarters.

Sir Francis was not without his critics. Sobersides of the Royal Geographic Society claimed that the project was spectacular, sensational, in short a "stunt" and not the sort of thing to be encouraged by a serious body such as the Society. They pointed out that the height, longitude and latitude of the mountain had been established; details could be filled in by a comprehensive survey of the lower slopes without going to the expense of placing a man on the summit. (Little did the critics of the time realize how many tens of thousands of pounds would have to be spent before this aim was finally achieved.) From the practical point of view no pocket of diamonds—or as we might say now, no uranium mine—was likely to be found at the peak height. Man was never likely to find himself compelled to work at such an altitude and the stresses imposed on the human body during the climb could be reproduced in more comfortable circumstances in the decompression tank of any well-equipped physiological laboratory.

Romantics among the mountaineering fraternity—and they were later to include some of the strongest challengers of the mountain such at the late George Lee Mallory and Eric Shipton—freely expressed the opinion that they would prefer to leave the mountain untouched in her splendor and untrampled by the foot of man. In his book *The Romance of Mountaineering,* R. G. Irving, the Winchester schoolmaster who first inspired the schoolboy Mallory to take up mountaineering, refers to the controversy as to the height Mallory did, or did not achieve during the 1924 attempt in which he lost his life and adds: "Does it really matter. . . . Do we destroy nothing by using all this mass of men and material to conquer Everest?" Mallory himself wrote after the failure of the 1922 attempt:

> When I call to mind the whole begoggled crowd moving with slow determination over the snow and up the mountain slopes, and with such remarkable persistence bearing up the formidable loads; when, after the lapse of months, I envisage the whole prodigious evidence of this vast intention, how can I help rejoicing in the yet undimmed splendor, the undiminished glory, the unconquered supremacy of Mount Everest.

In his book *Upon That Mountain,* (Hodder & Stoughton), Eric Shipton was later to write: "There are some even among those who have themselves attempted to reach the summit, who nurse a secret hope that Mount Everest will never be climbed. I must confess to such feelings myself."

It might be added here that as failure succeeded failure a third "tough" school developed that considered the ascent of Everest so monstrously divorced from what had hitherto been "the joyous sport of mountaineering," that it became fashionable among the men selected for the expeditions to joke grimly of "being condemned to climb the brute."

In his same book Eric Shipton quotes "a friend" (H. W. Tilman?) as saying: "For heaven's sake let's climb the wretched thing and get back to *real* mountaineering." Surely the epilogue for the "tough" school comments was written by Sir Edmund Hillary when he announced his triumphant ascent to his companions waiting below with the plain-spoken words: "We've done the bitch!"

But while the climb remained in the planning stage neither the criticism of practical men nor the scruples of idealists daunted Sir Francis. For to him the conquest of Everest remained the greatest of adventures; he was consumed with the explorer's urge to find the answer to an unsolved problem.

The Everest Committee—later to become the Himalayan Committee—got off to a good start. Its political strategy in gaining access to Tibet was sound. Colonel Howard-Bury was sent as the committee's emissary to India to solicit the support of the Viceroy. Here, Sir Francis' own great record as a Himalayan pioneer—though his work had been confined to passes rather than peaks—stood the committee in good stead. Support was readily forthcoming. More than that; it so happened that Sir Charles Bell, then Political Agent in Sikkim, was at the time on one of his periodic visits to Lhasa, where he was on good terms with the Dalai Lama. Sir Charles was instructed to intercede for an expedition and, after an anxious interval for contemplation and deliberation on the Dalai Lama's part, permission was granted. That was in December, 1920. All that now remained was to assemble the right men, provide the necessary finances and define the objectives of the expedition. It was unanimously agreed that the main object of the first expedition should be reconnaissance. Previously, no European had been within 40 miles of Everest. The first aim, therefore, was to probe the mountain's defenses and discover the weak spots through which an all out attempt on the summit could be launched with a reasonable chance of success. No attempt to reach the top was to be made unless terrain and conditions were found to be far easier than generally supposed. Here it may be said that any climb at extreme altitude, to be practicable, must be "easy," in the purely technical mountaineering sense. Owing to the paucity of oxygen in the air speed becomes essential, while strength is reduced and endurance curtailed. A steep "pitch" which may present only an interesting technical problem at 5,000 feet can be utterly insurmountable at 25,000 feet.

As regards recruiting the necessary personnel the Everest Committee met with two initial setbacks. It had been taken for granted that the nonclimbing leader of the expedition would be General Charles G. Bruce. He had been an Everest enthusiast for twenty years, he was a distinguished Gurkha officer beloved by his men, he knew Himalayan peoples and he was an outstanding character in every way. But pressing military duties demanded Bruce's presence elsewhere. An able substitute was found in Colonel Howard-Bury. The climbing party of four was to be a blend of youth and experience. Experiencc was represented by Harold Raeburn who had a fine record in the Alps and had also climbed in the Himalaya, and Doctor Kellas whose long record of high altitude climbing in the Himalaya was unsurpassed. The two younger climbers selected were George Lee Mallory and George Finch. Finch, however, was forced to plead sickness. His place was taken by G. H. Bullock. Both Mallory and Bullock were already known as brilliant Alpine climbers, but neither had previous experience of the Himalaya.

The party of nine—it was accompanied by four scientists who do not come into this story—left Darjeeling on May 18, 1921. On June 5, when still 100 miles from the mountain, Kellas, who had overstrained himself by too much high altitude climbing earlier in the year, collapsed and died of heart failure while surmounting a 17,000 foot pass. He was buried where he fell. A second disaster, though happily not so serious in its consequences, occurred shortly after. Raeburn was also taken ill and had to be sent back, an invalid, to Sikkim. The responsibilities devolving on Mallory and Bullock were now enormously increased and it says much for their great qualities that they were able to accept them. The party reached their first base camp at Tingri, to the north of Everest on June 19. The next five days were spent by Mallory and Bullock in following a false trail up the Rongbuk glacier. At a height of 18,500 feet both men were overcome with altitude sickness and turned back. That night Mallory wrote in his journal the rather forlorn entry: "the party is not fit." With hindsight, this seems a rather remarkable statement, for nowadays an approach march of over four weeks at heights seldom below 13,000 feet and occasionally lifting over 17,000 foot passes would normally be considered sufficient acclimatization for work at heights between 16,500 and 18,500 feet. But Mallory and Bullock were new to the work and could still be regarded as pioneers. Considerably higher climbs had already been made it is true but still little was known about the acclimatization of the body to altitude. Both were later to go far higher without noticeable ill effects. It may be that the hapless fate of Kellas bore upon them. Conditioning of the mind to altitude is almost as important as body acclimatization. Had Mallory known, as we now know, that man can exist for many weeks at 23,000 feet, without deterioration in health, provided he takes his heights slowly, he might have felt less discomfort.

It was not until the season was far advanced that Mallory and Bullock discovered the gap in the defenses of Everest—an inconspicuous branch of the Rongbuk glacier leading to a saddle later to be known as the North Col. On September 24, after a brilliant piece of mountaineering they stood on the

Col and looking up the North Ridge they felt confident that they had found a route to the summit which in favorable circumstances would "go." But on this occasion the blood-freezing autumn winds, blowing with cruel ferocity across the Col, were sufficient deterrent against pressing the attack farther. Wearied by months of exploratory work, but rejoicing in the positive outcome of their main mission, they turned for home. They had discovered the classic route which was to be followed by all subsequent expeditions which attacked the mountain from its northern approach.

The following year, 1922, a second expedition was organized with the declared aim of reaching the summit. Although the days of innocence were over, and the true magnitude of the task was beginning to be realized, the party assembled in a spirit of high optimism. General Bruce was now able to assume leadership and under him was gathered one of the strongest climbing teams which has ever faced Everest. They were Mallory, Captain George I. Finch, Howard Somervell, Major E. F. Norton, and Dr. Wakefield. They were supported by C. G. Crawford, Captain C. G. Morris and Major Morsehead, all experienced mountaineers who had been allocated various scientific duties, and Captains J. G. Bruce, transport officer, and J. B. Noel, photographer. Neither of the last named were trained mountaineers, but Captain Bruce learned so rapidly he was able to join an assault party. The expedition left Darjeeling on March 26 heading an immense train of three hundred baggage animals and sixty porters. They arrived at Rongbuk monastery on April 30. Here, General Bruce showed considerable wisdom in taking the entire expedition to be blessed by the chief Lama, a spontaneous and intuitive action which made the Lama the firm friend of that and all subsequent British expeditions until his death in 1950 at a very advanced old age.

The high hopes of the expedition were, however, soon to

be dashed. The oxygen equipment for high altitude work, which it had been decided, after considerable argument, should be carried, proved too bulky and none too efficient. Another factor, equally damaging to the chances of reaching the summit was the rate at which the expedition was compelled to expend its manpower. Some time before the party reached Everest it had been decided that Mallory and Norton, as the two strongest climbers should be held in reserve and spared the initial trail-breaking and pioneer work of establishing camps towards the summit, in order that they could remain in peak condition for the final supreme effort. But when the first reconnaissance party, having ascended the Rongbuk glacier, arrived at the foot of the 23,000 foot high North Col they found the entire aspect of the Icefall leading up to it had changed. It now called for ice climbing of the very highest order, and it was soon obvious that the best men would have to be brought forward to tackle it. This effort so exhausted the key men that they were not able to recover their full strength that year. When the final attempt came to be made Mallory, Norton and Somervell reached 26,983 feet without oxygen, having had to leave Morsehead, who was suffering severely from exposure, at Camp V (24,500 feet). A second attempt by George Finch and Captain J. G. Bruce, using improvised oxygen apparatus, pushed the altitude record up to 27,300 feet, the morning after weathering a nightmare storm at their own Camp V (25,000 feet). Captain Bruce, the comparative novice, had amply justified his inclusion in the party.

The two climbing parties now retreated right down the mountain to organize for a third attempt. They would have been better advised to leave Everest alone. All except Somervell, were suffering from dilated hearts, and Morsehead and Captain Bruce were frostbitten severely enough to require immediate evacuation to India. Also, had they but known it, the seasonal monsoon bringing snow which it was later to be found would make the upper slopes of the mountain utterly unclimbable, was already upon them. The third attempt ended in disaster; the entire party led by Mallory, Somervell and Crawford accompanied by fourteen Sherpas being overwhelmed by an avalanche before they had reached the summit of the North Col. The three British, and seven Sherpas, managed to extricate themselves, but the remaining seven Sherpas were killed. A curious fact is that the Chief Lama of Rongbuk foresaw this disaster in a vision and sent General Bruce timely warning of it. General Bruce can scarcely be blamed for ignoring intelligence of this nature, but it says much for the strength of character of the Chief Lama that, when informed of the dire news he forebore from adopting an "I told you so" attitude and expressed his intense compassion.

The tragedy, however, put an end to all further attempts on the mountain that year, and under the onslaught of the monsoon the expedition retreated down the East Rongbuk glacier abandoning considerable quantities of equipment and supplies.

The defeat of the second expedition by no means dampened enthusiasm, and preparations for a third assault were made in 1924 with optimism undiminished. It was thought that while the first expedition had discovered a feasible route to the summit, the second expedition had added most valuable data concerning snow, wind, cold and weather conditions generally on the mountain and had demonstrated that man could adapt himself to far higher altitudes than had previously been thought possible. The sum of this experience seemed to spell success.

In 1924 the expedition left Darjeeling on March 25 again

under the leadership of General Bruce. But the General early fell sick with malaria and was forced to return to India. Colonel Norton, a most able substitute, took command.

This third expedition proved the most ill-fated of all, although in general it was blessed with fairer weather conditions than any subsequent expedition was to enjoy until the successful British attempt of 1953.

The party had yet to learn that towards the end of May a lull of possibly two weeks can occur between the cessation of the northwesterly gales of winter and the onset of the southeast monsoon. They mistook the continued northwest winds of May to presage the early arrival of the monsoon (in fact it was to arrive far later than is customary) and they decided that no time must be lost in establishing the higher camps. It thus came about that a party of Sherpas became marooned at Camp Four on top of the North Col by a series of most violent northwesterns. As it had not been intended that the porters should remain on the Col after dumping their loads, they were wretchedly equipped to weather the storms and once more the services of the best climbers had to be called upon prematurely—this time to rescue the porters. This they achieved only after desperate exertion and although the men were all brought down safely two Sherpas subsequently died of frostbite. The rescue meant that the climbers had later to face the final assault with their physical resources reduced by previous effort.

The first bid, on June 1, by Mallory and J. G. Bruce ended at 25,500 feet where they were able to establish Camp V, but were overtaken by another storm and forced to return. They were followed by Norton and Somervell who, in improving weather, managed to place Camp VI at 26,800 feet. The next day Norton, with Somervell lagging slightly behind with chest trouble, climbed to 28,100 feet which was long to stand as a record.

The third and last attempt ended in great tragedy. It was made by Mallory and a twenty-two-year-old companion Andrew Irvine, of whom he was very fond, both using oxygen. They started from Camp VI in the early hours of June 8. They never returned and nothing definite is known as to their fate. N. E. Odell who came up in support from Camp V to Camp VI on June 8 reported that at 12:50 PM he saw both men through a gap in the clouds at about 28,000 feet "going strong for the top." It is extremely improbable that they ever reached the summit although one would naturally like to grant them the benefit of the doubt. When last sighted Mallory would have been something like four hours behind the schedule he had set himself. He can have had no hope at all of reaching the summit and returning before nightfall, and to spend a night unprotected on the exposed face of Everest would have meant certain death. Those who knew the rigid standards of self-discipline Mallory set himself find it hard to believe that he would have allowed himself to be betrayed into an act of supreme foolhardiness. It is considered more likely that either one of the two slipped, could not be held by his companion, and being roped together that both began sliding uncontrollably, finally to fall thousands of feet to be buried forever by the snows. The discovery of an ice ax at about 28,000 feet by members of the 1933 expedition tends to support this view. It was found under an overhang in a position where it could not possibly have fallen from above. About 250 feet above this position a "step" occurs which has been declared unclimbable by the members of subsequent expeditions and it seems likely that the accident occurred on the ascent to, or descent from, this step. To be more precise it probably occurred on the ascent, for once the step is reached an easier and safer route at once offers itself for the descent.

After the loss of Mallory and Irvine and frantic but fruitless efforts made by N. E. Odell to locate and succor them,

seventy men, supported by an airplane, were involved in the rescue bid which lasted over two nights and two days. When the two Nazis were finally hauled to the summit one was found to be suffering severely from frostbite, a punishment which one cannot help feeling he deserved. Fools may be suffered tolerantly, if not gladly, in many sports but they are a menace on a mountain. Certainly no man who casts aside self-discipline, ignores the rules provided for his protection and attacks a mountain in a spirit of blind folly is ever likely to get far up Everest.

The grim note on which the 1924 expedition ended did not deter the Everest Committee from making immediate preparations for another attempt. Against the cost in lives and money (about £40,000 had already been spent) could be set a rapidly growing dossier of experience gained. Having placed a man to within 900 feet of the summit the committee must surely have felt they were on the right lines and that one more effort would insure success. Actually it was to be nearly thirty years, and by a totally different route, that the summit was finally attained.

The immediate cause of delay was the attitude of the Dalai Lama. He felt the gods of the mountains were evidently displeased and that they should not again be disturbed. Eight years elapsed before the Dalai Lama could be persuaded to change his mind and not until August, 1932, could preparations for the next attempt be renewed. The interval had meant that the climbers of the previous expeditions had passed their peak—none could now be regarded as likely to be fit enough to reach the summit. But a new star had arisen, Frank Smythe, who must certainly be bracketed among the greatest climbers ever to attempt Everest. Smythe had already conquered the great peak, Kamet, 25,447 feet and had accompanied one of three German expeditions which had been sent to the Himalaya to attempt Kangchenjunga, 28,150 feet.

At thirty-three Smythe was at the very zenith of his powers. Supporting Smythe, were Percy Wyn Harris, L. R. Wager, J. L. Longland, an expert rock-climber and—for the first time on Everest—Eric Shipton. Shipton had already made a name for himself in the Alps, he had been with Smythe on Kamet and in East Africa had climbed Mount Kenya, Kilimanjaro and Ruwenzori.

It had been hoped to entrust leadership of the expedition to Colonel Norton who although no longer able to go high, would have been an ideal choice in every way. Norton, however, could not obtain leave, but once more an excellent substitute was found in Hugh Ruttledge. As an officer of the Indian Civil Service in charge of the District of Alomora, Ruttledge had acquired a profound knowledge of Himalayan peoples and being a gifted linguist could converse freely in the local dialects.

No expense was spared to ensure the success of the expedition. Equipment was lavished on the members and in the matter of tents, protective clothing and boots, was a considerable advance on anything provided hitherto. To counteract inevitable loss of appetite at great heights, which in its turn leads to loss of stamina, every conceivable delicacy was supplied.

The keynote of the expedition was to be "slow-acclimatization." In 1924 Norton had shown that, provided he takes his heights gradually, man can climb to 28,000 feet without oxygen. It was now thought that with even more careful preparations an extra one thousand feet was not utterly beyond the bounds of possibility. It was planned to carry oxygen as a reserve, but to dump it as high as possible on the mountain—somewhere over 28,000 feet if it could be managed—leaving the pair chosen for the final assault to make their dash to the summit unencumbered by the extra 30 odd pounds or so on their shoulders. On their return they could restore themselves from the cylinders before they came to tackle the main hazards of the descent. One of the main effects of lack of oxygen at high altitude is to impair judgment, thus betraying climbers into taking risks they would never normally run.

The vast train of pack animals left Darjeeling towards the end of February and after a deliberately leisurely journey so planned as to ensure adequate acclimatization, the expedition reached Rongbuk monastery on April 16. So great an accent had been placed on acclimatization throughout the march that Eric Shipton recounts (*Upon That Mountain*) that the members became "rather ridiculously self-conscious." Shipton adds:

> The average altitude of the plateau over which we were traveling was about 13,000 feet and several of the passes we crossed over were 18,000 feet high. We used anxiously to count our heartbeats and watch our breathing, while the doctors examined the reaction of our blood pressures and counted the red corpuscles in our blood. All this tended to produce a state of hypochondria and a sense of rivalry, which Ruttledge did his best to discourage. His was no easy task with such a large party of mountaineers—temperamental and individualistic creatures at the best of times—each passionately keen to justify his selection, and we owed a great deal to his sympathetic understanding.

The work of establishing the lower camps was undertaken with deliberate slowness and—hampered by worse ice conditions than had prevailed in 1924—it was not before May 15 that Camp IV was established on the North Col. A five day storm then set in and simultaneously the news was received that the southeast monsoon was already active in the Bay of Bengal—a good fortnight before it was due. Harried by gale after gale the expedition made desperate efforts to establish the higher camps necessary for the final assault before the monsoon—bringing the shroud of snow which would make further climbing impossible—should break upon them. But it was not to be. The nicely calculated plans had once more miscarried. As Sir Francis Younghusband writes in *Everest: the Challenge,* "If Ruttledge had planned to be early on the mountain so had the monsoon. And Everest herself was at her fiercest."

Nevertheless, by taking advantage of every lull, and weathering a succession of appalling blizzards Wyn Harris, Wager and Smythe all managed to reach a height of approximately 28,100 feet with Shipton climbing nearly as high. He had set out on the second attempt with Smythe, but being overcome by sickness was forced to unrope and return to Camp VI.

Defeat of the 1933 expedition highlighted the fact that the main imponderable militating for or against success was the weather. Although the argument between oxygenists and non-oxygenists continued—and still does—man had no longer to fear that reaching the summit was beyond his powers. Clothing and equipment had been developed to a high and adequate standard. Organization of camps in ascending stages, with the last camp pushed as near as possible to the summit in order to shorten the length of the final dash and reduce the effort required by it, had been perfected. Beneficial effects of slow "acclimatization" had been recognized and the subsequent speed of "deterioration" at high altitude assessed. But the fact remained that unless an expedition could be assured of a fine weather spell bringing with it windless days and bearable temperature at a time when the summit slopes were free of snow it could have no chance of success. After the 1924 experience it had been assumed that such conditions would invariably prevail yearly in late May after the northwest gales had swept the upper slopes clear of snow and then blown themselves out, and before the onset of the southwest monsoon. Failure of the 1924 attempt had been attributed to poor timing, excusable by lack of knowledge. The 1953 expedition showed that the longed for lull was entirely unpredictable both in its advent and its duration. Later expeditions were to find that the lull need not necessarily occur at all.

Immediate reaction to the 1933 expedition was the expression of doubts as to the advisability of continuing expeditions on the same colossal scale as hitherto. Critics who had already attacked the large expedition on psychological, moral and practical grounds were not slow to point out that if weather was to be the deciding factor it was folly to go on pouring out money on the grand scale on the off-chance that one or another year, chosen at random by the Dalai Lama, would find the mountain in perfect condition. The alternative suggested was to ask permission for small, more compact expeditions to visit the mountain in five successive years. It was argued that a dump could be established by the first expedition at Rongbuk monastery which could be used in the following years by the expeditions which came after. The success of this plan, of course, depended on the benevolent cooperation of the Dalai Lama. In 1935, rather unexpectedly, permission was received for expeditions to tackle Everest both in that year and in 1936. As 1935 was already rather too far advanced to leave time for the organization of a full-scale attempt, it was decided that the first expedition should be merely a reconnaissance. It was placed under the leadership of Eric Shipton. Shipton, a critic of the larger expedition policy, decided to make the reconnaissance an example of what the smaller expedition could do. Instead of calling for the average of £12,000 spent by previous expeditions, he budgeted for a total outlay of £1400 which worked out at about £200 per head including fares to and from

England. The objectives of the reconnaissance as outlined by Shipton in *Upon That Mountain* were:

> to try out new men and to give them some preliminary training in high altitude mountaineering, to examine snow and weather conditions on the mountain during the monsoon and to investigate the possibility of climbing it during that season; to experiment with equipment and food, to obtain further data regarding acclimatization, to train a nucleus of high altitude porters, and to carry out a stereophotogrametric survey of the glaciers lying to the north of Mount Everest and of as much of the surrounding country as possible.

A valued recruit of this party was H. W. Tilman who had been, and continued to be, Shipton's companion in numberless climbing adventures.

The main contribution of the 1935 reconnaissance towards the climbing of Everest was a closer inspection of the western approach to the mountain. The neighboring peak of Lingtren was climbed, the summit yielding a view of the 2,000 foot Icefall leading from the head of the Khumbu glacier to the wide basin contained by Everest and the Lhotse-Nuptse range to the south and known as the Western Cwm. (The Western Cwm was so named by Mallory who had first sighted it from afar in 1922. Mallory had done much of his climbing in Wales and gave it the Welsh spelling of the English word "Combe".) The 1935 party were of the opinion that if the Icefall could be forced—it was certainly a terrifying obstacle —a way might reveal itself of climbing from the Western Cwm to the top of the South Col and thence to the summit of Everest. But there was no way of conveniently approaching the Icefall except by the Khumbu glacier. This lies in Nepal territory and in that year the Nepali Durbar was still adamant in refusing permission for foreigners to enter their country.

In the light of subsequent events it is of interest that the

1935 expedition saw, for the first time among the Sherpas, Tenzing Norkey, then a youth just twenty-two years old.

The 1936 expedition—the last prewar attempt on the grand scale—again under Ruttledge, was literally swept off the mountain by the early approach of the monsoon before it had time to attempt any serious climbing. The climbers, Smythe, Wyn Harris and Shipton among them, merely succeeded in gaining a precarious footing on the North Col. They were speedily forced to retreat.

The ignominious defeat of 1936 swung opinion temporarily in favor of the light expedition. In 1938 when permission for yet another attempt was granted it was decided to avoid what has been described as the "majestic cumbrousness of preceding Himalayan tradition." This time command was given to Tilman.

It is difficult to judge whether Tilman or Shipton is the more ardent advocate of the advantages of the small expedition as compared with the large. The mountaineering fraternity are fond of retelling possibly apocryphal arguments between the two "as to whether a second shirt is or is not a superfluity for three months' rude travel," or as I have also heard it put "whether soap is lighter to carry than DDT powder." Tilman began by slashing the number of climbers to six besides himself. He also adopted the innovation of asking each member to make a small contribution to the funds as an additional incentive to economize. It was also a psychological move. The man who has a stake in an expedition is freer to judge what is and what is not a justifiable risk. Men climbing on other people's money (an innovation in itself for amateurs) may well, in a dangerous situation, feel compelled to overstep the normal limits of safety, in their anxiety not to disappoint their sponsors. This had been one of the main criticisms leveled against expeditions of the past. Tilman's total expenditure was to be a mere £2,360.

Unfortunately 1938 proved to be the year in which the essential "lull" between westerly gales and southeast monsoon never occurred at all. The argument between "light" and "large" expeditions was therefore left unresolved, possibly with honors even, for in spite of appalling conditions Tilman managed to place four climbers, Smythe, Shipton, himself and a newcomer Peter Lloyd, well over the 27,000 foot mark.

The Second World War now intervened to close another era of Everest climbing. The effects of the war were twofold. Firstly, repercussions in Asia apparently so preoccupied the Dalai Lama that postwar requests for permission to launch another attempt remained unanswered. In 1950 occupation of Tibet by Chinese Communists made all further requests superfluous. Secondly, during the enforced interval of thirteen years it had obviously been impossible to keep any nucleus of climbers in training. Of the remaining members of the magnificent teams recruited in the thirties none could any longer be reasonably expected to be fit to reach the summit—although both Shipton and Tilman were available as leaders if called upon.

The impasse regarding the approach to the mountain was, however, solved most unexpectedly by a sudden relaxation of the attitude of the Nepal government. It may be pointed out that this relaxation began before the overthrow of the Rana regime. It began gradually. Early in 1947 my wife and I received permission to visit Katmandu and the Great Valley of Nepal, on condition that we did not attempt to go outside it. In 1948 an American ornithologist Dr. Dillon Ripley, accompanied by a photographer Mr. Volkmar Wentzel, were permitted to leave the valley on a bird collecting expedition along the lower Himalayan foothills. The expedition resulted in the capture of a spiny babbler, a bird which had been thought extinct for nearly one hundred years. In 1949 the Everest Committee, now renamed the Himalayan Committee, received permission for H. W. Tilman to lead a small expedition through central Nepal to the Langtang Himal range about 80 miles west of Everest, the requested permission to visit Everest itself being withheld. In 1950 both French and British expeditions (the latter again led by Tilman) were permitted entry to Western Nepal, the French succeeding in a dashing and costly (in regard to injuries) attempt to climb Annapurna (26,493 feet), the highest mountain at that time climbed by man. In the autumn of 1950 permission was at last granted to visit the southern slopes of Everest. The favored party was a small American one led by Dr. Oscar Houston, which Tilman by "a bit of luck" was able to join. As time pressed Tilman and Dr. Oscar Houston's son Charles Houston, left the slower members of the party at Thyangboche monastery, about 12 miles from the mountain, and made for the Khumbu glacier. With only six days at their disposal they could make no attempt on the Icefall, at the head of the glacier but by climbing a subsidiary feature of Pumori opposite to it, they were able to look up into the Western Cwm. The key to a climb by the South or southeast ridge, the slopes leading from the Western Cwm to the South Col, remained obscured and Tilman's verdict that the route was scarcely likely to be a practicable one was based, as he freely admitted, largely on conjecture.

In the following year, 1951, the Himalayan Committee obtained permission to send out a fully organized reconnaissance expedition in the autumn. It was led by Eric Shipton and included in the party were Tom Bourdillon, Dr. Michael Ward, and Edmund Hillary, all of whom, in 1953, were to play a part in the final ascent of the mountain. The objectives of the reconnaissance were threefold: 1. to examine the possibility of an alternative route to the summit from the Western Cwm (always provided the Icefall could be forced); 2. to examine snow conditions on the upper slopes with a view to a possible post-monsoon attempt; and 3. to ascertain whether the extreme cold likely to be met with at high altitudes would make climbing impossible in autumn.

The Icefall proved quite as formidable as it had been thought it might be, and two attempts had to be made, culminating in some spectacular ice work by Bourdillon, before the party stood at the top. But here they were brought up short by a yawning crevasse—chasm would be a better word—stretching the entire width of the fall and being sometimes 100 yards in width and never narrower than 100 feet across. In a waterfall such a point would occur across the smooth curving wave made by the water at the summit of a fall before it takes its downward plunge. As ice will not bend readily, it splits from side to side at this point. In time, as the whole mass of an icefall moves downwards the crevasse will close again, but a second will open in its place. The only point at which this particular crevasse could be turned was, it seemed, in the extreme lefthand corner hard against the flank of Everest. But this corridor was under the constant fire of avalanches falling from the west ridge of Everest. While it was felt that one or two men might chance this passage and get away with it, it was by no means considered a route which could safely be traversed an unlimited number of times by laden porters. This then was the highest point reached by the 1951 reconnaissance party. They did not enter the Western Cwm, but enough of the snow slopes at its head had been seen to justify the belief they would be climbable and thus provide access to the 25,800 feet South Col. Once on the South Col, it appeared the southeast ridge would offer a practicable route to the summit. In his book *The Story of Everest* W. H. Murray, himself a member of the 1951 reconnaissance, sums up the advantages of the proposed new route over the old route as follows:

First, the main difficulties occur low down whereas on the north route they start at 28,000 feet, where the climber commands less energy.

Second, on the last three thousand feet of the southeast ridge the strata dip northward, in favor of the climber, and so should give better support from the snow, more tent platforms, and permit the last camp to be placed much nearer the summit.

Third, the route is protected from violent wind until close to the South Col (about 25,800 feet).

Fourth, the south-east ridge is broad and should give a wider choice of route than the northern line.

Fifth, on the north side the snow above 25,000 feet refuses to consolidate, and by remaining powdery makes climbing impossible until it is cleared by the northwest wind; whereas the fact that snow lies always on the southeast ridge, despite wind, would imply that there it does consolidate and *may* give satisfactory climbing.

Sixth, the slopes above the South Col are in sunshine from dawn, thus allowing climbers to make an earlier and easier start than from camps on the northerly side (where the old Camp VI was in shadow until 9 AM).

Murray lists three disadvantages:

First, at the narrows of the west basin (the Icefall) there appears a threat of avalanche from the flanking walls not present on the east Rongbuk glacier. . . .

Second, the traverse from the face of Lhotse (standing to the right of the head of the Western Cwn) to the South Col, although tactically good (granted good snow), is strategically bad. If the weather deteriorates while men are above the South Col their safe return is unduly compromised; powder snow falling in bulk on slopes so long and steep will create a dangerous situation. . . .

Third, an aerial photograph of the summit shows that the southeast ridge may become unpleasantly like a knife-edge along its last three hundred feet.

A final conclusion of the 1951 reconnaissance was that while the pre-monsoon lull in spring was still likely to provide the best climbing conditions, cold might not be so intense as to prohibit an autumn attempt after the cessation of the monsoon.

The results of the reconnaissance were considered so encouraging in London that permission was at once applied for to launch a full-scale attempt in 1952. It was then learned, with consternation, that the Swiss had lodged a prior application to mount attempts both in the spring and autumn of 1952, and that this application had been approved by the Nepalese government. It was a bitter blow. To a candid mind it savored very much of "poaching." There are naturally no hard and fast rules, but it had always been understood that once a nation had singled out a particular Himalayan peak for assault it remained "reserved" to them until either they had conquered it or announced they had abandoned the attempt. Everest had known none other than British expeditions and was therefore "British," in the same manner as Nanga Parbat was considered "Austro-German" (it was conquered in this year, 1952, by them) and Godwin Austin (K2), "American." Moreover no nation had sacrificed so many men, and spent so freely in money and material, as the British had done on Everest. It would be hard indeed if this dearly won and nearly completed pyramid of experience should be finally crowned by another nation. It was also an inescapable fact that no nation was as likely to succeed as Switzerland. While other countries had been preoccupied by the war, Switzerland had remained neutral and with fine natural training ground within her own frontiers she had been able, undisturbed, to build up a pool of mountaineers who combined youth and experience. The challenge was quite as formidable as that offered by Amundsen to Scott at the South Pole.

Everest is quite difficult and dangerous enough without the element of international competition entering into matters. A suggestion that a joint Anglo-Swiss expedition be organized was therefore made. Negotiations broke down over the problem of leadership. The British then withdrew leaving 1952 to the Swiss and staking a claim for one and if necessary two, attempts in 1953. In a sporting gesture, which in some measure repaid the generous help given to British climbers through the years by the Swiss Foundation for Alpine Research and other Swiss climbing bodies, the British offered all help and advice which they had at their command from past experience.

The Swiss excuse for their "intrusion," as outlined by Marcel Kurz in *The Mountain World, 1953,* is interesting in that it involves what a foreigner understands, or does not understand, when he uses the words "British fair play." Explaining the events leading up to the Swiss attempt (one must bear in mind that Britain renewed the assault on Everest as soon after the war as world events permitted her), Kurz writes:

> Hitherto the British had jealously kept the conquest of the Third Pole for themselves, to the exclusion of all other nations. The struggle was not free as was that for the real poles in former times. Everyone would doubtless have applauded a British triumph. None would have merited the victory more than Mallory who devoted body and soul to this great problem. But the struggle had lasted too long, the siege had dragged out too far.

It may be said that a group of Swiss climbers actually put forward proposals for a Swiss expedition in the year 1941. With Britain on her back and fighting for her life, two of the first three "considerations in favor of this proposition" were:

> The British sporting instinct will never admit that the Alpine Club holds a sole lease of Mount Everest.
>
> Such permission granted by the English to us Swiss would be highly creditable to the Englishman's sense of "fair play."

It is highly creditable to Dr. R. Schoepfer, the then President of the Swiss Foundation for Alpine Research, that he turned the proposals down flatly with the comment:

> *At the present time* to embark on such an undertaking is *wholly* out of the question. The British Empire is fighting for its existence. Who in Britain could sponsor an Everest expedition at such a time? *Sentiment* is decisive, and the heart will beat for the home country, not for an Everest expedition.
> Conclusion: We must not lose sight of the idea, but wait.[2]

The Swiss party of 1952, composed of eight climbers under Dr. Wyss-Dunant and two scientists, left Katmandu on March 29 and reached the foot of the Icefall towards the end of April. Direct assaults on the Icefall having failed, the Swiss then decided to pitch their Camp II high up in the fall itself and from this point chose the route hard under the west ridge of Everest. This was the corridor rejected as too dangerous by the British, but the Swiss could find no alternative. To minimize avalanche risks they restricted movement along the most perilous section to between the hours of 7 AM and 11 AM when the hanging glaciers threatening the route from thousands of feet above it could be considered to be at their most stable. Also, in the best Himalayan tradition, no parties of Sherpas were ever allowed on the corridor without a European escort. Camps were now established in orderly fashion across the floor of the Western Cwm and up the forbidding slopes at the far end until by a truly magnificent piece of mountaineering Camp VI was established on the 25,800 foot high South Col. Up to this point the Swiss advance had been orthodox and methodical but two mistakes had been made. The South Col had been attained too early to catch the pre-monsoon lull (for this the party could scarcely be blamed as the lull was now known to be entirely unpredictable). More culpable was the fact that too few Sherpas had been engaged for high alti-

[2] *The Mountain World: 1953.*

tude carrying. Of the four Sherpas who reached the South Col only Tenzing Norkey was in any condition to go further. The remaining three were sent back, sick, to Camp V. From this point onwards the Swiss judgment seems to have been at fault.

On May 27, Raymond Lambert, an Alpine Guide of great experience and tremendous strength, set off up the southeast ridge accompanied by Rene Aubert, Leon Flory and Tenzing on a rather indeterminate sortie which was apparently intended to be half reconnaissance and half an attempt to place a tent as high as possible. Tenzing carried the tent, the Swiss a little food. They had no sleeping bags, no air mattresses and no stove, indeed nothing which would make a night on the ridge even partly tolerable. But at 27,550 feet Tenzing suddenly put the tent down and suggested they spend the night there and make a dash for the summit on the following day. Lambert at once agreed. Accordingly Aubert and Flory turned back to the South Col leaving Lambert and Tenzing to weather the night alone. Such snap decisions are not without precedent in the Himalaya and have sometimes paid handsome dividends. A brilliant piece of opportunism whereby he suddenly threw his well-thought-out plans to the winds and telescoped three days' work into one, had enabled Frank Smythe to conquer Kamet. Everest did not prove so obliging. Lambert and Tenzing spent an appalling night, entirely sleepless and continuously buffeting each other to keep their blood in circulation. To still their raging thirst they fumblingly endeavored to melt snow over a candle. Morning found them so exhausted that the failure of the attempt was a foregone conclusion. Nevertheless by superhuman will power they managed to drag themselves step by step to a point estimated at 28,215 feet, the highest point then reached by men who have returned to tell the tale, but still nearly eight hundred feet below the summit. This very gallant effort, to be counted among the finest ever made on Everest, failed because the essential build up between Camps V and VII was virtually nonexistent.

On May 29, Dittert, Roch, Asper, Hofstetter and Chevalley mounted a second assault from Camp V but on reaching Camp VI on the Col they became stormbound. For two days no movement was possible outside the tents and by the third day altitude deterioration had set in to such an extent that none in the party was fit to go higher. On June 1, taking advantage of calmer weather Dittert called a retreat and managed to bring his men safely down to Camp V, counting himself lucky to have done so. It was the end of the spring attempt. As if to mock them, when the expedition reached Namche Bazar on June 6 on its homeward journey, the pre-monsoon lull arrived bringing with it fourteen days of perfect climbing weather.

In the autumn of 1952 the Swiss, now led by Dr. Gabriel Chevalley, returned to the attack. The party left Katmandu on September 10 and now met their first difficulties along the 170 mile approach march to Namche Bazar. The countryside was still saturated by the monsoon rains. Dank jungle paths seethed with thousands of leeches, rivers they were forced to cross were almost impassable. On the banks of the Dudh Kosi below Namche Bazar they were brought up short. The river was too swollen to be bridged. This meant a detour over high passes and when the rain turned to snow two coolies died of exposure.

Arrived at the mountain, conditions were considered slightly more favorable than in May and by October 26 Camp V was established at the foot of the Lhotse glacier. On October 31, when Chevalley and Spoehel and seven Sherpas were pushing on from Camp V towards the proposed Camp VI they were struck by an ice avalanche which killed Mingma Dorje, a promising twenty-five-year-old Sherpa, and incapacitated three others. After this accident the South Col track was rerouted farther to the right with the addition of two farther camps up the Lhotse glacier.

The proposed camp on the South Col now became Camp VIII. It was established on November 19 by Lambert, Reiss, Tenzing and seven Sherpas, but maintained only three days. On the twentieth the men set off for the southeast ridge but were met with a west wind so unbearably cold that they were forced to retreat at 26,575 feet. Two days later, when the wind showed no sign of slackening all further attempts were abandoned. On this occasion the Swiss had arrived too late to catch the fine weather lull which it is thought must follow immediately upon the cessation of the southeast monsoon.

(In view of the wild reporting that later attended the British attempt of 1953, it may be noted that towards the close of the second Swiss attempt an ebullient Indian newspaper correspondent back in Katmandu made a psychic bid for the result and announced that the Swiss had climbed to within 150 feet of the summit. As the only communication between Katmandu and Namche Bazar was then by runner the world remained in this belief for nearly three weeks when the true result became known.)

No history of Everest, however brief, would be complete without reference to four bizarre episodes—three clandestine attempts by individuals and a reported Russian attempt by the old northern route, in the winter of 1952/53 about which little is as yet known but which allegedly cost six lives.

The first secret attempt was made in 1934 by a former British army captain, Maurice Wilson. Wilson was convinced that he had found a new philosophy of life and his plan to bring it to the attention of the world was for himself to perform some truly outstanding feat. He chose the ascent of Everest. His first idea was to crash an aircraft high up on the slopes of the mountain, climb to the summit, place the British flag there and then return on foot. For this purpose he learned to fly, purchased a secondhand plane and actually flew it to India. There the plane was confiscated.

Undaunted, Wilson disguised himself as a monk and accompanied by three Sherpas and a pack pony crossed the frontier into Tibet and reached Rongbuk monastery on April 18, 1934. From Rongbuk, Wilson, although no mountaineer, managed to reach Camp III (21,000 feet) where his two remaining Sherpas deserted him. Wilson was now faced with the formidable ascent to the top of the North Col. He never made it, which is scarcely surprising. His diaries show that with failing strength but persistence and courage which would have been commendable in any other enterprise, he accepted defeat after defeat only to try again, until finally he collapsed and died of despair and exposure. His remains were found in his tattered tent by the Shipton reconnaissance expedition of 1935.

The second clandestine attempt was made in 1947 by Earl Denman, a Canadian, resident in South Africa. Denman states that he left Darjeeling on March 22 and disguised as a Tibetan, crossed the frontier into Tibet accompanied by two Sherpas, Tenzing Norkey and Ang Dawa. The climb went according to plan and a point was reached just below the top of the North Col. Here bitter gales and inadequate equipment forced the party to retreat. Marching by night as well as day—for Denman was apparently fearful of arrest—he arrived back in Darjeeling on April 28, having taken only five weeks for the round trip, thus setting a record which is scarcely likely to be beaten.

The third solitary attempt—again clandestine—was made in the spring of 1951 by a Dane, R. B. Larsen. Like his predecessors Larsen left from Darjeeling (on March 31) but he varied their itinerary by working westwards into Nepal, finally arriving at Namche Bazar. He was accompanied by seven Sherpas. An attempt to follow the Tilman-Houston route to the Western Cwm having been frustrated owing to deep snow and avalanches, Larsen turned north and crossed the Nangpa La (Pass) into Tibet finally reaching Rongbuk monastery after six days of forced marches from Namche. It seems that Larsen actually did reach the North Col, but there his porters refused to camp and Larsen was forced to admit defeat. He returned the same way he had come via Namche Bazar to Darjeeling—an interesting variation on the normal routes, but a long detour compared with them, and involving, in his case a series of forced marches which his Sherpas are never likely to forget.

News of a disastrous Russian attempt (obviously from the Tibetan side of the mountain), in December 1952, was published in the Italian Alpine review *Lo Scarpone* in the autumn of 1953, and must be treated with reserve until confirmation is available. A paraphrase of the article appeared in *The Times* (of London) of September 12, and runs:

> A number of climbers (Russian) were said to have been in training in order to provide the best men available. When the Russians learned that a second Swiss expedition was leaving in 1952 after the failure of the first, they apparently resolved to make a determined effort to anticipate them. The expedition is described as having consisted of thirty-five experienced climbers and five scientists, including Professor Antonyi Yondomnov, a geologist, and Dr. J. Nathael Dengumarov, a specialist in the study of human physiology at high altitudes, and it left Moscow on October 16. Five army aircraft transported the expedition and its equipment first to Novosibirsk, then to Irkutsk, and finally to Lhasa. From there the approach march was longer than expected, and the expedition is stated to have left Nasulan, its base to the north of Everest, a month later. It is stated to have returned to Nasulan on December 27 having failed in its objective and lost six of its members.
>
> According to Tibetan guides to whom the Russians last

spring entrusted the task of searching for the missing men, the disaster occurred at a height of 26,800 feet. The six killed were Dr. Pavel Deshchnolian, the Armenian leader of the expedition, who was regarded as the best Russian climber; Mr. Kazhinsky, Mr. Alexandrovich, and Mr. Lanitsov, all three of whom had accompanied him on ascents in the Caucasus; Professor Yondomnov, and Dr. Dengumarov.

Dr. Deshschnolian is said to have been in daily contact with Moscow by means of a portable wireless transmitter, and his last message was to the effect that the assault party had established Camp VIII on a ledge at about 26,800 ft., which it had reached without meeting unusual difficulties, and that it expected to reach the summit in the two following days if the winds were favorable.

After this no more messages were received, and Moscow immediately ordered a search. Search parties explored the mountain, going as high as possible, for 18 days, but found no trace of the missing men. Finally the search was broken off because of the arrival of the monsoon (*sic*), and further search made in the spring was equally fruitless.

It is assumed that the members of the assault party were swept away by an avalanche not far from Camp VIII.

The organization of the expedition is said to have been criticized in Russia. Its equipment is said to have turned out to be too heavy and the expedition to have been sent out rather rashly. Native porters are said to have been used to transport equipment to the base camp on the Rongbuk glacier, but at higher altitudes the services of Tibetans who had taken part in expeditions on that side of Everest are said to have been refused.

After this macabre interlude behind the Iron Curtain it is time to return to our own story, only pausing to remark that there is nothing incongruous in the fact that the Russians may have attempted to climb Everest from the northern side, or, if the above story is a complete fabrication which seems unlikely in view of its detail, that they may attempt to do so in future. In his book *China to Chitral,* (Cambridge University Press), published in 1951, H. W. Tilman, after a study of Russian climbing literature, points out that since the war "they [the Russians] have been doing a great deal more high mountaineering than we have," although usually, as Tilman adds, "to a jarringly loud accompaniment."

In London, news of the failure of the Swiss attempts of 1952 caused efforts to ensure the success of the British 1953 expedition to be redoubled. The old controversy—"light" versus "large" expeditions—was settled irrevocably in favor of the larger. No expense was spared. It was to be the biggest, best equipped and probably costliest expedition ever sent to the mountain. This called for planning on almost a military scale and an ideal leader and administrator was found in Colonel John Hunt, C.B.E., D.S.O. Colonel Hunt had done much climbing in Sikkim before the war, including some notable midwinter ascents, and during part of the war had served as Chief Instructor (under Frank Smythe as Commandant) of the Commando Mountain and Snow Warfare School. His preparations included frequent visits to Switzerland to test new equipment and to consult with the Swiss Everest climbers, by whom he was most cordially received. In assembling the British party no concessions were made to sentiment and no account taken of superstition. The completed party numbered thirteen—the main body left for Nepal on February 13.

I must now add a few words regarding the financing of the British expeditions in order to explain my own presence in the theater of operations round Everest during the 1953 attempt. In the early 1920's when the first expeditions came to be organized, The Royal Geographic Society and the Alpine Club found themselves without sufficient funds for the purpose and with the difficult question of publicity still to settle. In return for a contribution towards expenses it was decided to award the copyright of stories and pictures of the expedition to *The*

Times of London. This practice has been followed ever since, with the single exception of 1933 when the concession was bought by *The Daily Telegraph.* Thus, (with one exception), through the years, in return for continued and generous support, *The Times* has had exclusive rights of a gripping serial adventure story distinguished more often than not by fine writing. This situation has, I think somewhat naturally, been resented by other newspapers who would have been prepared to match or excel the monetary contribution of their favored rival, and who, in their efforts to supply their readers with news of what, after all, is a national interest, have been betrayed into inaccuracies which *The Times,* by reason of its monopoly of "inside information" has been able to avoid. This has led to the legend among mountaineers that: "only *The Times* is interested in climbers actually climbing mountains; other newspapers are merely interested in climbers falling off them."

Many climbers quite genuinely resent publicity—unless it be in *The Times.* One can well believe H. W. Tilman when he writes in his book *Mount Everest: 1938:* "A feeling that the eyes of England are upon you may be very bracing before a battle but it is not conducive to sound mountaineering." It should, however, be added in fairness to the popular Press, that by voluminous correspondence, syndication services, supplement and serializations, no newspaper has done more to publicize the ascent of Everest than *The Times.* One cannot have it both ways.

In theory, it is no more possible to copyright the actual fact of the ascent of Everest by Sir Edmund Hillary, than it is possible to copyright the actual fact of the ascent of the Nelson Column by that eminent steeple jack Mr. Sydney Larkin. In practice, however, while a couple of thousand or more reporters can watch every inch of Mr. Larkin's progress from the comfortable security of Trafalgar Square, the copyright of the ascent of Everest is defended by the three major factors which so long defeated the climbers and would obviously and inevitably defeat any independent reporter, namely: magnitude, altitude and inaccessibility. Prior to the war, even if he disguised himself as a monk and made his solitary way across the freezing Tibetan plateau, and even if he were to emulate a Wilson, a Denman or a Larsen, and reach a point on, or just below, the North Col—he would certainly not have got farther—an "outsider" would still find the events which interested him occurring, invisibly, thousands of dizzy feet above his dizzy head.

After the war the problems of magnitude and altitude remained for the reporter, but that of inaccessibility appeared slightly, very slightly, easier. The barriers round Nepal were relaxing. In my case I had been permitted to visit Katmandu in 1947; it was not impossible that I might be permitted to do so again. Left to myself, it would never have occurred to me to ask to be sent there, for I knew that while Katmandu is only two days by Comet from London, it is three weeks by foot from Everest and from Cairo, where I was stationed, it did not look a workable proposition. But in newspaper parlance Katmandu is a sure-fire "date line" conjuring up as it does a vision of temples and green eyes of little yellow gods, kukris, Gurkha soldiers and fields of blue poppies, with Everest, of course, looming in the background. My own foreign editor, Mr. Leonard Curtis of *The Daily Mail,* was the first in Fleet Street to think of the idea of sending a correspondent there during the period of the British climb. I was selected for the task, but it was some weeks before my visa to enter Nepal was granted. Even then I was well ahead of the field, for correspondents who tried to follow me experienced similar visa delays. In the end, thanks to the British Ambassador, only five British correspondents succeeded in reaching Nepal during the actual period of the climb, and of these two were from *The Times.* What nobody seems fully to have realized at the time was that Katmandu already had a considerable and very active corps of Indian newspaper correspondents who suffer no visa difficulties. Thus during the British ascent there was no lack of news, and particularly of rumors. Because of the physical impossibility of breaking the copyright and the vows of silence imposed on the members of the expedition, much of this reporting tended to be anti-British. Communist agitators in Nepal, and unfortunately there are a number, were quick to exploit this situation, as they were later to exploit the dispute as to whether Sherpa Tenzing is an Indian or a Nepalese subject. But I anticipate. My immediate objective is to introduce Nepal—the country.

CHAPTER II

NEPAL

> The country is wild and mountainous and is little frequented by strangers, whose visits the King discourages. Marco Polo

I USED the above quotation to preface an article I wrote in *The Daily Mail* after returning from a visit to Nepal in 1947. It remained true in that year and, although the political regime has now changed, it remains true, to a lesser degree, today.

Nepal—it is an independent kingdom, not an Indian state—continues to be the largest inhabited country in the world virtually unexplored by Europeans. Unlike Tibet, it has never been penetrated by an expeditionary force. When during the Nepalese War of 1816 a 13,000 strong British column under General Ochterlony threatened to outflank the Nepalese Army and reach Katmandu, the Nepalese came to terms and thus preserved their capital inviolate. Since that time only a few hundred Europeans have been permitted entry and these singly, or at the most in twos and threes (the climbing parties admitted since the change of regime in 1950 are exceptions).

The vast majority of visitors have been British and they have entered Nepal for military, official, or antiquarian purposes. Certainly, up to 1947, no journalist had ever been there.

I owed my visit to the courtesy of the British Envoy in Katmandu, Colonel George Falconer (later Sir George Falconer) and his wife, who invited my wife and myself to be their guests. Even then, a special dispensation was required from the Maharajah, the then hereditary ruling Prime Minister, and at New Delhi I waited in trepidation until this favor was received, for I was enthralled at the prospect of visiting the country. Nepal is one hundred miles wide and five hundred miles long and occupies the central third of the Himalaya range which is almost 1500 miles across its entire width. Besides the southern slopes of Everest it contains scores of majestic peaks which climbers have for decades yearned to attempt but are only recently being allowed to visit.

Nepal's richest possessions are the long, narrow strip of fever-haunted, jungle-fringed land called the Terai, which edges the southern frontier with India, and the twenty-by-twelve mile valley basin buried in the heart of the mountains surrounding Katmandu.

In both these areas the land is very fertile, well-tended, and carefully cultivated or forested. In addition the Terai provides some of the world's finest big-game shooting. Nothing has exceeded in splendor and magnitude the shooting parties which past Maharajahs have arranged for their most valued guests. Probably the height was reached in December, 1911, when Maharajah Chandra Sham Sher entertained the late King-Emperor George V to a week's shooting following the Delhi Durbar. Months were spent in preparation and six hundred elephants collected—including a number borrowed from India—to compress all beasts of prey in a sixty mile stretch of forest into a reasonably compact area. The pressure of dangerous animals was so great that what can only be described as a "counterattack" was feared and King George's camp at Sukibhar had to be protected by barbed wire entanglements. A little way away the Maharajah's camp held accommodation for twelve thousand followers, besides the elephants and two thousand attendants upon them. After five days' shooting, King George's personal bag included twenty-one tigers, ten rhinoceroses (regarded in Nepal as the royal game *par excellence*) and two bears. The total of his party was thirty-seven tigers, eighteen rhinoceroses and four bears.

In other respects the Terai is a notorious place not only because for six months of the year it is the origin of a particularly deadly form of malaria known locally as "awal," but because in times past, impenetrable parts of the forest have provided refuge for criminal fugitives from the law. The most infamous of these was Nana Sahib who after the Indian Mutiny massacre at Cawnpore, and his subsequent defeat at Tantia Topi, fled to the Terai taking with him a priceless collection of jewels. Exactly what happened to Nana Sahib has never been discovered. It is believed probable that he died in 1859, but rumors that he was still alive persisted (as such rumors are apt to persist in the East) until the beginning of this century. Certain of his jewels passed into the possession of the Maharajah's family; notably an emerald 3¼ inches long which was later to be incorporated into the gem-encrusted headdress worn by Nepal's hereditary Prime Ministers until their regime was brought to an end. The emerald is set to the right of the magnificent central brown, orange and white bird of paradise plume. Another of Nana Sahib's acquisitions which passed to the Maharajah's family was the famous "Nau-lakha," a long necklace of pearls, diamonds and emeralds which has been described as "perhaps without a rival in the world." It was subsequently sold back to India and is now, I believe, in the possession of the Maharajah of Dharbhanga.

Nowadays, the journey across the Terai over the foothills and into the Great Valley of Nepal to Katmandu can be accomplished comfortably by air in forty minutes from Patna. But as late as the early 1920's the journey was an adventure, not lightly undertaken, which took many days. Having arrived at the guest house set in dusty mango trees beside the railway station at Raxaul on the Indian frontier, one proceeded on elephant back through the dread Terai jungle to Amlekhganj thirty miles to the north, where one arrived lucky to have escaped a bout of "awal." One then plodded upward on pony back a farther 27 miles to Bhimphedi where one dismounted dejectedly and faced a further two days on foot—and sometimes on all fours—over the Sisagarhi and Chandragiri Passes down into the Valley. Travel was speeded up in 1927 by the opening of a single track railway between Raxaul and Amlekhganj and later by a truck service between Amlekhganj and Bhimphedi, but the last mountain stage has remained (until this autumn when a "Jeepable" road was opened by Indian Army Sappers) a matter for one's two feet.

In March 1947, when my wife and I arrived at Bhimphedi, we were fortunate enough to find that the Maharajah had sent two of his own ponies and a guide—a handsome fellow with a tall feather in his cap—to meet us. But even with a pony beneath one it was a grueling enough trip and I still recall with a shudder heaving and slithering up and down gradients as steep as a quarry face and occasionally balancing precariously on the edge of chasms. But there are compensations along this final section: glasses of hot sweet tea in the teahouses of the red brick and thatch villages one passes; sudden exciting glimpses of the scarlet and vermilion flash of rhododendron trees in the gorges below; the liquid trill of the golden oriole; cascades of pale cream orchids hanging down amid the maidenhair fern from the dark walls of the mountain springs.

Along this track in both directions, crawling like ants under immense burdens threads a never-ceasing chain of diminutive coolies toting packing cases, grain sacks, and the palanquins of the wealthier Nepalese. It is not until one reaches Katmandu and gazes in amazement at the numerous cars and trucks, the huge pieces of powerhouse equipment and the bulky luxuries such as grand pianos and full-sized billiard tables, all of which have been carried over the mountains by coolie labor, that one realizes what prodigious weightlifters the Nepalese are. Standard practice for carrying a motorcar is to detach all removable parts, lash poles beneath the gutted chassis and engage coolies who man the poles like galley slaves and move upwards a few hundred yards at a time between prolonged and well earned rests. Pride of the coolie population must undoubtedly be the valley's two huge steam rollers built by a British firm in 1910. However far you take a steam roller to pieces its dismembered parts must still represent the heaviest and most awkward loads men's backs were ever meant to carry.

An electric rope railway opened in 1925, which ascends in giant strides over the mountains between Bhimphedi and Thankot in the valley, and contains one huge span of 1300 feet, carries baggage loads of up to 500 weight in each sling and offers some relief for coolies, although the most cumbersome and weightiest articles obviously must remain in their charge.

The rope railway also offers little solace to the foot-traveler as he sees sling after sling sailing over his head, its only live passengers a flock of joy-riding birds.

The valley of Katmandu may be considered the center of Nepalese civilization. Ringed by mountains which have only one exit, remote and utterly unlike anything in India, this green and smiling valley lies open to one's eye as one stands panting on the summit of the final 8,000 foot high pass of

Chandragiri. At this point, triumphant, one's guide points out Katmandu, rose-red and white, set in dark clumps of trees. Then Patan and Bhatgaon, the two other towns of Nepal, this great temple and that famous shrine, the two rivers, the sacred burning ghats of Pashpatti, and, above them all, hanging like a frozen, foamy wave glittering against the cobalt blue sky, the snowy peaks of the Himalayas.

Another sliding four miles down the mountainside brings one to the first village and one's first surprise; a sleek saloon car stands waiting for the last nine miles.

Reading over the article I wrote in 1947 I feel certain extracts are worth reproducing—together with notes I now append, for together they give some indication of the changes which have taken place in the last six years.

In 1947 I wrote:

"Katmandu itself is the second surprise, with its broad smooth roads flanked by high red-brick walls surmounted by white stone copings reminiscent of Georgian England; a vast lawn-like parade ground round which stand huge white stucco palaces, hospitals, schools and the Nepalese University.

"This city center is the one part of Nepal which can be called modern, though it is still unspoiled. The capital has had electricity since 1911, and an abundant water supply through the efforts of generations of the Royal House; it has also a certain amount of modern plumbing; X-ray apparatus for the clinics, and, it is said, private cinemas in some of the palaces of the generals and princes.

"There are no public cinemas or theaters, no advertisement billboards, no radios, no airplanes, no beggars."

Check! There is now a rather blatantly obvious public cinema showing Indian films. There must now be hundreds of radio receiving sets and a radio transmitting station broadcasting very well thought out programs. There is now an airfield and a regular air service to India, as well as an *internal* air line operating over what must be some of the most terrifying country in the world. There are still very few beggars except a posse at the airport to whom I later refer. I might add that there is now a large hotel—which there was not until very recently—and, although this may seem hard to believe, a night club.

"There are now two or three hundred motorcars in the valley and a thousand or so bicycles, but no carts and no pack animals, for nearly all freight-shifting is still done by man."

This remains true.

"The people are small, compact, sturdy-legged, deep-chested, with a Mongolian cast of countenance; the women pretty and dainty, with flowers fixed in their sleek, black hair; the men all wearing their traditional dress of cotton jodhpurs and wrap-over jerkins, with the kukri knife-dagger stuck in a waist sash, and a little lopsided Phrygian cap on their heads."

A fashion change is that the student class now tend towards the Western style zoot-suit jacket in place of the wrap-over jerkin.

"Stepping off the main streets into old Katmandu is like stepping into a picture book of Marco Polo's travels. Exquisitely carved wooden pagodas, their many tiers crowned by gilded finials, stand shoulder to shoulder beside gleaming hemispherical temples, all guarded by lions, griffins, and other fantastic animals in wood, stone or brass. Everywhere there are flowers."

The pattern of the multi-tiered pagodas of China is said by certain archaeologists to have originated in Nepal.

"One building which combines the ancient with the comparatively modern, is the Maharajah's Durbar—or reception hall. Outside, it appears to be just another well-proportioned, nineteenth century palace. Inside, one is back again in the fourteenth century. The roof is supported by shimmering pillars coated with white-gold leaf; the floor is laid with superb tiger skins; on each side of the scarlet plush and gold throne stands a shoulder-high gilded lion, winged and spurred like a griffin and lit internally so that it may appear to breathe fire.

"Nepal has a King, whose position is that of supreme figurehead. The entire administration of the country is in the hands of the hereditary Prime Minister, at present His Highness the Maharajah Sir Padma Sham Shere Jung Bahadur Rana.

"The succession to the Kingship is from father to son; that to the office of Prime Minister, which is normally held for life, from brother to brother. On the death of the youngest brother it goes to the eldest son of the next generation.

"The present Maharajah, who received me in his private palace (I was to meet him again later, informally, during a picnic with Sir George and Lady Falconer), is a shrewd, dignified, and courtly man of sixty-six, with a flowing gray mustache, and because of it a faint resemblance to Bismarck.

"He adheres to the traditional policy of preventing the exploitation of Nepal by foreigners, but he is anxious, so far as finances permit, to introduce such Western inventions as will improve the lot of his people without corrupting them. He is adamant against the importation of foreign political systems, and is rigid in his exclusion of all missionaries."

Very little of the above remains true today. The Maharajah's regime with its adherence to tradition, its distrust of Western methods, and its rather vague ambitions was swept away in 1950. Full powers of government were restored to His Majesty King Tribhuvan who is assisted by a Council of State which in its turn is advised by very able officers of the Indian Civil Service. It is His Majesty's desire that Nepal become a democracy in the best sense of the term. Political parties have been introduced and progress is being made towards the holding of general elections. American agricultural experts of the Point Four Program, a Swiss geologist and an Indian Military Mission have now been invited to Nepal in an advisory capacity—while one of the best loved characters in Katmandu is an Irish-American missionary, Father Moran. The Nepalese are mostly Hindus with a strong minority of Buddhists mainly concentrated along the northern borders. In certain parts of the country there is an interesting and unique mingling of the two religions.

Under the new regime Nepal's economic problems remain the same as under the old:

"Coming from the poverty and dissension of India (I must make it quite clear again that I wrote this in 1947, at the height of the political turmoil which attended the handing over of power by Britain), at first sight Nepal seems the Happy Valley. But she, too, has her troubles. She is not self-supporting and largely depends on India for her supplies of cloth, kerosene oil, gasoline, salt and sheet iron. As a result of the war, the cost of these imports has risen, and this rise cannot be offset by Nepal's own exports, the official list of which begins with "jute, timber, rice," and ends with "talking birds, falcons and yaks' tails."

"But the chief of Nepal's exports is mentioned in no official list. He is the Gurkha soldier.

"Anyone who has served with the Gurkhas will talk for hours of their courage, endurance, good nature, and honesty. From the time of the Indian mutiny they have flocked to the British standard in time of trouble; out of Nepal's total population of a mere 6,000,000, 2,000,000 Gurkhas came forward to fight for us in the 1914-1918 war, 120,000 fought in this last war, while in the years between many thousands saw action on the northwest frontier. Hillmen from the mountainous regions still closed to Europeans, they are hardy, self-reliant, and fiercely proud of their difference from races to the south. The agreement under which these men have so far been recruited is between the British and the Nepalese."

I then went on to outline the problem which would arise when India became an independent nation—namely *to whose* army would future Gurkha soldiers be recruited. This is now past history and need not be recapitulated. A compromise was reached whereby a proportion of Gurkhas are drafted to the Indian Army and a proportion direct into the British Army for service overseas. Under this arrangement India gets the lion's share, but as British recruits have to pass through her territory as she is geographically in a position to seal off Nepal at will—and is under some Communist pressure to do so—Britain has no strong case for complaint. How long the arrangement will last is another matter. Pandit Nehru reiterated this year (1953) that it cannot last for ever.

Comparing my visits of 1947 and 1953, the chief difference that strikes me is the complete liberty of movement I enjoyed under the new regime. This was so pronounced that it was difficult to get used to when I remembered my previous experiences. In 1947 my wife and I were virtually confined to the compound of the British Legation (now the Embassy), known rather grandiloquently as "The Lines." Apart from official visits and brief sight-seeing excursions under escort, we were only allowed outside "The Lines" when accompanied by the Envoy. As Sir George had much work to do our promenades together were confined to a sedate evening stroll round an upland parade ground where we hoped for a view of Everest but were always denied it owing to cloud. We did, however, manage one very pleasant picnic in the woods where quite by chance we encountered the Maharajah.

At that time, besides the Envoy and Lady Falconer, there were only three other British residents in Katmandu—enough that is, with one reserve, to make up a bridge or tennis four. The three were Lieutenant-Colonel "Sandy" MacClure, the Gurkha Recruiting Officer who lived in "The Lines" and whom we met only fleetingly as he was proceeding on leave, and Mr. and Mrs. Roy Kilburn. Kilburn was Engineering Consultant to the Maharajah. He was responsible for the valley's electric lighting system and for many other projects and amenities. Being a Scot and a sportsman he also strove manfully to create a golf course out of a nightmare example of soil erosion which adjoins the present airfield. He died last year.

The series of buildings which have housed Her Majesty's representatives in the past, have been described scornfully by Mr. Perceval Landon (*Nepal* vol. i, Constable) as "unfortunate" and "undignified" and the less admirable because of contrasting so unhappily with sumptuous homes of "even the junior members of the Maharajah's family." The original residency was, according to Landon, "an edifice of brick and plaster of the 'churchwarden' Gothic type"—whatever that may mean. Of the legation which replaced it, Landon states that "a sanatorium in Switzerland must have been taken for a model." The third building of the series—the legation of 1947 and the embassy of 1953—while not exactly "undignified" (although it does remotely resemble a concrete chest of drawers) can be considered "unfortunate" in that it was resolutely built with its back to the finest view in the world.

The latest building—which was constructed from funds derived from the revenue of British India—will shortly be taken over by Mr. B. S. Gokhale, the Indian Ambassador. Alternative accommodation is now being built for the British Ambassador on an adjoining meadow, it is to be hoped with more success than has attended our efforts hitherto.

This is no book in which to include a summary of the history of Nepal, fascinating and incident-packed though it has been; nor would it be courteous to include a critical analysis of politics, for it was not for that purpose that I was granted permission to enter the country. Suffice it to say that whatever regime she adopts, Nepal will continue to have my heartfelt wishes for her prosperity and the continued welfare of her people.

When I left Nepal in 1947 for India I was enchanted by all that I had seen—it would be impossible to be disappointed however fantastic one's preconceived dreams—but never for a moment did the thought enter my head that one day it would be my good fortune to return.

CHAPTER III

NEPAL AGAIN

IN MID-FEBRUARY, 1953, the news came through to Cairo where I had just returned from Kenya, that my visa for a second visit to Nepal had been granted and was waiting for me at the Nepalese Embassy in New Delhi. With it came instructions by telephone to be off to Katmandu as soon as possible. The baggage party of the British Everest Expedition it seemed, was due in Bombay any day. In vain I pleaded that we were being unnecessarily hasty, no serious climbing would be done for at least another two months. The voice at the other end of the wire was inexorable: "It doesn't matter, we want you in Katmandu in good time to beat *The Times.*" A horrifying thought crossed my mind: "I say, you don't expect me to gatecrash the expedition, do you?"

"Exactly," said the voice, "and the best of luck to you." I rang off with very mixed feelings indeed. That I should cover the expedition had been suggested some weeks before, but until this telephone call I had buoyed myself with the comforting illusion that we must have come to some financial arrangement with both *The Times* and the expedition. It had not occurred to me that even the hardest hearted editor could expect anyone not on the "inside" to get much out of a story due to take place three weeks on foot across the worst country in the world from the nearest cable head and many thousands of feet above his head when he got there. Had I known how vigorously the copyright was to be defended I should probably have chucked my hand in straight away. As it was various well-meaning friends beguiled me into it with such trite remarks as: "You'll see, it'll be all right when you get there" and "Go on, they can't eat you." Nevertheless, in my profession there are "winning" and "losing" stories. An ideal "winner" provides excellent food, accommodation, transport and communications facilities. "Color" and the latest hour by hour developments are doled out to the reporter by his humble servant the public relations officer and the final result reflects great credit on all concerned. The "loser" generally costs a great deal of money and effort, yields a very stony harvest indeed, and the reporter slinks away from it abashed, suffers agonies compiling his expense account, and fervently prays that no other "loser" will come his way at least until he has had a chance to restore his tarnished reputation. If ever I saw a "loser" looming—and I have suffered many—this was it.

However, out of some trunks in the attic I dug the only suitable kit I possessed—a weatherproof, reversible, kapok-lined Commando jacket, a war relic—a fleece jerkin with windproof jacket to match and a pair of woolen khaki pants bought for the Korean War from the US Army PX store in Tokyo, and a down sleeping bag with waterproof cover purchased from the same source for the same purpose. It was too late to order anything from London, deficiencies would have to be made up in India.

I left Cairo on February 23 aboard a Qantas aircraft bound for Karachi, as depressed as I have ever felt when facing a new story, except perhaps when returning to Korea after a week in Tokyo. In Karachi there were the minor irritations of finding that Egyptian money was not acceptable in Pakistan—just as I later found that Pakistan money was not acceptable in India—and that, because we had been flying east, only two or three hours remained for sleep before the local aircraft left for Delhi. Spirits revived, with the returning memory of past associations, as we flew towards the Indian capital and as we circled the city I viewed with astonishment building additions which had been made since I was last there. On the vast area beyond the racecourse, Delhi is in process of adding an eighth city to the seven which have already stood within her boundaries.

Spirits were immediately dashed again when on arriving at the Imperial Hotel, where I had cabled for a room, I was told firstly that it was a "dry" day (it was a Tuesday) and secondly that there was no room available. Three of a long list of scientific conferences which now occupy Delhi's winter months were in progress, a cosmopolitan horde of learned men had descended on the capital and in no hotel in either New or Old Delhi was there even bathroom or corridor space for the tired traveler. A downtown pension having been uncertainly suggested and promptly rejected on viewing, I drove to the Swiss Hotel in Old Delhi and appealed to the mercy of manager Mike Michaeloff. A room was a pretty considerable favor to ask even of an old friend, but Mike magnanimously insisted that I should share his own apartment, his hospitality extending to a tot or two—measured to a scale of about three fingers to the inch—of that which was not obtainable elsewhere. In Mike's dressing room I slept solidly for twelve hours. Later Mike offered me a room which had been vacated by a man who had been rushed to the hospital with polio and had just died there—and such being the congestion I considered myself very lucky to get it.

The next morning things began to look up a bit. It is

always pleasant to be recognized, after a long absence, by an acquaintance. When I walked into Thomas Cook's to draw some money that had been cabled to me, the clerk behind the cashier's desk scarcely glanced up from the bundle of notes he was counting: "Quite a long time isn't it Mr. Izzard (it was five years); I have your money waiting for you."

My next encounter was with my former Hindustani teacher, a young agile, bespectacled Hindu named Sood. Sood came clattering off his bicycle outside Cook's office, face beaming, spectacles sparkling: "I was bicycling along Queensway when I said to myself: 'I bet you, Mr. Sood, that is Mr. Izzard, isn't it?' and so it is."

My first official call was at the Nepalese Embassy where I was most courteously received by the Ambassador, General Bijay. My visa was ready for me, the General politely inquiring whether I should like it extended to include my wife—unfortunately she was not with me. The General also gave me some valuable travelers' tips regarding Katmandu. I should find the city much changed since my last visit; taxis would be available at the new airport (I had imagined I should have to walk and had inquired whether I should find any porters waiting there). Accommodation might be difficult; the state guest houses were fully occupied, perhaps I could ask the British Ambassador to put me up? Knowing the size of the embassy from my previous stay, I pointed out that Mr. Summerhayes—to whom I was however, bringing a letter from the Cairo Embassy—was likely to find himself more than fully exercised providing room for all thirteen of the British Expedition; while at the same time, the presence of an "outsider," interested in, but not "of" the expedition, was likely to be an embarrassment for everybody. There was, the General continued, the Nepal Hotel, not of course up to European standards but possibly I would find it adequate. (It proved far more adequate than anyone could possibly expect in such a remote place.) The Nepal Hotel was there and then decided upon, the embassy kindly suggesting that they send a signal announcing my impending arrival.

After the embassy, I drove to the best bookshop and gutted it of all books I could find on Everest. There were few enough: Tilman's *Nepal Himalaya* and *Mount Everest: 1938,* and Younghusband's *Everest: the Challenge*. With these I retired to the hotel and, it being uncommonly hot for the time of year, spent the afternoon reading on my bed.

That evening I was invited to two parties which, besides refreshment, provided cuttings (by courtesy of Dickie Williams of the BBC), of articles written by Colonel Hunt for *The Times,* concerning the expedition. These I had not yet seen, and although I was not at liberty to quote from them as they were protected by strictest copyright, they would obviously repay careful study. I also heard the news that Adrienne Farrell, Reuters Delhi correspondent, was planning to follow the expedition as far as Namche Bazar. This news seemed to commit me irrevocably to launching a one man expedition of my own. Miss Farrell had been in Katmandu the previous year and if she, as a woman correspondent considered the trek possible, a male correspondent could not, with honor, lag behind. (Eventually Reuthers' Peter Jackson made the trip on her behalf.)

My mind having been made up for me, the next problem was to assemble supplies. This was no easy matter for in Delhi, one of the hottest capitals in the world, the shops are naturally not stocked with cold weather goods. A methodical man would write out a long list of requirements covering every possible contingency and probably take a day doing it. My own list would obviously contain so many items that were unobtainable that I forbore to make it and contented myself with browsing round the shopping center buying up anything I could see which could be reasonably considered essential.

I drew an immediate blank over a lightweight tent; most vendors had never heard of such a thing. I acquired a mosquito net—which I never used—and an air mattress of robust local manufacture (my subsequent memories of it were that it seemed to take half the night to get the air into it and the other half to get it out again). Climbing, or even stout walking boots, were out of the question. Being a large-footed man in a neat-footed nation I could find no boot or shoe to fit me in any shape or form except a single pair of sneakers or tennis shoes in a Bata store. These I bought as slippers to wear about camp, but in the end I marched nearly 400 miles in them, over the roughest possible going, before finally throwing them away (they were retrieved by one of my coolies who is probably still wearing them). Medical supplies I purchased in abundance not so much for myself (I was only to use Paludrine) but to patch up the coolies when necessary and because, nowadays, all Europeans traveling through the wilderness are expected to administer a pill or a plaster to all who happen to need them whom he may meet by the way. Other odd items were needles of all sizes, darning wool, thread and twine, buttons, three or four mouth organs for barter or presents, two or three flashlights with spare bulbs and batteries and a solid reliable cigarette lighter, with extra flints and a tin of lighter fuel. Normally I never carry a lighter, but it is the best insurance against a cold supper when on trek. Matches are bulky to carry and it is astonishing how easily they are wasted especially when slightly damp; while there is always the possibility that one's whole supply will be spoilt by a coolie overbalancing in a mountain torrent. For bulk provisions I relied on Calcutta and Katmandu, but seeing some good chocolate I bought enough to insure me one big slab per day for six weeks, and I also bought what I considered was enough cigarettes for the same period. In practice one never has enough cigarettes, for the obligations of the trail being what they are, one gives away far more than one would ever dream of smoking. These, and a few other odd purchases, made up my Delhi list. I had been working entirely on my memories of past experiences and I later discovered only three important omissions: a compass, which would have been useful but did not prove essential; a pair of dark glasses—a shocking omission this, for which I was to pay painfully with snow blindness; and a thermometer. Possibly I was as well without the thermometer, for when I later went down with fever my temperature reached such a height that I might have frightened myself to death had I been able to read it.

This partial collection of stores took some days, interrupted as it was by two days which the shopkeepers took off to celebrate the Hindu Holi festival. Holi is an occasion which the wary traveler avoids, for the sprinkling of colored water being an essential rite of the festival, the overcurious must consider themselves fair game and may well end up splashed from head to foot with indelible red ink by ecstatic merrymakers.

I booked my seat in a plane for Katmandu on Tuesday, March 3. I then learned that Colonel John Hunt and Tom Bourdillon, the expedition's oxygen expert, were due to arrive in Delhi on Sunday, March 1. It so happened that their plane was delayed twenty-four hours and thus, by pure coincidence, it came about that we were to fly into Katmandu together.

The peremptoriness with which air lines treat their passengers in most parts of the world, requiring them to be at an airport at any hour of the day or night, often hours before the aircraft actually leaves, finds no exception in India. Some ghastly hour before dawn therefore, saw me sitting blear-eyed on my baggage at the airport once more heartily wishing I could abandon the whole project, as long term policy—and go back to bed as a short term one. As soon as there was light enough to see I turned over the local newspaper to discover a statement Colonel Hunt was alleged to have made on his arrival in Delhi the previous night: "We are hopeful of success. We are optimistic largely because we are the latest in the field and are lucky to benefit by all past lessons and particularly by the experience of the Swiss. They have brought to light a lot of problems and we think we can cope with them. But," he added, "there is always the weather—an unknown factor." Hunt had apparently refused to accept Swiss criticism that the British oxygen equipment was heavier and bulkier than that used by their own climbers during the two attempts of the previous year. "We are no more heavily loaded than they were," he had said, "we have not yet reached the ideal in oxygen equipment, but it is a great improvement over anything used on Everest before." The press interview had then apparently drifted to the "Any questions?" stage, which had opened the door for the emergence of our old friend the Abominable Snowman. Here my Indian colleagues had elicited some worthwhile comment: "I consider the Snowman to be a hitherto unknown creature and feel that sufficient reliable evidence has now been established to merit launching a separate scientific expedition to trap it. Should we come across footprints, we will not allow ourselves to be distracted from our main task."

I was brooding over the various accounts of this interview when Hunt himself appeared, accompanied by Tom Bourdillon and attended by Arthur Hutchinson, *The Times* Delphi correspondent. Rather shamelessly taking advantage of my old friendship with "Hutch"—we had worked together on various stories in the past and had served under the same Command in the Navy—I introduced myself forthwith. Hunt had been well primed for the encounter. Leaning forward on his ice ax, which both he and Bourdillon were carrying in lieu of walking sticks, he eyed me shrewdly and said: "We might as well get this straight at the start. We can't take you along with us; we are not equipped for that sort of thing; all our kit and provisions have been worked out exactly. Also, there is nothing to prevent you reporting facts, but you must understand that as part of our agreement with *The Times* I am forbidden to tell you anything, and that applies as well to all members of the expedition." At this, Hutch, in the background, politely stifled a "Well played, sir," which must have nearly choked him. I replied that this was no more than I expected, and that I had no intention of making a nuisance of myself. Hunt then inquired, I think with genuine curiosity, what I *did* intend to do. I answered that if I could get the necessary permission, which was by no means certain, I might follow the expedition as far as Namche Bazar, but he would understand that there was little point in a solitary individual going farther. Hunt received this reply rather dubiously as if he thought that a real man—say a Shipton or Tilman—traveling alone, could accomplish quite enough to be an embarrassment. He would probably have been more reassured had I told him that I barely knew one end of an ice ax from the other, and had never climbed even a minor peak in my life. This interlude was cut short by: "Passengers for Allahabad, Lucknow, Patna and Calcutta on board please," and the three of us embarked, leaving Hutch with his copyright anxieties on the tarmac.

No conversation was possible in the aircraft for both Hunt and Bourdillon, who had been traveling almost continuously since Sunday, settled down to sleep immediately. At Allahabad Hunt was accosted by an American traveler and I saw no opportunity to interrupt the talk. It so happened that in the plane I was reading Tilman's *Mount Everest: 1938* and during the next stage I came upon the passage where the then Major Hunt describes in a letter to Tilman the Abominable Snowman footprints which he had found while climbing the Zemu Gap in Sikkim in 1937. Hunt had assumed at the time that the steps had been made by a German party who had been climbing in the neighborhood, but he was later able to ascertain that *they never went to the Gap at all.* He ends the letter with the query: "What on earth is the explanation of these tracks?" This seemed a fitting time to ask Hunt whether he had subsequently come to any conclusion himself, and at Lucknow I did so. Hunt now appeared convinced that the author of the prints must have been the Abominable Snowman, although he qualified his previous impression that the creature had cut steps down the farther side of the Gap, as he had suggested in the Tilman letter.

At Patna, where we changed planes, Hunt and Bourdillon were greeted by a party of Jesuit missionaries and retired to the Aero Club waiting room, while I fortified myself with a large bottle of beer for the last stage of the flight. To those who dislike air travel as I do, the mere thought of flying in a beeline into the heart of the Himalaya is sufficient to make the scalp prickle, and the only thing to commend this particular journey is its comparatively short duration of forty minutes. We were soon over the tortuously winding Ganges, had crossed the Terai and were into the tree-clad foothills.

On a clear day the whole range of the northern Himalayas would now have stretched before us like a foamy wave and Everest herself would have been visible nearly two hundred miles away to the east. But on that day low clouds driven by high winds reduced visibility to nil; the aircraft, veering and bucketing alarmingly, occasionally giving us a glimpse of a tree top or two just below the windows. At this time, when I was heartily wishing myself on the ground, Hunt remained peacefully asleep. I was only to discover later that our pilot Captain "Ravi" Randawa, a bearded Sikh, was probably the best Indian National Airways possesses, and was generally reserved for such important missions as taking Mrs. Pandit, the Prime Minister's sister, to Peking. Ravi, a cheerful supremely competent and confident character, and I, were to become very good friends and later he proved of great comfort and assistance to me. Happily, on this occasion, the flight was soon over and we dropped through the clouds and touched down on the airfield.

Katmandu airfield, nonexistent during my previous visit, is built on the only stretch of level ground to be found on the undulating and terraced floor of the great valley, and it resembles a giant aircraft carrier in that it drops sheer for a couple of hundred feet at each end of the runway. This fact is best discovered on alighting.

The arrival of the aircraft being one of the main events of the day, quite a sizable crowd had turned out to greet us. The majority were Nepalese clad in the uniform dress of the middle classes; twinkling white cotton jodhpurs, Western style jackets and waistcoats, and cloth "pixie" caps, but a small group in European dress turned out to be some members of the American Point Four Mission come to see one of their number off on the return flight, and Mr. Christopher Summerhayes, the British Ambassador, who had come to greet Colonel Hunt. While we waited for our baggage to be off-loaded Hunt courteously introduced me to the Ambassador, a tall gaunt figure with an iron gray mustache, who gazed at me rather bleakly—I learned later that I had unwittingly committed an unforgivable sin by not applying through the British Embassy for my visa (that it was scarcely likely to have materialized had I done so was another matter). Mr. Summerhayes regretted that he had no accommodation available for me. He then left me to my own devices.

The impact of modern democracy upon Nepal has been so sudden that somewhat naturally the growth of the Civil Service has been unable to keep up with it. Thus passport formalities and Customs clearance at the airport are still rather sketchy. After my passport had been held upside down for some time, my name was duly entered in a school exercise book and I was passed on to Customs. Here I announced firmly and with repeated emphasis that I had two bottles of whisky to declare. No one understood me. In a bamboo shelter, there has not yet been time to erect permanent buildings, all my belongings were turned out on the floor—more I think out of curiosity than in any hope to find dutiable goods —while I still pleaded to be allowed to declare the two precious bottles. Eventually—and seemingly to my shame—the whisky came to light amidst triumphant cries which were echoed by a rapidly assembling multitude. Two hundred per cent was the duty payable upon the two bottles, but this was reduced to 100 per cent when I argued, quite truly that they were for personal, medicinal, use only. In return for my money I was given as receipt a beautifully inscribed roll of locally manufactured rice paper which I still treasure. My bags having been accorded the necessary hieroglyphics, I was surrounded by a horde of beggars some of whom required bakshish for carrying the bags and others of whom merely required bakshish. All cheerfully exposed shocking deformities, notably legs grotesquely swollen by elephantiasis. Katmandu itself is by no means a beggar-ridden town, in fact they are scarce there, and I feel the authorities would do well to clean up the airport contingent, for the impression they make on the newcomer is not a good one. I am told they are an overflow from that natural affliction of the earth's surface, the Katmandu golf course, which adjoins the airfield, where they perform as caddies during the week ends.

I was fighting a losing battle to prevent my bags being scattered in all directions, when my sleeve was politely plucked and I turned to find at my elbow a neatly dressed man of middle age wearing gold rimmed spectacles, who announced he was the manager of the hotel. The manager now took charge and having beaten off the clamorous cloud of indigents we set out in a battered sedan for the city. The manager's English was remarkably good taking into account the fact that probably less English is spoken in Katmandu itself than in the hills where Gurkha troops are recruited, but nevertheless conversation was stilted. The manager deprecated the amenities of the hotel adding: "We are doing our level best," a phrase I was to hear a few hundred times before I paid my last bill there. I expressed my admiration at the incredibly neat manner in which the fields on either side of the road were cultivated to which the manager, who was clearly flattered, replied, "Yes, we Nepalese are a very laborious people." When I told him, in answer to a question, that I came from Cairo, he supposed that Cairo was "somewhere between Katmandu and London."

On my suggestion, we headed at once for the Telegraph Office for I was anxious to insure my communications. Be it ever so good, a newspaperman's "story" can never rank as such until it is safely put to bed in his own head office. I had heard dire tales that all cables had to be sent down by runner to Raxaul, a journey of two days. Over this I was pleasantly surprised. The Office stands within the British "Lines," but is now run in a most efficient manner by the Indian Embassy. Press cables could be accepted and in normal circumstances they would not take more than five hours to reach London. As a five hour time lag operated in our favor, they would thus be received in England at roughly the time they were dispatched. The one snag—which was removed later—was that all overseas messages had to be handed in by midday of the day they were to be sent which meant, as it was now mid-afternoon, that there was nothing I could do until the following morning. Returning down the road the manager pointed out to me two elegantly attired young Indians whom he described as "colleagues." I stopped the car at once and introduced myself to Roy of the Press Trust of India and Harish Srivashtava of *The Statesman* and the Associated Press. There is a freemasonry of the Press which safeguards traveling correspondents, and more or less obliges "old stagers" to "fill in the picture" for new arrivals, a reciprocal service which operates the world over—and I no longer felt so helpless as I had done hitherto. We arranged to meet on the following day.

We now headed, myself with some curiosity, for the Nepal Hotel, which lies some six miles out of the city. I had been anticipating anything down to a mud hut and was therefore quite taken aback when we turned in past tall lodge gates, swept up a drive flanked by purple bougainvillea and flame trees and came within sight of a most imposing palace which would not have been out of place in Monte Carlo. This truly enormous edifice, which stretched far behind its stuccoed front, had been the palace of a former Prime Minister, the later General Joodha. The building has now fallen into a state of some dilapidation and disrepair—large areas of primrose plaster were flaking from the walls—but to say it was more than sufficient for my own needs would be a crass understatement, if only for the fact that I soon discovered I was the only guest there. Inside the palace proved to be a museum piece of Nepalese court elegance of a bygone era. Having paid off our ancient vehicle with about £3—a sum which I then considered outrageous and now consider reasonable in view of the vastly higher sums I was to pay later—we entered the cavernous entrance hall. This was entirely given over to trophies of the chase. Two stuffed leopards grappled in a death lock in the center of the floor. A crocodile leaking sawdust lay against one wall and a rhinoceros head, sawn off behind the ears, served as hatrack. Tiger heads and skins, many of them magnificent, filled or covered most of the other available space. Here, four servants dressed in jodhpurs and hobnailed boots fell in behind us and we clumped across the hall up the central stairway, through a sumptuous salon hung with refulgent chandeliers, across the first floor verandah flanking a courtyard which served as a ready-use locker for the supply of chickens and eggs for the kitchen, up a spiral staircase at the far end, back along the second floor verandah and into my apartments. These consisted of a living room laid with expensive rugs and furnished with sofas and occasional seats in the French Empire style, plus an ormolu-decorated table bearing some ageing English illustrated magazines and instructions on how to dance the rumba, and a bedroom within which stood a commodious four poster bed totally enclosed by a mosquito net. A startling feature running round the whole, was a frieze of pink snakes with skinny legs, tufted tails and Groucho Marx mustaches—a local touch designed to protect me from greater evils. Here the manager discreetly withdrew while my four henchmen ranged themselves against the wall and waited for further orders. It is impossible to appear casual with four pairs of eyes watching your every move, and soon I sent all four of them packing. They did not, however, withdraw farther than the verandah, where they squatted down smoking and chatting, occasionally pausing to spit over the balustrade. The slightest sign of activity on my part brought all four clattering back to my bedroom to await the next instruction. In the end I called for a bath, expecting something of the hip-tub variety which is still common all over India outside the big cities, but once again I was agreeably surprised. My suite, it seemed, included a bathroom fitted with every modern plumbing convenience and supplied with limitless hot water. This I soon discovered when, having filled the bath overfull, I pulled out the plug before getting in it, and was sent howling for the door with scalding water pouring over my bare feet on its way to a drainage hole in the center of the floor.

It was now time for dinner, and followed by my escort in line ahead we made our way down through the building to the dining room. The splendor of this room exceeded anything I had seen hitherto. Formerly it had served the late Prime Minister as audience chamber. A gilded and canopied throne stood at one end while high at the other was a Ladies' Gallery fronted by an ornamental lattice. Richly carved Chinese and French cabinets containing porcelain, objets d'art and general bric-a-brac stood round the room, the walls of which were hung with over life-sized portraits of the General, his relations and the ladies of the court, all of them in massive gilded frames. The two chandeliers were even more magnificent than those of the salon, but as each was lit by one dim bulb only, the general effect was one of gloom so intense, it was scarcely possible to see across the hall. I sat down to my solitary dinner—and an excellent one it was, including a superb Chicke a la Kiev—with my escorts standing guard and occasionally smacking their lips loudly to indicate politely what a lucky man I was to be provided with such palatable fare.

The meal being finished, we all trooped back to my apartments where I indicated that the performance was closing for the night as I wished to go to bed. The mattress proved hard as a board and the bolster hard as a rock and I remained sleepless for some time. The surprises of the night were not over. Alone, in this vast building, I had just fallen into a doze when I was brought wide awake by the opening chords of a very tolerable jazz band. This din so intrigued me that I lay awake for some hours proposing to myself, and rejecting, one fantastic theory after another to account for it. It seemed to me I must have come to some haunted castle dreamed up by Jean Cocteau, fully peopled, where life pursued its normal course, and only I was denied the eyes to follow it. At this, the snakes round my bed appeared to move forward three feet in unison, and I shut my eyes to banish the thought and finally fell asleep. To crown what may be described without exaggeration as an unusual night, I was awoken in the early hours by the roaring of tigers outside my window. Morning brought the answer to both riddles. A zoo, and a good one, adjoined the hotel. We were reminded of this some weeks later when the Manager casually announced that four cobras had escaped from their cage, one of which was subsequently killed in the hotel grounds.

The jazz band also had its explanation, if a rather bizarre one. After breakfast, a rather more adventurous exploration of the immense building brought me to a door upon which was pinned a notice in English:

> Rendezvous Club
>
> Admission Five Rupees at the gate (it was on the first floor). Night dress essential. Full supply of alcoholic drinks is now available at cheaper prices. The cooperation of the guests is solicited.

Within the door was a night club furnished in a style befitting London, Paris, or New York—red-plush settees, burnished mirrors, spotless tablecloths and speckless glasses. During my long stay in the hotel hardly a soul ever visited the club. The band practiced assiduously throughout the morning and played on bravely through the night, many times more often than not to an entirely deserted floor. Some time ago certain high personages had designed to visit the club; it was thus kept in perfect running order in case it should once again be so favored.

I spent that morning writing my first dispatch—a brief account of my arrival in the valley with Colonel Hunt, including a brief quote or two from the interview he had given in Delhi. My taxi not having arrived, a boy on a bicycle was sent to fetch another and with this venerable conveyance, one of whose front wheels was splayed at an angle of 45 degrees, we set off for the city.

The road from the hotel is part of the main east to west route from Katmandu to Thankot at the head of the rope railway leading up from Bhimphedi. It is rough and unmetaled until it enters the city, but quite motorable. Immediately outside the hotel, the road crosses a wide expanse of turf like an English village green where ducks puddled contentedly in a central pond. The road then curves through a small village typical of those to be found throughout the valley. The narrow red brick and timber houses are fronted with intricately carved wooden balconies after the manner of Swiss chalets. Each parapet bears geranium pots and upon most balconies standing olive-skinned maidens braiding flowers into their hair. There is one temple, daintily proportioned, guarded by two bronze lions, faced with colored tiles, and covered with a curly-eaved roof carrying bells like a jester's cap. Beyond, the road runs downhill between high red brick walls capped with white stone copings and bearing stone cannon balls at intervals giving the avenue a Georgian aspect —a motif which reoccurs frequently in other of the more modern sections of the city and to which I have already referred. Here, the avenue ends in another small village, conspicuous for a large stone image of Hanuman, the monkey God, daubed with vermilion powder, smeared with red paint and rather forlornly holding a tattered cloth umbrella over its head. A steel cantilever bridge now leads over the river, the banks of which are lined with stone steps to facilitate the washing of clothes. The river was almost dry at this, the end of the rainless season, but sometimes a sharp rise in the water level would give a good indication of weather conditions in the high Himalayas. Beyond the river the road turns sharply to the left and passes Jang Bahadur's temple of Kalamochan, a square solid building of white stone with a golden dome, protected by gilded lions, dragons, griffins and other fabulous animals. Perceval Landon, a purist regarding Nepalese architecture, considers this temple almost an anachronism compared to the other splendors of Katmandu, and I display my own deficiencies as a connoisseur by saying that I found it enchanting. A short stretch through a suburban bazaar, where dogs lie heedlessly scratching themselves in the dust of the road and where sacred cows amble majestically about the pavements, brings one with a jolt to the beginning of the tarmac. Here, where there is a traffic round-about, one passes on the left the five State guest houses standing behind another high Georgian wall. Guest house No.1 is reserved for visitors of royal blood or guests of honor of the king; No.2 for diplomats and numbers 3, 4, and 5 for less distinguished visitors. At the time of my arrival numbers 3, 4 and 5 were jam-packed with Indian newspaper correspondents. The tarmac leads rapidly on to the great central maidan, a tremendous expanse of level turf known at the Tundi Kehl to record the legend that the work of creating it was paid for by the gold which, by a miracle of digestion, replaced maggots in grain. Concerning it, Landon (*Nepal*, vol. i: Constable) adds: "The story is too fantastic to retell, but the maker of the plain, in the first lease of it—it was to an ogre—stipulated that three bricks were never to stand one on another upon the Kehl. Except for the double plinth surrounding the famous tree, this condition has nearly been kept to this day." The famous tree referred to stands in the center of the plain and the plinth is traditionally used as a platform by orators during times of national emergency.

The maidan is used as a parade ground; officers exercise their chargers there; regulars and recruits in mufti march and countermarch, while the populace looks on. Ball games have not yet been widely introduced in Nepal and when there is no military activity the general aspect of the recreation ground with its family parties and pairs of youths strolling staidly hand in hand over the turf is that of a Victorian print of a Sunday afternoon in the park.

On the southern side of the maidan stands the two hundred foot tall, thin "round tower" erected as a whim by General Bhim Sen Thapa, Nepal's first Prime Minister, early in the nineteenth century. This shaft is no object of beauty, but it has its place of affection in the hearts of the Nepalese owing to the legend that General Jang Bahadur Rana, the Warrior Maharajah, once jumped his horse from the summit, remaining unscathed although his mount was killed. It may be added that the General died as recently as 1877, so that the leap must have been made almost within living memory. He is himself commemorated by a fine equestrian statue which stands near the tower. This statue, made of bronze, weighs seven and a half tons and is believed to be the heaviest single load ever carried over the mountains and into the valley by coolies.

Halfway across the maidan and to the left, there is an archway leading to Joodha Street, which has now become the city's main business and shopping center. On the far side the road again enters an avenue between the walls surrounding the King's palace on the right and the palace of General Kaiser, the King's Chief Counselor, on the left. The road then leads over a brief stretch of open country into the British "Lines" with, standing just outside them, the temporary buildings housing the Indian Embassy Post Office and the Pensions Office. The latter is another great center of activity for all day and all night it is beleaguered by the relations and dependents of dead, disabled or demobilized Gurkha soldiers, waiting to draw their relief money.

The Post and Telegraph Office was greatly overloaded with work, with the result that the reliable inquirer was handed all incoming cables and post and requested to hunt out what might concern himself. It thus came about that while the security of outgoing cables was guarded more satisfactorily, we of the newspaper world were daily cognizant of each other's business as far as it related to instructions from our head offices—we also learned a good deal about the affairs of the expedition which did not properly concern us. Far be it from me to criticize, especially as I, myself, had little enough to conceal. In fact, the cable office, with the normal resources of a small provincial town, strove manfully and efficiently to cope with an ever increasing flood of Press messages which, at its height, may well have totaled very many thousands of words a day. The service never broke under the strain, no cable or letter to my knowledge ever went astray, and no one could complain that any outgoing cable was ever subjected to unreasonable delay.

CHAPTER IV

TO WORK

OUTSIDE the Post Office I again met Roy and Harish Srivashtava. The three of us bundled into my taxi and we set off for Joodha Street to discuss a mutual plan of campaign. The features of Joodha Street are a garage and taxi rank on the left, the Air Booking Center, which daily received a supply of newspapers from India and was therefore an obligatory calling point, the Himalaya Hotel which is best dismissed as a "one star" establishment but was definitely more convenient and central than my own for those pressed for time, the United States Reading Room and the British Reading Room which faced each other across the street (that of the United States being better frequented as it was on the ground floor and open to the street, while that of the British was on the first floor and approached through a chemist's shop), a few antique shops, a cinema showing Indian films and relaying the sound track to the world at large over a loud-speaker fixed above the entrance, and the Rangana Café. This café became our town headquarters and this is where the three of us went.

So many Europeans had visited Nepal since I was last there six years before, that I was no longer an object of curiosity except for my height of six feet four inches. The Nepalese are a stocky race—which explains their tremendous capacity for weight lifting—and cannot average much above five feet. (I have been told that some of the boy cadets recruited into the Gurkha Brigade of the British Army are some inches under five feet on arrival and have to have furniture specially made to fit them.) The Rangana Café was certainly not made to fit men of my size and I never entered it without cracking my head either ascending the narrow staircases, or on one of the low lintels across the doorways. The establishment had, however, much to commend it and in future years, when the city is more developed, it will be able to claim justly that it was the first enterprise of the kind ever to be opened there. Progress was already such that a brave attempt had been made to translate the bill of fare into English. Unfortunately most of the translations had slipped out of juxtaposition with their originals. Thus "chops" proved to be a rissole fried in potatoes; "omelette" a single egg baked in a tiny casserole and "bread" a piece of marzipan striped in the Indian Congress Party colors and topped with a piece of silver paper. Flies, of course, were everywhere but these were kept at bay by a boy armed with a Flit gun who sprayed chairs, tables, guests and food with equal abandon.

Tea having been ordered, and coffee served, we got down to business. From Harish I learned that besides Hunt and Bourdillon four other members of the expedition had already arrived. They were Doctor Charles Evans and Alfred Gregory who had got in the previous Sunday, and Major C. G. Wylie, organizing secretary and Tom Stobart, film cameraman, who had turned up that morning. As all four were quartered within the walls of the ample British Embassy compound it was agreed that little could be done about them. Both Roy and Harish were convinced that our chief hope for an interview lay with Tenzing. They knew him well, but there was a strong possibility he would not be able to join the expedition as when last heard of he had been seriously ill with malaria. We then discussed ways and means of "scooping" the final result, that is to say Harish and Roy propounded theories and I listened. This was an unfailing topic of conversation among the "outsiders" (who included myself) and continued with infinite variety and new suggestions, and entirely inconclusively, for weeks. Harish, however, was well worth hearing upon the subject. He had had a good beat on the previous year's success of the first Swiss expedition, although he had come sadly unstuck over the second, announcing it to have climbed within 150 feet of the summit of Everest, when it barely reached the South Col. Harish said he was at a loss to account for this slight error, after the careful preparations that had been made, but he was still confident that if enough money was spent, no such mistake would occur again. Personally I was not in favor of paying out money to a second party, or third party, until I was satisfied that the matter was beyond my own individual efforts and resources.

As I had been too busy to visit the embassy during the morning, I now had to wait till evening and Harish, Roy and I agreed to meet that night. At dusk I was stopped at the gates leading through the wall of the embassy compound by the two Indians who were now the center of a milling throng of Sherpas newly arrived from Darjeeling where they had been handpicked for high altitude work by Tenzing. Gathered under the pines they were a gay, colorful bunch clad in a motley assortment of climbing gear—the souvenirs of past expeditions—and including balaclavas, striped pull-overs, breeches, football stockings and boots or tennis shoes. There is an infectious gaiety about Sherpas which is one of their chief charms and in first meeting you they pump your hand so vigorously, beam with smiles and appear so genuinely glad to see you that you feel you have known them all your life. With the party were a number of women destined to carry loads for their menfolk to Namche Bazar, while the menfolk carried loads for the expedition. These women are handsome if rather solidly built, their round olive skinned faces touched with a little color in each cheek, their hair either braided across the crown or hanging in a single long pigtail down the back. All wore prettily striped skirts, strings of amber, blue and coral pink beads, and embroidered red felt Tibetan knee boots.

The glad news had speedily been spread that Tenzing himself had at last decided to join the party.

"Where was he?" The embassy sentry pointed down a narrow path which ran to the left outside the compound wall. Harish, Roy and I followed this path for some time and rapidly came to the conclusion it was leading nowhere. It was then we came to a gap in the compound wall. Here I hesitated. Having lived in the building (which was out of sight behind a group of trees) I was in favor of a frontal approach, rather than be caught as a trespasser sneaking over the back wall and having to explain myself. Harish, however, showed more enterprise. He was through the gap like a weasel, and after him went Roy, leaving me to decide whether I should forgo my interview or risk being challenged and shown off the premises. In the end I followed Roy. We passed through a copse and came to a row of stables in a corner of the compound. One of these had been allotted to the Sherpas—there were about thirty of them—and it was quite clear they were none too happy about it. This accommodation would have sufficed before the war, but since the war top-ranking Sherpas have been treated with such easy familiarity by the expeditions of other nations that they now consider themselves rightly or wrongly, for better or worse, a corps d'élite who demand and expect better treatment than the humble, uncomplaining coolie who is quite content to lay his head on a stone and count it luxury. There have been a number of versions of this incident, including the story that Tenzing complained to Colonel Hunt that this was not the way other expeditions made their arrangements and he, for his part, was moving to an hotel. I do not know whether Tenzing ever did say such a thing, but I *do* know that he spent that night loyally with his people. As it was, the evening was too far gone to remedy matters. The next day the Sherpas—bless them—were roundly taken to task by the embassy for dirtying the ground in front of the stable, and then were moved in a body under canvas in the Nepalese Army Lines near the neighboring town of Bhatgaon. This first incident was unfortunate, for it undoubtedly got the expedition off on the wrong foot with its Sherpas, caused them to be overcritical of other arrangements and led to a number of further complaints. It says much for the tact and diplomacy of Major Wylie—who speaks Gurkhali and other Himalayan languages with remarkable fluency—he is the grandson of a former British resident in Katmandu—that the breach was slowly healed until finally it could be said with justice that no expedition was served so faithfully and well by its Sherpas.

When we came upon Tenzing he was in the midst of soothing ruffled tempers and counseling his followers to make the best of things. With his innate sense of propriety, he made no mention, at the time, of the cause of the trouble, either to myself, or to my two companions who would have had no compunction at all in exposing an injustice.

My first impression of Tenzing was of a man of medium height, slender and very finely drawn—there was, in fact, much evidence in him to support the stories that he had overtaxed his strength with the two Swiss expeditions of the previous year and had been further pulled down during the winter by malaria. It was, in fact, difficult to believe that this was the man capable not only of almost superhuman stamina and endurance but also of prodigious feats of sheer muscular strength. But an inner fire burns in Tenzing and never is it better displayed than when his eyes flash and his face breaks into his brilliant smile, a smile adorned—as by no means is always the case with Sherpas—by two rows of strong, perfectly set teeth. Tenzing was dressed in a "terai" hat decorated by a peacock feather, khaki bush shirt, neatly creased khaki shorts, stockings and climbing boots. His immediate task was that of Sirdar or porter "boss" of Sherpas and coolies on the approach to the mountain. Once there he was to take his place with the climbing parties.

As Tenzing had nearly completed his rounds he readily agreed to accompany us down into the town. Accordingly we all trooped out of the compound, clambered into the waiting Jeep and drove off to the villa where Harish had taken rooms. Here as we sat on a low divan drinking tea, Tenzing told us about his past and his plans. He spoke for fully an hour. Now thirty-nine he had been born at the village of Thame in the Everest district of far eastern Nepal. Here his parents had settled after immigrating from Tibet. Tenzing had left Thame in 1953 for India, and was now living in the Toong Soong Busty at Darjeeling with his wife and two daughters Pem Pem and Nima who attend the local Nepali Girls' High School. This was to be his sixth Everest expedition—his first had been the 1935 reconnaissance led by Eric Shipton. Besides Everest he had accompanied many other important Himalayan expeditions notably to Tirch Mir, Nanga Parbat, Bandar Punch, Satopanth, Kedernath and Nanda Devi. He considered the French attempt on Nanda Devi of 1951 the most difficult and dangerous expedition he had ever undertaken. During the war he had served as both mountain guide and ski trainer with the Operational Research Section of the Indian Army. Unquestionably the greatest experience in Tenzing's life had been his climb the previous year to 28,210 feet on Everest in company with Raymond Lambert. Tenzing is devoted to Lambert whom he describes as undoubtedly the greatest climber he has ever been with. (He ranks the late Frank Smythe as the finest British climber.)

Understanding between Tenzing and Lambert is complete and also uncanny for neither can speak more than a word or two of the other's language. Tenzing manages a very little French which however, he pronounces almost perfectly having learned entirely by ear. Ever since their climb together Tenzing and Lambert have remained in correspondence with one another and it is a safe forecast that if ever Lambert returns to try Everest again, Tenzing will be with him.

For some minutes Tenzing described his night with Lambert in the tiny tent at 27,800 feet with little food and no sleeping bags. "We punched each other continuously to keep warm. As the sun went down the shadows lengthened upwards until finally a dark red glow only was left round the very summit. This lasted a long time. At dawn a dark red glow again appeared, lightened and spread downwards. We had not slept; we were too cold to go far; if we had just one cup of hot tea it might have been different, but we had no means of brewing it." (For this climb Tenzing was awarded the Nepal-Pratap-Bardhak Medal by the King of Nepal.)

The most charming trait in Tenzing's character is his complete modesty. He never distorts or exaggerates, thus when he told us: "This time if the weather holds nothing can stop me reaching the top," it was meant as a plain statement of fact, delivered without a trace of boastfulness or affectation. He emphasized that even he would need oxygen for the last 1000 feet (with Lambert he had been without it) and he was careful to add that though he considered himself strong enough to reach the top it would be entirely up to Colonel Hunt to decide the composition of the final assault party and that it would never occur to him to question the Colonel's decision. Here Harish, who had abounding faith in Tenzing's prowess, interjected the question whether he would go on alone to the top if he were selected for the final assault and found his companion failing in the later stages? Tenzing pondered this question for some time and finally answered diplomatically that such a situation was possibly conceivable, but that he would never disobey orders.

Tenzing then spoke in glowing terms of the Sherpas he had recruited. They were a young team but no less than nine of them were "Tigers," that is they had already carried loads up to 25,800 feet.

This led to a general discussion about the organization of expeditions. Tenzing made it clear that he infinitely preferred a numerous heavily equipped party to a lightly equipped one. He said: "In a light expedition the porters are the first to suffer from any shortage of food or equipment. Our morale sinks. There is less fear of shortages with a big party." This led on to the arrangements made by different nations and here Tenzing said quite openly that he preferred working with the Swiss or the French to the *previous* British expeditions he had been with. This was again a plain statement of fact, delivered in no apparent spirit of criticism and with no reference whatsoever to the current dispute within the compound. "The Swiss and the French treat their Sherpas on a footing of full equality regarding food, clothing, and equipment generally. This has not been so with the British. Consequently the British generally have to encourage us and boost our morale. Last year with the Swiss, because of our treatment, we were in such good condition that it was finally we Sherpas who were encouraging the climbers."

I have included these remarks here, as I included them in an interview I wrote for *The Daily Mail,* because it is just as well that the Sherpa's viewpoint be known, especially when it is expressed by a man of good judgment and sound common sense like Tenzing. The standards set by the British had served very well in their day, and had certainly achieved outstanding results in discipline, performance and loyalty. But Sherpas are very human beings indeed and if other countries come along and raise the standards there is no putting the clock back, and all countries must conform to the new higher standards or expect dissatisfaction. Our talk lasted till nearly nine o'clock that night when Tenzing insisted that he must get back to the embassy as he had to go into conference with Colonel Hunt. It was arranged that the four of us should meet again the next day. We then drove him back to the embassy, whereupon Harish, Roy and I retired to compare notes, which had been jotted down in a mixture of Hindustani, English and Tenzing's few words of French.

Early the next morning I wrote out my interview, and joining forces with Harish and Roy filed it at the cable office. One or two cups of tea along the way had delayed us and as the morning was rapidly passing I felt that I could not possibly longer delay my first formal visit to the embassy. Accordingly it was decided that I should pay my respects to the Ambassador while Harish and Roy hunted out Tenzing, and that I should join them later.

Mr. Summerhayes received me in his office—it had been the drawing room in my day—looking thoroughly bewildered, as well he might, for the building had been modestly designed for two or three guests at the most, and the sudden descent of thirteen men, collectively generating intense activity, had overtaxed its capacity so that even the corridors were cluttered with camp beds.

Mr. Summerhayes read my letter from the Cairo Embassy, folded it and again apologized that he had no accommodation for me (this was hardly necessary). He then invited me to come to him if I needed anything but he added quickly after I had outlined my plans: "You cannot expect any special help such as getting up to Namche Bazar, as I understand *The Times* has paid a lot of money for this story." I pointed out that surely it was unethical to discriminate between newspapers on a purely monetary basis. I had never known such a thing before and, in any case, as far as money was concerned, had it been acceptable, my own newspaper had been quite prepared to match the contribution of any other to the expedition funds. I felt it to be entirely incorrect that I should be deprived of the assistance which any British subject on lawful business has a right to expect from Her Majesty's representative in any country in which it happens to be his lot to work. Mr. Summerhayes was quite adamant on the point and for the first time I had an inkling of the unswerving loyalty to one particular newspaper which he was to pursue throughout the coming months and which finally caused him to be dubbed—I consider deservedly—by my Indian colleagues—"The extra-special correspondent of *The Times*." The Ambassador changed the subject to the difficulties of Gurkha recruitment, and the growing influence of Communism within the valley, about which he spoke entertainingly. I left with an invitation to cocktails on the lawn at noon on the coming Saturday: "to meet the members of the expedition," and with nothing else, except a certain relief that I should not have to compose the fulsome phrases of flattery with which most travelers feel compelled to interlard their accounts of meetings with their ambassadors in far away places, in return for favors received.

As I was in the embassy, I took the opportunity to introduce myself to Colonel R. R. Proud of the Brigade of Gurkhas who combines the offices of Counselor and Gurkha Recruiting Officer. He is a neat figure of a man with close clipped mustache and iron-gray hair, and on this occasion he received me very civilly and listened with sympathy to my intentions.

He asked me if I had previously traveled in the Himalaya and after I had outlined my past experience in Lahoul and Assam he warned me I should find conditions in Nepal more difficult (in fact I found them no worse and often easier). He then led me to an immense wall map (none are available in handy size) and sketched out my route, inviting me to return and make notes when I was ready to leave. He explained how coolies were obtained from the bazaar and thought it possible that I might also recruit an odd Sherpa or two who might be returning home to Namche Bazar and could act as guides. He advised me to buy a case of tinned provisions in Calcutta—this last advice later puzzled me for I would have had to pay an inordinate amount in air freight to get the case to Katmandu where I soon discovered tinned goods of every conceivable variety were available in ample supply. This conversation was, however, helpful and considerably encouraged me to pursue my plans.

I had spent longer in the embassy than I had intended and after I had walked down the long winding drive to the gates of the compound I was not surprised to find that the interview between Harish and Tenzing was over. I therefore went in search of Harish and found him quite willing to let me use his notes. According to these, Tenzing had been told at the night conference that he was to become a member of the final assault party—if he was fit at the time. He had also been assured that if he found himself within reach of the summit and his partner failed, he could push on alone, provided he felt he could make the climb and return safely. It was also decided at the conference to establish eight camps up the mountain, the topmost final assault camp to be between 27,000 and 28,000 feet. As it was obviously futile to try and check this interview with Colonel Hunt I had to take it for granted. On the face of it, if the aim of the expedition was to place a man on top of the mountain, it seemed logical enough. In 1924 Norton had pushed on alone without Somervell, as had Smythe without Shipton in 1933. If Tenzing proved to be in a class by himself he could hardly be denied his reward. I hastily scribbled out a cable and filed it as an addition to my earlier message.

As I was to be denied the official support of the Embassy in getting to Namche Bazar my only recourse was to make a direct appeal to the Nepalese government. I confess I did so with some misgivings. I had lived long enough in India, and had learned enough from my visit to Nepal, to know something of the depth of religious susceptibilities. I had always been careful to respect them scrupulously, but I knew that I was asking something of the Nepalese which, had I been in their place, I should have refused myself. Nepal's policy of isolation is very shrewdly explained by Perceval Landon in the preface to his book *Nepal,* vol. i (Constable).

> This is not merely the policy of a very able Prime Minister. Even less has it been suggested by the Government of India [the book was published in 1928], though it welcomes the barrier thus created. It is ingrained in every Nepalese. It is a faith not a foible. The presence, even the look, of a stranger is to them fraught with evil influenuce; his intrustion into the woods, hills and rivers, temples, pools, and springs of Nepal is often scarcely less than sacrilege. All of them are instinct with a divine immanence that the Nepalese would not, and perhaps could not, explain to a foreigner.

Upon the particular route I was choosing to follow, part of the main trunk road between Darjeeling in the east and Kumaon in the west, Landon is even more forbidding:

> It is a bad route from the start obstructed by many steep ascents and descents, and during flood time practically impassable. . . . A small party might perhaps push its way through in spite of all difficulties, with the help of local assistance in the matter of rope bridges, ferries, and other means of crossing

> swollen rivers. But the entire length of the route runs through the under features of the Himalayas—under features which, in any other country, would be hailed as mountains of importance—and the pace is necessarily slow. Nor is it possible without previous arrangements, to secure provisions locally. On the whole a fair number of Nepalese *powahs,* or lodging places are to be found. It need hardly be said that any attempt to use this road without the permission of the Nepalese Government would be entirely impossible, and that *such permission would certainly not be given to a European under any condition whatever.*

It is true that Landon was writing twenty-five years ago, and that restrictions had been considerably relaxed since, but it occurred to me very forcibly that while permission might be granted to a well-organized party under responsible leadership and formally supported by its government, it might still be very properly refused to an entirely unsponsored, ill-equipped and inexperienced individual like myself. To the best of my knowledge no solitary European had yet been allowed out of the great valley unescorted, and I could not help feeling that my own mission hardly merited the trouble and expense that the Government would incur by providing an escort for me. Additionally, I had to ask another privilege. It would be impossible for me to set out on such a journey without first completing my equipment and supplies in Calcutta. This would mean applying for yet another visa to re-enter the country and it was by no means certain it would be granted. But as there was no sense in making any further plans until both concessions had been reviewed and judged, I decided to present my case forthwith.

The Nepal Foreign Office is now housed in the palace of the former hereditary Prime Ministers. It is a truly magnificent building, of vast extent, in the French style and fronted by a colonnade of creamy Corinthian pillars. This building would be impressive in any setting, but to discover it buried in the heart of the Himalaya can only evoke amazement. Of the sumptuous reception hall Landon writes:

> Its rich decoration may seem to many too rich, but it is only right to say that there is not in all India a hall of such magnificence. One wonders how all these enormous mirrors, these statues, these chandeliers of branching crystal were brought over the mountain passes of Sisagarhi and Chandragiri. But unlimited human labor will achieve almost anything in the way of transport.

The living chambers are so commodious that Landon writes that in his day, with two exceptions, all the sons of the Maharajah, with their wives and families, were easily accommodated in the building.

On this occasion I entered through a side door in the immense right flank of the palace, soon lost myself, and was then politely escorted to the office of Mr. Dixhit, the then Secretary for Foreign Affairs. Mr. Dixhit's welcome could not have been more heart-warming and my anxieties were at once dispelled. A staunch friend of Britain, he had served in London during the war and although not strictly required to do so, had remained at his post throughout the "blitz." He had more than a working knowledge of Fleet Street and listened with sympathy to my requests. Regarding my proposed visit to Calcutta, he asked for my passport and promptly endorsed it, with his own hand, for as many trips in and out of Nepal as I cared to make throughout the duration of the expedition. My rather hesitant request concerning permission to travel to Namche Bazar was dismissed with equal cordiality. I had been given permission to come to Nepal to write about the expedition; that meant I could certainly go as far as Namche Bazar. "There is nothing to prevent you going to the top of Everest," added Mr. Dixhit, at which we both laughed heartily. To confirm this permission Mr. Dixhit then introduced me to his senior officer, Mr. Khadgaman Singh, then acting as Foreign Counselor to His Majesty. The Counselor was equally affable. The road to Namche was open for me all right but it was a difficult and arduous one. "For my part," said the Counselor, "I should consider it a penance rather than a pleasure." I expressed my thanks profusely, and we parted on very friendly terms. Outside the palace I could have skipped with elation. The maze of red tape which I had envisaged had proved entirely imaginary and the success of my own little venture now depended alone on my own resource and endurance.

The next day brought two new additions to the strength of the expedition. From the Far East came the New Zealand climber Edmund Hillary and from the Far West came Dr. Griffith Pugh, the expedition's physiologist whose advice on acclimatization and altitude deterioration was to prove invaluable.

The rumor spread round the Press circle at noon the next day that Colonel Hunt would talk on the expedition that night in the British Embassy Reading Room in Joodha Road. At first I understood that this talk was to be a Press conference, but on arriving in the room I found it to be an impromptu lecture, arranged by Colonel Proud for the benefit of the local population. The close-ranked school forms were packed and the serried rows of "pixie" caps bobbed expectantly, but no place in the room was more crowded and none was surrounded with more excitement than the Press bench. This was a development which Colonel Proud had not expected, and had he known about it beforehand I doubt if Colonel Hunt would have gone on with the talk, for it is impossible to hold a public meeting "off the record." Of the Press, I was the sole European among a dozen or so Indians and Nepalese. As this was the first opportunity I had had to study Colonel Hunt at close quarters and to listen to him speaking at length, perhaps I may be forgiven for inserting here my impressions and a short life history as I came to know it. A man who knows Colonel Hunt well has told me of him: "He may not have been born brilliant, but he has achieved brilliance because he has always worked three times as hard as ordinary men." His career has been an impeccable one, moving steadily and consistently from one success to another and holding every promise of future additional responsibilities. By design, it would seem, rather than by accident, he has managed to "marry" the two ruling passions of his life—the mountains and the army. At forty-two, Hunt—by his own standard—is too old for an "Everester," but his clear eye and complexion, steady hand, poise and quiet confidence all speak of perfect health and physical condition while his strength of will, as his performance on Everest shows, must at least equal that of Tenzing.

Like other great Everesters before him—Generals Bruce and Norton, and Colonel Howard-Bury—Hunt comes from an Indian Army background. He was born in India in 1910, where his father was a serving officer. (His father was killed in the 1914-1918 war.) Hunt had begun climbing in Switzerland before he went to Marlborough but here he came under the influence of a young master, E. G. H. Kempson, who was a passionate mountaineer and was later to be a member of Eric Shipton's reconnaissance party which went to Everest in 1935. (Other Old Malburians with the 1953 party were Dr. Michael Ward and Major C. G. Wylie.) Hunt continued climbing during his school holidays. At eighteen he passed first into Sandhurst, later to pass out first with the King's Gold Medal and the Anson Memorial Sword. He was commissioned to the King's Royal Rifle Corps then stationed at Lucknow. During the 1931 Civil Disobedience Campaign he played a role which might have come straight from Kipling's *Kim*. A natural linguist, he asked to be seconded to the Indian Police and although fair-haired and blue-eyed he wrapped himself in a "dhoti" and squatted in the Calcutta bazaar, talking and listening sympathetically to all he heard.

Hunt's first major Himalayan expedition came in 1935 when he accompanied James Waller's party to the Karakoram for an attempt to climb Peak K36. In 1937 he led a winter expedition through Sikkim to the Kangchenjunga *massif*, making an ascent to the Zemu Gap (19,000 feet) where he first found traces of the Abominable Snowman. On this expedition he was accompanied by his wife, Joy, (they have four daughters).

His climbing ability was put to good use during the war and in 1942 he was appointed Chief Instructor, under Commandant Frank Smythe, of the Commando Mountain and Snow Warfare School. Commandos I have talked to describe him as a hard taskmaster indeed, sometimes driving his men to the limit just to see how much they could stand, but they ungrudgingly admit that he never worked anyone harder than he was prepared to work himself.

Hunt returned to his regiment in 1943 and fought through North Africa and Italy. Here he was given command of the 11th Indian Infantry Brigade following which, his exploits in the mountains of Italy won him the DSO.

When asked to lead the 1953 Everest Expedition he was serving at H.Q. 1st Corps B.A.O.R. His leadership of the expedition will not only be remembered for meticulous planning and administration and the clockwork precision with which the program was carried out, but for the heroic part he, himself, played during the final stages of the climb. Nothing typifies Hunt's character better. He gave himself and two Sherpas the appalling task of carrying a camp from the South Col to 27,800 feet which was to be used as a final jumping off point by Hillary and Tenzing. On the South Col one of the Sherpas dropped out owing to altitude sickness, leaving the other—Da Namgyal—and Hunt, with what he modestly describes as "an unexpectedly heavy load." It consisted of the tent, food, fuel and their own oxygen equipment. Hunt, with the valves of his oxygen equipment frozen and working imperfectly, and Da Namgyal struggled up to 27,350 feet where they were forced to dump their loads. They also unstrapped their oxygen equipment leaving what remained in the bottles for the benefit of the climbers who were to follow. Thus, without oxygen they faced the descent. They reached the limit of exhaustion in the steep upper part of the couloir, above the South Col, now an agonizing ordeal which Hunt dismisses by merely saying that here they were both very tired and were taking great precautions to prevent a slip, "not entirely with success."

Hunt's truly remarkable feat in carrying an extra heavy load to such a height with little aid from oxygen on the way up, and none on the way down, entitles one to ask the question whether he, himself, might not have reached the summit had he had the same assistance he was prepared to give others. In my opinion he might well have done so, but he deliberately denied himself the chance, refusing to push himself forward in case he disrupt the harmony of the team. It was team spirit which Hunt wished above all to foster and preserve, as he wished, vainly as far as Asia was concerned, that the ascent of Everest should be recognized as a team victory.

What impressed me most on the occasion of his lecture was the simple language which Colonel Hunt chose to explain the involved problems relating to the climb to an audience who cannot have had much English between them.

Colonel Hunt began by posing himself a question (a good one as far as the Nepalese were concerned): "Why do we wish to climb Mount Everest—your mountain?" He continued: "This is a very difficult question to answer. It is an urge to find an answer to an unsolved problem. It is a challenge to our skill and experience. Mount Everest epitomizes this urge we have." Colonel Hunt then outlined his hopes of success: "We have been tremendously benefited by the experience of the past—this is the tenth expedition to be going to the mountain in thirty-two years—but in particular we shall benefit from the experiences of the Swiss expeditions of last year. We also have modest confidence in the preparations we have been making. Great thought, time and trouble has gone into producing and thinking out our equipment, which is the best of any so far used. We have a strong team with plenty of experience and very well knit together. We have confidence in our Sherpas and shall rely greatly on their team which will be led by Tenzing. (Shuffling of feet and applause.) We now have twenty high-altitude Sherpas, who will be completely equipped and we expect to recruit fourteen more at Namche Bazar for low altitude work who will be less well equipped." Colonel Hunt then introduced the British team by name (none were present). "We are bringing ten climbers; one doctor climber, one film cameraman and one doctor physiologist."

The party consisted of Colonel Hunt himself; Dr. R. C. Evans, F.R.C.S., aged thirty-four, "a brain surgeon and a famous climber"; Alan Gregory, forty, managing director of a Blackpool travel agency; Major C. G. Wiley, thirty-three, organizing Secretary of the Expedition, "A Gurkha Officer who speaks very fluent Gurkhali and will thus be a very useful linguist for us"; Dr. Michael Ward, twenty-eight, expedition physician and an experienced climber; Tom Bourdillon, twenty-nine, "a scientist who designs jet engines and has helped to perfect our oxygen apparatus"; M. H. Westmacott, twenty-eight, President of the Oxford University Mountaineering Club and now a statistician at the Rothampstead Experimental Station; George Band, twenty-four, President of Cambridge University Mountaineering Club, "rather young perhaps—we think the best age for Everest is between twenty-five and thirty-five—but he is possibly the finest climber in Britain today"; Edmund Hillary, thirty-four, ex-RNZAF pilot from New Zealand—"very tall, he is six feet four inches. He nows keeps bees and makes honey"; W. G. Lowe, twenty-eight, "He also comes from New Zealand where he is a schoolmaster"; C. W. F. Noyce, thirty-five, a schoolmaster (Charterhouse) with considerable Himalayan experience; Dr. L. G. C. Pugh, forty-three, physiologist, a long distance skier who competed in the 1936 Olympic Games; Tom Stobart, thirty-five, film camera-man and zoologist, who had accompanied expeditions in many parts of the world.

Colonel Hunt then stated the problems of the climb—altitude, magnitude and weather (which I have summarized in a subsequent chapter). He then gave us his tentative program: "We shall leave here on the tenth and eleventh of March for Namche Bazar and establish our first Base Camp for stores at Thyangboche monastery. There, we shall spend three weeks climbing in the surrounding mountains—but not on Everest—acclimatizing ourselves by going higher and higher first to 15,000 and 16,000 feet and then to 18,000 and possibly 20,000. This will get us strong and give us training with our equipment and practice in using oxygen. In the second or third week in April we shall move our Base Camp to under Mount Everest and finally up the mountain to 23,000 feet." Colonel Hunt concluded by saying: "We are not pessimists; but we must have fine weather when we need it."

As Hunt finished speaking Colonel Proud rose with the customary and purely formal remark, "Any questions?" At once there was a clamor from my Indian Colleagues on the Press bench: "What is the weight of your oxygen equipment?" "What's its endurance?" "How many camps are you going to make?" "Who's going to make the final bid?" and so on. Hunt struggled bravely for a question or two, then, realizing that this was an attempt to break the copyright, he appealed to Proud who rose and promptly applied the closure. I had not asked a single question, and as he was leaving the room Hunt took me in kindly fashion by the arm and said: "You realize, don't you, that I have not said anything here tonight which I have not already written in *The Times*?" I agreed at once, but this could not alter the fact that I now had a notebook full of direct quotations which I was now at liberty to use whenever the opportunity offered.

This meeting served to introduce me to a number of other Indian newspapermen notably Tribhuvan of *The Times of India* and Narendra Saksena of *The Hindustan Times.* I took an immediate liking to both. Saksena, or "Sax," and I became great friends and we were soon to agree to a mutual assistance pact which I never regretted. Sax had been educated in England and at the Dehra Dun School which is one of the finest establishments of its kind in India. He had also served in the Indian Army as a Signals Officer. Young and intelligent he was an all-round sportsman having shot his first tiger at sixteen and was a passionate follower of English cricket and no mean exponent of the game himself. Above all he was level-headed and scrupulously honest in his work, that is, he never touched a story which he did not firmly believe to be true at the time. This integrity never even failed him when Katmandu was swept with a tide of conflicting rumors as the progress of the expedition was reaching its climax. Sax had applied for work as a correspondent in Katmandu to be near his wife who was a doctor attached to the female wing of the local hospital.

An absentee at the meeting who was to become another good friend was Balram Tandon, also of *The Times of India.* Balram had a roving commission and was in the habit of making lone excursions into the Nepal countryside. This showed considerably more enterprise than most of the other Indian correspondents in Katmandu. He was now away on another of his missions, some of which lasted for weeks, but Sax assured me he would soon be back and would be invaluable in helping me to organize my own expedition.

The following noon all of us turned up on the lawn of the British Embassy for the promised cocktail party. Most of the expedition members had now arrived in the city but all had been so sternly warned of the penalties for breaching copyright that most of them shied away in horror whenever I approached them. A brave exception was burly Tom Bourdillon who actually introduced himself to me—we had not talked during our plane journey together—prefacing his remarks with a lighthearted: "I shall probably be shot if I am seen talking to you." Tom agreed with me at once that there was no sense in my stopping in Katmandu and that now I was there I would be foolish not to get out and see something of the mountains. He said he thought I should have no difficulty at all in getting to Namche Bazar and if I really wanted to, I might get quite a distance beyond. I explained my difficulties about boots and the lack of a tent and he comforted me by assuring me that as far as Namche I could have nothing better to wear than tennis shoes, but as the going was very rough I had better take at least two pairs. As regards the tent, he said if the worst came to the worst I could probably do without by sleeping in the villages. He did not advise this because his wife, who had accompanied him on a trip in the Sherpa district the previous year, had gone down with typhus after sleeping in one of the cottages. This reminded him that I had better get a typhus "shot" if I had not already had one. He also gave me many useful tips regarding what food was likely to be available if I intended to live largely off the land. All of this was good sound practical advice and later I put it to good effect.

Also at the party I met David Haye-Neave, second Secretary of the Embassy who became a very pleasant companion, and Jan Fletcher the wireless operator—an ex-naval Warrant Officer with whom I had also, at one time, served in the same Command. I no longer felt such an utter stranger in Katmandu.

The expedition land party, escorting its seven and a half tons of equipment, had now arrived at Thankot, at the head of the valley, after traversing the passes from Raxaul on the Indian frontier. They had been generously helped by the Indian Army who had transported much baggage along completed sections of the new Jeep road which sappers are now building between Bhimphedi and Thankot (the road was opened in autumn 1953) and again in the valley where Indian Army trucks were waiting to carry the equipment from Thankot to the Nepalese Army lines outside the town of Bhatgaon. Things were now moving at an increased pace, for only three days remained before the first section of the expedition was due to move off to Namche Bazar.

Returning to the hotel that evening I had a strange encounter. At the entrance the manager greeted me in a state of delighted agitation and announced that three "Dutchmen" had arrived. He then led me to the register where I read the names of two men and one woman, all New Zealanders (a pardonable mistake on the manager's part). The four of us met at dinner and they had a curious story to tell. Believing them to be guests of importance, for the net permitting entry to Nepal is still very fine, I had set the ball rolling by asking them how long they intended to stay in the country. To my astonishment they replied "twenty-four hours." My curiosity getting the better of me, I expressed surprise that they should take so much trouble to get visas—it is often a matter of many weeks—for such a short stay. It was their turn to be astonished. They had no idea visas were necessary; they firmly believed that Nepal was part of India. They had been on a tiger shooting excursion—with some success—but being also keen photographers they had been determined to get some pictures of the Himalaya. They had looked up the nearest big town to the mountains served by an airline and without further ado had climbed into a plane and come here. Apparently at the airfield there had been so much confusion attendant upon the arrival of further expedition members and their luggage, that they had walked through the barrier unchallenged and had pursued their innocent way to the hotel.

With some relish I told them they could consider themselves highly privileged people to be in a country which was still the most seclusive kingdom in the world yet unexplored by Europeans. They received this news partly with delight—for this was an adventure with which they could entertain their friends for years—and partly with horror at having unwittingly contravened the most rigid of regulations. We sat far into the night, they telling me of their tiger shooting adventures and I telling them as much as I could of Nepal, its magnificent temples and palaces, its wild rugged scenery and its charming people. The next morning their luck held. They rose early and climbed to the roof of the hotel to take their pictures. They found that the clouds which had hung over the valley since my arrival had lifted. The rich green undulating valley floor lay before them in all its enchanting beauty, the sunlight glinting from the gilded temple finials of Katmandu, Patan, and Bhatgaon and lighting up the slopes of the encircling mountains, while away to the north, in sharpest outline, was the whole stretch of the snow covered high Himalayas, with, no doubt, Everest visible away to the east. This I did not confirm, for at the time they were setting up their cameras, I was still soundly asleep below.

They left at noon, three ardent enthusiasts for Nepal and no one a wit the wiser for their coming.

That morning Saxsena, Harish, Roy and myself joined

forces, clambered into a taxi-Jeep and drove the ten miles out to Bhatgaon to view the expedition's rapidly growing mountain of baggage and equipment. The road skirts the airfield, then dips down to cross the river and passes through the village of Themi which is the valley's industrial center for the manufacture of glazed and unglazed earthenware pots, heaps of which stood outside every cottage door. A constant procession of coolies jogged in either direction along the side of the road loaded either with a single carrying basket on their backs, supported with a headband, or Chinese-style with a yoke across their shoulders from which a pannier was slung on either side. Weight alone seems of little concern to these men, and it is no uncommon sight to see a load such as a bag of rice being carried in one pannier and balanced by a heap of rocks or bricks in the other. Thus a double load is made out of one which, by a little extra trouble, could be carried as two halves.

This was the marriage season and we were constantly stopping to allow the passage of festive processions in the center of which were either a young girl prettily decked out with silks, ribbons and flowers, and carried in a canoe-shaped litter, or a solemn youth, hung with garlands and sitting uncomfortably on an apathetic but gaily caparisoned pony. Behind the girls the males of the family struggled with dowry chests, while each wedding party had music of some sort to add to the rejoicing.

At this season, across the fields and down the roads one might often hear the sounds of a dozen bands all performing at the same time. A single pipe and drum might be all the humbler families could afford, but the richer weddings might be accompanied by a full brass band, accommodated sometimes in an ancient car which teetered and groaned along in bottom gear while the blaring bells of the battered instruments projected from the windows and occasionally stuck out through the roof. Music, dancing and general jollification often continued throughout the night and in some cases festivities are continued nonstop for two or three days.

We located the expedition's supply dump on a lawn-like stretch of turf next to a huge artificial tank, or cistern which stands about half a mile from the main gates of Bhatgaon and where the citizens were either washing themselves or their clothes or drawing drinking water. As everyone was frantically busy accumulating the store dump, we drove on into Bhatgaon which, in my view is possibly the most impressive sight of the valley. The mass of its beautifully carved and wrought architecture is concentrated in the Darbar Square of which Landon (*Nepal,* vol. i) writes that it is "of those places of which the sight only will convince, for it contains a group of marvels hardly less splendid than that of the great square of Patan," (the third city of the valley—which has, however, suffered more damage by past conquest). Landon continues:

> Of them the most beautiful and best known is the golden door of the palace. As a work of art this is perhaps the most exquisitely designed and finished piece of gilded metalwork in all Asia. There is nothing in Lhasa or Peking that can rival this piece of superb craftsmanship. . . . To the right and to the left and in front of it are the walls of temples and palaces wonderfully enriched with moulding, knop and trellis, with deep-set carvings, with strutted roof imposed upon strutted roof, with plinths and pillars, and with windows of characteristically elongated lintels and sills, laden with incised pattern and arabesque. . . .
>
> Elsewhere in the city are many beautiful things. Of them the long wooden façade of the royal palace, a triumph of ornamental grating, bracket, strut, eave, and sill and the "five roofed temple" are perhaps the most conspicuous. [Both form part of the Darbar Square.] The latter [the temple]—which, by the way, is dedicated to an unknown god—is a fine example of the pagoda work of Nepal, and famous far beyond it as the

best example in the country of a terrace plinth of which the stairway is attended on either side by symbolic figures. In this case, there being four terraces and the lowest figures being set upon the ground, there are five pairs. These lower figures are of two famous heroes who are locally believed to be Jaya Malla and Phatta, two champions of a Bhatgaon Raja, each of whom is said to have had the strength of ten men. Above them are two elephants which were estimated to be ten times as strong as Jaya Malla and Phatta. The third pair are lions reputedly ten times as strong as the elephants. The fourth are sarduls or dragons, ten times as strong as the lions. The last and mightiest pair of all are the two "Tiger" and "Lion" goddesses Baghini and Singhini, whose strength is supernatural.

We spent some time in the square working out angles which would provide the most picturesque backgrounds for photographs when the expedition marched through (unfortunately they were to by-pass the square). Having my camera with me I took a number of shots chiefly to test the reaction of the local inhabitants to photography. I had thought there might be some objection; but this was by no means the case and there was no lack of willing posers. The only demur came when our rascally Jeep-driver, without my bidding, climbed the giant steps of the stone platform whereon stood a mighty bell, five feet in diameter, and slung beneath a curly-eaved canopy of tiles. He was speedily sent packing—it probably being feared he might sound the bell which might well have been heard in Katmandu. We then adjourned to a teashop where we drank innumerable cups of the sweet, soupy liquid offered us.

That afternoon a heavy thunderstorm broke over the valley—in fact a fine morning and a wet afternoon had been almost the rule since my arrival. Rain, even of the force which we generally experienced it, was not a major anxiety for the expedition, but it was a matter of some concern, for the water absorbed by baggage, canvas gear and cardboard containers appreciably adds to the total weight to be carried. Rain also renders the mountain paths greasy and more difficult, it encourages the emergence of such unpleasant things as leeches in the jungle patches which have to be traversed, and it adds to the chance of sickness among the coolies.

Under the supervision of Major Wylie and Dr. Evans, preparations for the move to Namche Bazar were completed at Bhatgaon on Monday the ninth of March. Once more we drove out there and I asked Wylie for permission to take some pictures, which he gave, adding that he had no instructions on the subject. I confess I was astonished at the vast mountain of material which had been assembled for the ascent—one of my Indian colleagues promptly dubbed the expedition the "expeditionary force." With a fairly practiced eye I made a rapid mental calculation that the "lift" would probably require about 500 coolies. (I was not so far out; I was working on the assumption that an average load would be 40 pounds. In fact loads were nearer 60 pounds and 350 odd coolies were needed.) I wondered, without making comment, how long the morals of a country where theft and petty crime were almost unknown—and its local economy—would withstand the impact of vast armies of coolies repeatedly marching through it. There were four major expeditions in Nepal in 1953.

Coolies are paid three shillings and sixpence (roughly half a dollar) for a day's work, out of which they are expected to find their own food and lodging along the route. Although the economy of Nepal is on a higher standard than that of Tibet, where the passage of a large expedition can strip a whole district of its food, the remoter villages are not normally accustomed to grow more grain than will suffice for their immediate needs and will tide them over the winter and spring. Good silver rupees were paid for this grain, but more than one headman has eyed an overflowing money chest ruefully and said: "You can't eat silver coin; all this does is to make my neighboring headmen jealous whose villages don't lie on the route."

Another evident source of corruption is the presents and the litter of locally valuable debris such as empty bottles and tins which an expedition liberally scatters in its wake. These give rise to disputes and jealousies with the result that the unsatisfied in a previously uncorrupted community may soon resort to filching what they have not been given or "won." (The inventive peasant living in primitive conditions can seemingly find a use for any piece of discarded rubbish. A proof of this is the fact that when I came to follow the route of the expedition to Everest I found not even as much as a thrown away empty matchbox to mark its passage. That is, until I reached an altitude where there were no longer any inhabitants, and where there was litter in plenty. I even picked up a package of dehydrated mushroom soup which had been left behind by last year's Swiss expedition and which proved very palatable.)

An urgent cause for anxiety for the authorities is that hundreds of foraging porters, passing from village to village, may spread disease—a serious matter in outlying districts where smallpox, typhus, cholera and even plague can occur in epidemic form.

A balancing factor, to the advantage of the government and to the distress of most expeditions, is that competition for the best Sherpas and porters (as the number of expeditions increases) has led to an almost 100 percent rise in their wages compared with prewar levels. But taking things all in all, I do not think it will be long before the government demand a substantial license fee before they permit the passage of future expeditions organized on a major scale.

The other point that I found for comment was that the expedition was apparently expected to climb the mountain on army rations. These were the standard "14 in 1," that is each container holds sufficient for fourteen men for one day—there being seven variations for each day in the week. The ascent of a giant like Everest is so far removed from the sport of mountaineering as most climbers know it, that many men invited to join an expedition have spoken jocularly of "being condemned to climb the monster." To be condemned to climb the monster on army "Compo" seemed to me, and no doubt would seem to most men who have existed on army fare for months on end, a particular refinement in the self-mortification of the flesh. The problem of food for high altitudes, where appetite is almost nonexistent, has never been satisfactorily solved and, owing to transport difficulties, may well never be. The earlier Everest expeditions had been provided with a Lucullan diet of palate-tickling delicacies—albeit all of them in tins. There are a number of objections to an exclusive diet of tinned foods. The obvious one is the weight of the tin, but apart from that it is questionable whether tins preserve the necessary nourishment to sustain one over a long period. The Shipton-Tilman school had introduced the basically carbohydrate diet, supplemented by dried meats, cheese and fresh provisions where they can be obtained. (The purchase of yak's milk, butter, eggs, chickens and a yak or sheep carcass makes no strain on local economy.) I prefer such a diet although I would carry a certain number of tins to add piquancy to special occasions.

On the food question Eric Shipton is worth hearing (*Upon That Mountain:* Hodder and Stoughton):

> There is no doubt that food embalmed in tins, however cunningly, lacks some essential quality, and when one is fed on nothing else one very soon becomes heartily sick of even the most elaborate delicacies. I believe that to be one of the reasons why we found it so hard to eat enough at high altitudes in 1933. That year I had been given the job of running the commissariat. At first everyone was loud in praise of the fare, and I was always having to emerge from the mess tent to open

another tin of this or that to satisfy rapacious appetites. Long before we had reached the Base Camp this enthusiasm had died down; before the expedition had run half its course the complaints against the food were bitter and endless, and to these I had lent strong support. Actually the quality of the tinned food could hardly have been improved; we had every conceivable variety—half a dozen different kinds of breakfast food, bacon, ham, beef, mutton, chicken, lobster, crab, salmon, herrings, cod-roes, asparagus, caviar, fois gras, smoked salmon, sausages, many kinds of cheese, a dozen varieties of biscuit, jam, marmalade, honey, treacle, tinned and preserved fruit galore, plain, nut-milk and fancy chocolates, sweet, toffee, tinned peas, beans, spaghetti—I cannot think of anything that we did not have. And it was supplied in such quantities that, rather than transport what was left all the way back from Base Camp we threw away scores of cases of provisions. And yet, one and all, we agreed that the food was wholly unsatisfying. It seemed to me that the conclusion was obvious—and it was amply confirmed by my subsequent experience. But it was by no means universally accepted, and the majority were inclined to blame the firms that had supplied the food.

In 1935 I went rather too far the other way; it was bad policy to force people who were quite unused to rough food to make such a sudden and complete break with their normal diet. Taken in moderation, tinned food undoubtedly has its uses, particularly when—as on Mount Everest—transport presents no particular problem. But it should be used to supplement fresh, salted or dried food, rather than as the main diet. A perfectly simple compromise is possible on an Everest expedition. If, for example, the party were kept on a diet of fresh food supplemented with untinned ham, bacon and cheese until it reached a point well beyond the Base Camp, such things as tinned brisket of beef and chickens' breasts would then provide a most welcome change of which people would not tire, at least during the critical weeks of the actual climb. I would dispense altogether with caviar, lobster, crab and the like. These are no doubt very delicious when eaten in the suitable surroundings, properly served, washed down with the appropriate wine and followed by a comfortable cigar; but I find that they lose all their charm when eaten as a mangled mess out of a battered tin on which someone has probably cut his finger.

The advantage of army rations is that it can be told at a glance exactly how much food will be required by any number of men over any given period; an oversimplification which can only be described as the easiest way out of a complicated problem. The disadvantages are that most of it is, indeed, tinned, and that even a seven day a week variation can become deadly monotonous. One soon finds out one's pet likes and dislikes with the final result that, in a unit where rigid self-control is not exercised, the routine is broken by ditching the "dislikes." Where the routine is strictly adhered to, men eventually begin to miss certain meals altogether. I have existed for long periods on both British and United States army rations and personally I find the American tastier, although the British is supposed to be more sustaining—at any rate for a British stomach. As far as I could judge from captured supplies the German army ration had much to commend it.

It is true that in this year's expedition the climbers switched to a superior ration (the army "assault ration") when they went really high and that in the end the "summiters" were given freedom of choice in making up their packages for the top, but the diet by no means suited everybody. This brings us back to the fact that at such altitudes, it is unlikely that a diet ever will be found which is satisfactory to all.

Returning to Katmandu I had a surprise which was to have some embarrassing consequences. The morning papers had arrived from India and I discovered that *The Statesman* of Calcutta and New Delhi who were subscribing to *The Times* syndication service for news of the Everest expedition, had also bought the rights to reproduce the dispatches, articles and pictures which I was sending to *The Daily Mail.* This put Harish Srivastava, *The Statesman*'s local correspondent, and me, in the curious position of being colleagues and rivals at the same time. In one edition considerable space had been given to my interview with Tenzing; it had, in fact, been thrown into undue prominence, for on that day the Indian newspaper carried no contribution from *The Times.* I was soon to learn what the expedition thought about the interview. Towards four o'clock I was just leaving the cable office when I met Colonel Hunt as he was coming out of the side gate of the Embassy compound. Colonel Hunt at once expressed his displeasure. He objected to the passage where Tenzing had stated he preferred Swiss or French expeditions to British (for this I could not blame him although, to be fair, I had quoted Tenzing's exact words) and he took particular exception to the additions which Harish had received from Tenzing on the morning after our original interview. He denied that any special conference had taken place on the evening we had mentioned. It would never occur to him to allow Tenzing to go to the top of Everest alone. There was no plan to establish eight camps up the mountain (some weeks later Colonel Hunt announced that it was to be an eight camp assault—but it was obvious that this plan had not yet been decided on when he was speaking to me). Hunt concluded: "If the weather is bad we may not even get up the Icefall." I was duly contrite and explained that it was no particular pleasure to me to accept news at second-hand but if the main actors in a drama which was, after all, of national interest, refused direct comment, there was no other course open to me. Hunt thought I should refrain from writing anything at all, but I pointed out that while this might satisfy *The Times* it was scarcely likely to please *The Daily Mail.* The temper of Colonel Hunt—an even tempered man if ever there was one—can hardly have been improved when, on arrival at the Post Office where he had been summoned to answer a telephone call from London, he found that the call was not from the Himalayan Committee, or *The Times* as he must have imagined, but from my rival newspaper *The Daily Express*.

It was small consolation for me that Hunt, in his anxiety to correct my interview, had given me a few more quotable lines which would make another story even if it conflicted with what I had already sent. Looking back over one week's work I gave myself nil marks for diplomacy. A week ago it might be said that I was on friendly terms with the expedition so long as certain subjects were avoided. Now we were barely on speaking terms, which was a much more serious state of affairs for me. I must make it quite clear that, all along, the last thing I wished to do was to be a nuisance to the expedition in any way and I particularly did not wish my presence to increase their work or anxieties. I can truthfully say that no one wished more sincerely for their success than I did. The same can hardly be said for some of my Indian colleagues. In the first place it would be foolish to imagine that Britain—or any other Western power—enjoys any particular popularity in Asia (Nepal is a happy exception, but I am not at the moment discussing the Nepalese). In the second place, for Indian newspapermen, Katmandu is not a particularly productive news center. Good stories are few and far between and it is not too easy to make ends meet. A major international expedition, in given circumstances, can be a gold mine yielding pay increases and promotion. The Swiss and French had proved amiable, affable and cooperative as later, in overwhelming measure, were the Japanese. The British were aloof, abrupt in refusing to answer questions and inconsistent in later requesting newspapermen not to take pictures while permitting other British and American civilians to do so. All this rankled. From that very first week, in the Indian mind,

Tenzing began to emerge as the real hero of the expedition and it was not long before, in guest house and teahouse, the tip was being freely given "Tenzing to beat the British."

If the embassy had had its wits about it, it would have noted this trend which was to lead to the most unfortunate political complications—for the Communists were not slow to sense the rift in the lute and exploit it—and a quiet word to Colonel Hunt might have remedied matters. A brief communiqué reporting progress issued from time to time would probably have halted the trend and could scarcely have affected *The Times* whose right to the magnificent personal adventure stories and action pictures to be obtained on Everest itself was never in dispute. The embassy chose to ignore the trend and even aggravated it by becoming more jealous of expedition news than the members themselves.

My own temper that afternoon was not improved by my first open dispute with the Katmandu taxi-owning fraternity. These gentlemen are a law unto themselves. There are a certain number of Jeeps, all nearly run into the ground and a number of heroic veterans which have survived dismemberment, transport over the mountain on coolies' backs and reassembly by none too expert hands in the valley. The standard of driving is appalling, the roads outside the city shocking, spare parts unobtainable and service and maintenance nonexistent. Probably the best method of insuring a safe passage from point to point is to hire the oldest and slowest vehicle in the rank knowing full well that though it may collapse of its own weight, it will never again proceed fast enough to be a menace either to oneself, to a pedestrian or to a sacred cow, the killing of one of which still nominally incurs the death penalty.

None of the above is written in a spirit of criticism for the mere fact that a taxi can be obtained high in the heart of the Himalaya can never cease to be a source of wonderment to me. What I would endeavor to improve is the morals of the drivers. When I was in the valley, temporary repairs to the electric ropeway had necessitated a corresponding temporary introduction of gasoline rationing. Gasoline coupons could be obtained readily by all who had legitimate business. There were two systems of hiring a taxi. Either the passenger paid an exorbitant "all in" amount which included gasoline supplied by the driver, or the passenger paid half that amount and produced his own coupons and paid for the gasoline. Theoretically this alternative was the cheaper, especially as the drivers would wail that they themselves could only obtain gasoline at blackmarket prices. In practice both methods were equally costly for Jeeps which were capable of a comfortable ten or twelve miles a gallon on driver's gasoline would suddenly be found to be capable of only three or four miles a gallon when passenger's gasoline was used. A frantically flourished dip stick had to be taken as proof of this voracious appetite—leaving the crestfallen passenger to draw the obvious conclusion that as soon as his back was turned his Jeep was whisked round a corner and drained of most of its fuel—which would then be presumably resold to him against the surrender of more coupons.

Whichever the system the passenger adopted both grew daily more expensive on the "we'll just see how much the poor mug will stand" principle. Soon or later the poor mug, according to his means, would cry "Enough!" and dismiss his driver with abuse and acrimony. The driver would accept this development philosophically and wait at the back of the rank until those higher up the line had proved themselves bigger rogues than himself.

That afternoon saw my own patience exhausted. I had taken every step open to me to reduce my transport bill and instead of halving itself, as I had a right to expect, it was doing exactly the opposite. Saksena, who had manfully accompanied me to the hotel—another storm had broken and the rain poured over us in sheets as we slithered up the road from the city—proved of little help. Whatever may be the relations between Britain and India and Britain and Nepal, those between India and Nepal remain delicate. Because of this the Indian Ambassador, Mr. B. K. Gokhale, had very wisely advised all Indians resident in the capital on no account to become involved in altercations with the local inhabitants. Sax therefore stood glumly by while I rated the driver, paid him what he demanded, and ordered him never to come near me again. (He was soon back and gratefully accepted.) When the victorious expedition re-entered Katmandu they were presented with an illuminated address by the Taxi-owners Union. I often wondered whether anyone took the trouble to translate this address. It might well be found that it was in reality a vote of thanks addressed to the Press corps which by that time had assembled in force. Certainly in the short time we were there we must have presented the members of the union with enough money to buy new vehicles all round. When affairs reached their climax anything up to ten pounds sterling per day was asked and given a rate which must have worked out at something like £1 per tortuous mile. I may add that the Indian correspondents had long since taken to bicycles, except for the most pressing engagements.

The next morning all of us were out early at Bhatgaon to see the first half of the expedition off on its way to Namche Bazar. One could not say "bright and early" for it was a dull day, low cotton wool clouds shrouding the valley and barely clearing the foothills of the encircling mountains. By 7 A.M. long straggling lines of porters with their carrying baskets were squatting in rows on the turf beside the piles of equipment and stores waiting their turn to be signed on by Major Wylie. Dr. Evans and Tenzing were much in evidence making up loads and checking the weight of each to as near sixty pounds as possible on a spring balance hung on an improvised bamboo frame. As soon as this work was completed Wylie began a pay parade for the Sherpas and those of their womenfolk who had been engaged as temporary carriers. Each Sherpa received an advance of thirty rupees, bending low as the silver was placed in their two palms by Tenzing and then permitting his thumb to be dipped in red ink and pressed on to Wylie's account book by way of receipt.

At eleven o'clock the expedition had assembled in force and Mr. Summerhayes, Colonel Proud, Haye-Neave and a number of American officials of the Point Four program and their families arrived to join forces with Nepalese and Indian dignitaries in saying farewell to the members. All this time I had been dodging among the dwindling piles of luggage and the groups of porters and Sherpas helping each other to adjust their loads, with my camera, for I wanted a good informal portrait of each of the members. This was by no means easy to achieve for some members—Hillary, Lowe and Gregory in particular—were "camera-shy," and others were far too busily occupied to pose for photographs.

As the preparations neared their end, Colonel Hunt drew the Press aside and asked our indulgence to enable their official photographer—Gregory—to take a group photograph without our presence. One could not well refuse this request—as a consolation prize Colonel Hunt laughingly agreed to allow me to take a picture of himself—but it seemed a scarcely necessary one for no restrictions as regards photography were placed on civilians other than pressmen and I have no doubt that pictures taken by, say, the Americans, would have been available to us if we had asked for them later. The request, which had seemed harmless enough at the time, was described as "discourteous" in the Indian press.

At 11:30, an hour after the scheduled time, whistles were blown, Tenzing marshaled the straggling porters into some sort of line and the first half of the expedition moved off headed by Dr. Charles Evans and with Tenzing as porter boss bringing up the rear. The day's march was to be as far as Banepa, a distance of about five miles over easy country, except for one short climb just beyond the town of Banepa at the eastern extremity of the valley. To my distress the porters by-passed the main Darbar Square of Bhatgaon but by pounding on ahead of them I managed to get a not entirely contemptible shot of them as they wound down a picturesque side street.

The next day, which saw the departure of the second half of the expedition was largely a repetition of the first. Ambassador Summerhayes, clad in knickerbockers and Tyrolean hat, arrived bringing Colonel Hunt in the embassy car and after satisfying themselves that all was well they drove on the remaining miles to Banepa.

The expedition had proved a lucky break for seven sepoys on home leave from Major Wylie's regiment, the 6th Gurkhas, now serving in Malaya. The men were granted an extra four weeks' leave on expedition pay to escort the expedition's cash boxes and the "avalanche gun" (an adapted three inch mortar) and ammunition, up to the first base camp.

Soon all the porters were on their feet and moving, the rear this time being brought up by Major Wylie, and Drs. Ward and Pugh. I watched them go with some emotion. Uppermost in my heart was somewhat naturally, a schoolboyish yearning to be one of that gallant band—an accepted member not merely a "parasite" as I was. Then professionally I felt dismay that my "story" was literally vanishing before my eyes. Only by acting immediately and energetically could I ever hope to catch up with it. As a matter of fact I had already made my plans. I was booked to leave that day on the noon plane for Calcutta.

CHAPTER V

MY OWN PREPARATIONS

As I HAD an hour or two to spare I decided to call on Colonel Proud and inform him of my plans. It proved an unwise decision, for where Colonel Hunt had been aggrieved over my Tenzing interview Colonel Proud chose to be indignant. From his attitude I might have thought he expected that at any moment a hostile crowd would arrive and stone the embassy windows. There were a good deal of unpleasant variations on a central theme—an accusation of "bad taste." This I was not prepared to accept, for although there may be no accounting for tastes, the truth is seldom unpalatable to an unprejudiced person. In this case exception was only taken to those parts of the interview I had heard from Tenzing's own lips. My "sin," if such it was, lay in the fact that I had reported accurately the simple opinion of an honest man. Guile and deceit are the last two vices of which Tenzing could ever possibly be accused. But the Colonel and I made no progress whatsoever towards reconciling our views and it was not long before he said that although at first he had been inclined to help me, I could no longer expect any help from him in reaching Everest. As I had been received in such kindly fashion by the Nepalese, this was no longer such a hard blow as it might have been a week before. I cannot help adding that I left with the impression that the embassy—regarding me as an embarrassment whatever I did or wrote—had been happy to find an excuse to wash its hands of me. How completely I had been officially cast into the wilderness I did not discover until later when my wife informed me that letters which she had sent me from Egypt marked "C/o British Embassy," had been returned to her inscribed "Has left the country," which the author responsible must have known to be palpably untrue. So it was with a "Heigh ho!" and the feeling of another bridge burned behind me that I climbed aboard the aircraft to Calcutta, burdened with a story of the day's events which I had not yet written, and a good deal of undeveloped film. Captain Ravi Randawa, who vows he is passionately fond of mountain flying, was again at the controls. We had just got over the "hump" and I was offering up a silent prayer of thanks, when he poked his jovial, bearded face into the cabin and announced that as one fuel pump was out of action we would not be flying farther than Patna that day. Passengers who wished to proceed by train might do so. As this meant arriving in the early hours of the morning in Calcutta this was no good to me, for I still had my story to file. I therefore elected to spend the night at Patna and travel on by plane the next day. No one stays a night in Patna if they can possibly avoid it, for although it is the capital of Bihar Province it has yet to witness the establishment of a first-class hotel. The building I was driven to was in an advanced state of disrepair and was in every way a depressing comedown even after that haunted castle, the Nepal Hotel. The air of the plains was hot and steaming after the hills and mosquitoes were so thick one had almost to brush them aside before entering one's room. By the time I had finished my story—sustained by two bottles of bootleg beer, for it had been a long day—I was ferociously bitten.

I was late for supper which was a scratch meal and not a particularly appetizing one, but my gloom was relieved when I noted a British couple sitting at a neighboring table. There was something familiar to me about the man, who was also glancing at me as if he recognized me. We were soon in conversation and then, of course, I remembered—they were the MacMillans. He and I had met in 1950, in Pusan, during the hectic days when North Korean troops were pouring down the peninsula towards the port. Employed by the Public Works Department, he had there been erecting temporary buildings to accommodate what remained of the British staff who had had to evacuate the Legation in Seoul. Now, with his wife and their son John, he was on his way to Katmandu to supervise the building of a new British Embassy (the present building will shortly be taken over by the Indians). Some queer quirk of fate had decided that we should not meet in Piccadilly, or Times Square, or on the terrace of the now defunct Shepheard's Hotel in Cairo—the three places where all travelers are, or were, supposed to meet at some time in their lives—but in two of the remotest places either of us had ever been to. MacMillan prudently had a flask with him—Patna being nominally "dry"—and again what had promised to be a dismal evening was retrieved with good conversation and reminiscences of our many mutual friends. We said farewell at the airport the next morning and were very shortly to meet again.

In the meantime, the irrepressible Ravi had repaired his plane and as I was the sole passenger remaining, he flew me down in solitary state to Calcutta.

The heat and humidity in Calcutta was terrific, it was an unusually hot summer, and the process of passing my films through Customs and freighting them off to London was a long and laborious one. Films are tricky things to ship at any time, for each has to be in a fireproof metal container and Customs officials the world over are chary about letting undeveloped films go out of their countries, particularly when it is acknowledged they come from a touchy frontier district. Here, the words "Everest expedition" proved the magical means for insuring the indulgence of the officials even if they did not speed up the process of form filling, rubber-stamping and signature appending. Together with the fact that I motored out again to Dum Dum airport to see the films safely on a London-bound plane, this occupied me for five hours, so that when I finally arrived that evening at Spence's Hotel I was sweat-soaked and exhausted. Four days later—it would have been three days had not a Sunday intervened—the pictures occupied the whole of the back page of *The Daily Mail.*

The next day being a Friday, and a public holiday, there was little I could do, but the following morning I at once endeavored to set my affairs in order. My first appeal was to the Himalayan Club. The club had helped me most generously over a previous expedition I had made in 1948 and I feel they will not mind it being put on record that their help and advice is never refused the bona fide traveler in the Himalaya even though he be a nonmember. What I required was a tent—a lightweight one—and a good Sherpa or two (the most reliable of these carry a Himalayan Club service book containing their past record and the comments, favorable or otherwise, of their successive masters). This time I drew blank and quite understandably so. Apologetically Crawford of the Himalayan Club informed me at once that the year was seeing so many Himalayan expeditions of all categories that the club's store cupboards had long since been bare. The Sherpa situation might well be no better for there had been such a run on the Sherpa community that it was doubtful whether any experienced men remained. This could only be ascertained by reference to Darjeeling which would require three or four days.

As regards the tent, in my helplessness I turned to Darrell MacMahon, the very able chief reporter of *The Times of India,* another old friend and I use the word in its truest sense. In 1948, when I had stupidly broken a collarbone and it seemed that I should have to abandon my expedition before it had begun, Darrell had collected all my gear together and personally escorted it up to the foothills of northern Assam thus allowing me two valuable extra weeks for my injury to heal. But our combined efforts failed to produce a tent. We searched from bazar to brustee, to fashionable Chowringhee, but never a tent did we find unless it be an affair designed to be carried by an elephant. Tents of the kind I desired were to be had in India—but at Cawnpore—so we flashed off an urgent cable and then sat down to wait. Another delay occurred over the matter of a typhus inoculation. I had had so many during the war that it had never entered my mind that typhus serum might not be obtainable in India. Such is the case; it was possible some might be found, but not immediately. It seemed everything I touched entailed a delay of four days or so, and I was getting anxious. I had planned to spend only two days in Calcutta, and that included the purchase of further stores and all sorts of essential camp paraphernalia beside the tent. Now here was I becalmed, while the expedition was passing steadily out of reach, no doubt increasing the length of each day's march towards Everest as it swung into form.

During this doldrums period a request came from London for an Everest "curtain-raiser." This is what I wrote (*Daily Mail,* March 19, 1953: "It's a Race for Life on Top of Everest"):

"The man who aspires to climb Mount Everest must contend

with three major problems—magnitude, altitude, the weather. The sheer size of the mountain is its first defense. It dwarfs the Swiss Alps just as the Alps dwarf the peaks of Snowdonia. Compared with Switzerland its technical difficulties and obstacles are magnified to such an extent that experienced mountaineers viewing them for the first time have confessed themselves appalled. Unlike Swiss peaks most of which, by using permanently established huts, can be climbed up and down in a day, it is impossible to "rush" Everest in even a few days. Any expedition must be a carefully planned siege, gradually pushing itself forward and upward, establishing camps as it goes (as many as eight may be needed), and, above all, insuring the safety of its lines of retreat.

"This leads to a snowballing process in the porter train—porters to carry food and shelter for porters carrying the expedition's equipment and so on—until finally it is estimated that to place two men near the 28,000 foot mark, ready for a dash for the summit, food and accommodation for nearly twenty men (it proved to be more) will have to be provided at about 23,000 feet.

"The magnitude of Everest leads to altitude problems. If you or I were suddenly transported to the summit (29,002 feet) we should be dead in 90 seconds. (On April 15, 1875—three aeronauts, Crocé Spinelli, Gaston Tissandier, and Georges Sivel, set out to explore the upper layers of the atmosphere on the balloon *Zenith,* reaching a height of 27,000 feet. Tissandier, as they came down, emerged from a deep coma to find his two friends dead.) We should last approximately 12 minutes at 25,000 feet and a quarter of an hour at 23,000 feet. But one of the most valuable lessons learned by previous expeditions is that by taking heights gradually man is capable of prodigious feats of acclimatization and adaptation to lack of oxygen in the upper air.

"In 1787, when de Saussure led a party of twenty to the

top of Mont Blanc, they reported themselves reeling and staggering like drunken men. It was believed for some years that Mont Blanc's 16,000 feet was near the limit of man's capacity for surviving in rarefied air. But we now know that hundreds of thousands of Tibetans live almost their entire lives at this height, and think little of carrying loads over 19,000 foot passes, and, above all we have the records of former Everest climbs to study. Three times climbers have bivouacked for the night at more than 27,000 feet, and last year the Swiss Raymond Lambert, together with Sherpa Tenzing Norkey actually spent a night near the 28,000 foot mark, though both admitted they were more dead than alive at the end of it.

"However, it appears to be established that properly acclimatized man can survive for weeks at 23,000 feet, without his physical condition deteriorating and this Colonel Hunt, leader of this year's expedition, intends to do, waiting for a favorable opportunity to push his final assault parties forward to the summit.

"Above 23,000 feet the effect of lack of oxygen on a man's body becomes increasingly marked. His muscles waste, he suffers complete loss of appetite—he can no longer sleep. Mentally he is overcome by deadly lethargy and suffers a decreasing sense of judgment which can endanger both himself and his party.

"His upward progress therefore becomes a race between his waning capacities and the task in hand. Quite apart from weather conditions, speed becomes an important factor.

"It is to try to boost this essential speed in the last phase that this year's expedition will again be carrying oxygen equipment. This is better than anything so far devised, and weighs no more than 28 lbs. But there are still doubts whether this additional burden on a man's back will compensate for the relief it is likely to give his lungs. Mountaineers are divided both on the benefits of oxygen and the ethics of using it. Purists say that when a man needs the artificial aid of oxygen he has reached a point where he can go no farther and must concede victory to the mountain. Members of the oxygen school feel that while it may be preferable to climb a mountain without oxygen it is better to climb with it than not at all. (I might have added here that a chief objection of the non-oxygenists is that a successful ascent of Everest with oxygen will only set the ball rolling for a whole series of attempts without it. Personally I think this is an inevitable development just as it is inevitable that some day we shall have to acclaim the first *woman* to ascend the mountain.)

"The remaining great factor vitally affecting Everest attempts, and causing the utter defeat of at least two of them, is the weather. Except for freak conditions, Everest is only climbable towards the end of the latter half of May. (This may not be strictly true. Some climbers believe that the post-monsoon period in the autumn may provide a possible alternative, but a majority of experts consider that cold would be too intense and winds too fierce at this time.)

"For most of the winter season bitingly cold northwest winds sweep the mountain so ferociously that no man could climb it and live. The arrival of the southeastern monsoon, generally in early June, nullifies this condition, but it deposits a blanket of snow which fails to consolidate at that altitude and leaves the rocks of the summit technically very difficult and desperately dangerous.

"It has, however, been noticed in some years a lull occurs between the winter wind, which sweeps the summit clear of snow, and the onset of the summer monsoon. This lull may last as long as two weeks—or it may never occur at all.

"It is, however, Colonel Hunt's only hope. To take advantage of it he must have his main party firmly established and acclimatized at 23,000 feet by mid-May. Then as a break in the weather presents itself, he may launch his assault parties, probably in successive pairs, up the last 6000 feet. The problem of who shall have the ultimate honor of reaching the top can only be decided at the time. Given equal climbing ability, it will depend entirely on physical condition for high altitude men can become far more affected by lethargy than boxers gone stale. This lethargy is difficult to shake off, for between spells of lung-bursting activity they may have to spend days in sleeping bags waiting for a gale to blow itself out. (Eric Shipton describes bed sores, both physical and mental, as a little known but very real 'occupational disease' among mountaineers.)

"This expedition has the immeasurable benefit of being built on a pyramid of experience created by all previous expeditions. But it will still need a most generous portion of good fortune. As Hugh Ruttledge, one of the greatest of Everest experts, wrote: 'When we can synchronize four consecutive days of fine weather with the perfect simultaneous acclimatization and training of six men, possibly two climbers will reach the summit.'

"To this opinion Sir Francis Younghusband, father of a number of Everest attempts, comments: 'This is a rather too nicely calculated estimate, for it is quite certain that six perfectly trained and acclimatized climbers never will meet with four perfect days on Everest, and at that rate the mountain never will be climbed.'

"But Ruttledge himself is sure it will be. So there must be a flaw somewhere."

I need hardly add that most of the above article—which still seems to stand up pretty well—was based on notes I had taken during Colonel Hunt's lecture in Katmandu.

Towards the middle of the week I began to hear the answers to a number of personal questions. Darjeeling replied that all Sherpas on their books had already been engaged by other expeditions. This applied to all experienced men and it was such a man I required. I did not need to be told that an untried, unknown Sherpa might prove worse than useless, for most Sherpas have sweet wills of their own and do not take readily to discipline. Darjeeling added that there was still a chance I might pick up a Sherpa in Katmandu. The "close" season for climbing was still hardly over and during this period some Sherpas make pilgrimages down into the valley to satisfy their spiritual needs at the great Buddhist shrine of Bodnath, which stands a few miles from Katmandu. My last hope for a Sherpa therefore rested in Nepal.

Typhus serum proved completely unobtainable so I shrugged my unpunctured shoulders and decided to do without it.

A cable arrived—somewhat tardily—from Cawnpore saying that while mountain tents were made there, there were none in stock. One could be made to order but it would take a fortnight. This was far too long, so I promptly canceled it. Once more Darrell MacMahon and I set out on a tour of the bazaars and at last, in a corner of a go-down in a remote and insalubrious bustee, we met with some success. Army surplus tarpaulins were sold here and apparently, at some time, in response to an order which was never fulfilled, someone had started to make a tent. It was an impressionistic piece of architecture, built to no particular design but faintly resembling the "cottage" type tent. And it was only half completed. This last defect, the owner explained, was a matter of no importance, as he once demonstrated. He clapped his hands, and while Darrell and I sat down on a pile of sacks, a company of needlemen descended on the tent and finished it before our eyes. The fabric was probably light enough to satisfy the most exacting of the lightweight specialists but we had yet to find the complementary poles. I had wanted something of the jointed bamboo type, but all that could be produced were two massive posts solid enough to support a billiard table. A little carpentry reduced the poles to two sections each and the addition of a cumbersome and rather insecure nut and bolt system enabled each pole to be reunited as a single imperfect whole. It looked, as Darrell remarked, a very *collapsible* sort of tent. But it did place me a step nearer Everest.

We were about to leave when the owner, who had been rummaging about behind a mound of rotting canvas—scattering rats in all directions—announced that he might have something else to interest us. He did, for his researches finally brought to light a pile of one-man tents of the U. S. Army "Ranger" type. These were pretty far gone in all conscience, for they had been made by an American toy firm in 1943 and for most of the years since must have lain in the bustee exposed not only to the rats, but to the ravages of one of the dampest atmospheres in the world. Many of them came apart in our hands as we dragged on them, but fairly low down in the pile we came upon one which was still in *comparatively* —I stress the word—good condition. True, the sides had shrunk so that later the snow was to whistle in underneath them, and there were holes in the roof through which one could almost tell the time by the stars, but mercifully as it turned out, I decided to purchase it as well. Not even the owner had enough face to ask much for it. It proved its worth ten times over and I salute the makers.

We now set about collecting the remaining necessary camp gear. It was again an appallingly hot and sticky afternoon—almost too hot to think, and after the first half hour all I had in my hands was a fine spring jackknife which I had bought for sentimental reasons for it was obviously an antique relic of the windjammer days. By chance, however, a turn round the next corner brought us to another area of the bazaar devoted to the sale of army surplus goods and here our purchases came thick and fast—aluminum cookings pots, pans and plates, a kettle, a huge mug, forks and spoons, padlocks I never used, a hurricane lamp and two canvas buckets one of which was later discovered to have a nest of lice in it. All this and a good deal more we stowed into some old army kit bags. I was now ready for Everest and I admit, when I inspected my kit, I felt more like a clown than a climber. Early the next morning, before the break of dawn, I returned to Katmandu, once more piloted by Randawa—it was my good fortune that right up to my last flight from Nepal, by pure chance, he always happened to be at the controls.

It was now March 19, I had lost a full week, and the expedition with a full eight days' marching behind them must be over halfway to Everest. Yet there was still much for me to do before I could leave Katmandu. Apart from Sherpa hunting, coolies had to be engaged, my bank notes had to be changed into silver coin, provisions had to be bought for a minimum of six weeks, and beyond all this a host of other minor preparations had to be made.

Back at the Nepal Hotel I found I had company. Some prominent guests had arrived from India and were now occupying my former apartments. On a lower floor I found Arthur Hutchinson of *The Times*. "Hutch" had been whisked up to Katmandu as a countermove to my own activities, but hardly had he arrived when he had the misfortune to go down with glandular fever and he was now miserably bedridden. Although we were competing against each other we talked the same language—namely Press "shop"—and we could offer each other some company.

The next day, being Friday and the Hindu sabbath, was again a dead loss for me. The next morning I had a long conference with Saksena. I had decided to ask him to act as "backstop" for me during my absence from Katmandu. It was essential to have some man at base in case I ran out of money or supplies and to handle my dispatches when they arrived by runner. Normally I should have offered the job to Harish Srivastava, as Hutch would have done in similar circumstances, but as his newspaper was now linked to both *The Times* and my own it was impossible—as it would have been unfair—to ask him to serve two enemy camps simultaneously, and he thus fell between two stools. I was much relieved when Sax accepted my offer and he at once began to knock some sense into my arrangements. Together that evening we visited the Buddhist colony at Bodnath where we hoped to find my Sherpa.

At Bodnath, the immense and splendid stupa is entirely surrounded by a circle of colonists' dwellings, each containing numerous tiny cells which provide shelter and solace for the traveler. The base of the great white dome of the stupa is itself surrounded by hundreds of prayer wheels which spin almost continuously as they are stroked by passers-by. Surmounting the dome is a square white plinth upon which are painted four pairs of strangely arresting eyes, one pair staring with formidable penetration out over the valley to all the cardinal points of the compass. As Perceval Landon says (*Nepal,* vol.i), "scarcely less questioning is the '?' which stands where the nose should be." He would be foolish indeed who would hope to sin within range of the eyes and escape detection. The plinth itself is surmounted by a four-sided gilded pyramid which leads in steps to the base of an immense gilded umbrella. From the topmost point—the ferrule of the umbrella—streamers fully one hundred yards long and each hung with scores of fluttering prayer flags, lead down in every direction to the roofs of the circular row of dwelling houses after the manner of the ribbons of a maypole. Links between Bodnath and Lhasa are still strong and besides Sherpas Bodnath still receives many pilgrims from Tibet, in spite of the Chinese Communist occupation of that country.

Students of comparative folklore may be interested in one of the legends concerning the foundation of the Bodnath shrine as related by Landon (quoting Waddell's *Lamaism*):

> A little girl named Kang-ma, of supernatural birth, having stolen a few flowers in Indra's heaven, was rather rigorously punished by being reborn on earth as the daughter of a swine-herd in the valley. She married, and being left a widow with four children, she maintained herself and them as a goosegirl. Having accumulated much wealth in this unlikely way, she was seized with the desire to build a noble temple in honor of the Buddha Amitabha. So she went to the king and asked him for as much ground as a hide would cover. The king replied, "Jarung," which is equivalent to "Can do." So, using the conventional trick, she cut the hide into thin strips and of them made a leathern cord. Stretching this out in the form of a square, she claimed and, in spite of local jealousy, was allowed, the land, whereon she began to build Bodnath.

In the light of the dying sun, Sax and I found the Chief Lama seated cross-legged on a kitchen chair outside his dwelling. As was to be expected he proved a singularly enlightened and intelligent man who spoke more than a little English and, who, in forbidding us to take off our shoes, displayed a liberality of view which did not, apparently, obtain in Landon's day. As soon as he heard of our mission he sent off a number of youths to scour the surrounding buildings which serve much the same purpose as those of a university quadrangle. While this search was proceeding he apologized for his lack of knowledge of the current affairs of the hostel explaining that he had just returned from a pilgrimage to Tibet. With a shy smile, as if confessing a minor peccadillo, he told us that as his legs were no longer as strong as they had been he had used an airplane for the stages to and from Calcutta. Colleagues of an eminence equaling his own would no doubt consider such an action to be daringly sophisticated.

In fact "sophistication" was the last word one could apply to this benign character who gave one an overwhelming impression of benevolence and desire to be of service. Unfortunately, to the Chief Lama's distress, the search for a Sherpa proved unavailing. We did, however, pick up the incidental intelligence that a Japanese expedition which had arrived in the city on its way to attempt the 27,000 foot peak of Manaslu to the west of Everest, had ordered seventeen Sherpas. It was rumored that they would no longer require so many and might possibly have one or two to spare. Returning into the city we were suddenly hailed from the roadside by Balram Tandon the mercurial Marco Polo of the local Indian press corps. In an old stained battle dress and an equally ancient balaclava he looked every inch the experienced traveler, and, indeed, by sleeping in any hut he could find and foraging for food as he went he traveled a good deal lighter than ever I should have cared to have done. This time he had just returned from a long trek through the Terai. I took an immediate liking to Balram who was an old school friend of Sax's. He was small in stature but a bundle of energy, merry of eye and quick of wit. His sound judgment equaled that of Sax, and above all he had a limitless fund of good advice to give me concerning my own journey.

The next morning the three of us called on the Japanese who were lodging in an empty house next to the former royal palace in the heart of the city. While the British had remained aloof behind the embassy walls, the Japs proved to be "at home" at all times, were all bows and smiles and invariably presented guests with a jointly engraved visiting card which was a collector's piece. A notice on the door requested guests to observe that visiting hours were between the hours of three and five, but neither the guests nor the Japs ever paid any attention to this. Kit inspection was invited and it looked remarkably efficient to me—needless to say all was Japanese made. The Japanese leader greeted me very warmly and questioned me closely, and at length, about the British Expedition and its gear. He was particularly curious about our oxygen apparatus, about which I knew nothing—but he astonished me by saying that their own oxygen apparatus weighed no more than ten pounds—if I understood Colonel Hunt aright this being less than half the weight of the British. On the face of it, as the value of oxygen apparatus at high altitudes is largely governed by the additional weight a man has to carry, it would seem that the Japs would score heavily. But the Japanese leader—whose name I have unfortunately forgotten—added that he was dubious; he had been told by experts in Calcutta that his bottles were too lightly constructed and might burst and he added, rightly, that it was better to err on the side of safety, for a failure at extreme height could obviously be lethal. We were then joined by the expedition's doctor. He also asked me a large number of questions relating to physiological matters which I found very difficult to answer. His especial interest was the height of members of the British team. When I told him that Hillary was 6 ft. 4 in. in height and at least four other members of the team—Band, Stobart, Noyce and Wylie—must also be six footers, he gasped with astonishment. With apologies to me, for I stand as high as Hillary, he told me that current opinion in Japan was that tall men were no good on high mountains, and for that reason they had selected small men for their own team. (The fact that the British climbed Everest whereas the Japs failed to climb Manaslu is, I feel, of little significance in this respect!) Talk then turned to inoculations and when the doctor heard I was still lacking an anti-typhus "shot" he seized my arm and inoculated me on the spot. We had some difficulty over the correct translation of "typhus" and "typhoid" but as I subsequently caught neither I consider myself well served.

Only over the matter of the Sherpas did we draw blank. The Japs had, indeed, cut down their own Sherpa team to fourteen men, but the three "rejects" had promptly been engaged by the British Embassy for a third British party which was shortly to leave for Everest. This was news to me—it is often in such an unexpected and roundabout fashion that a reporter gets his information. I subsequently learned that the third party consisted of porters carrying additional oxygen equipment. It was escorted by Major J. O. M. Roberts and James Morris and left about ten days later, by which time I, myself, was well on the road towards Everest. As regulations forbade commercial airlines from carrying such equipment, the apparatus was very courteously flown into the valley by the Indian Air Force.

An elegantly dressed young man who had appointed himself unofficial agent and interpreter to the Japanese now suggested he should act in a similar capacity for me. He promised that given two days he would produce the perfect Sirdar cum-servant, cum-cook, cum-interpreter. As by now I had given up hope of finding even a small and insignificant Sherpa left in Katmandu I agreed to this offer. Thus a further two days were wasted. What I imagine must have happened was that the agent's original choice proved unavailable, but being a man of resource, and not wishing to lose a fat commission, he had managed to drum up a substitute. This proved to be a scrawny, zoot-suited youth with much the furtive air of a racecourse pickpocket. Highly embarrassed, he was pushed to the forefront and beseeched by the agent to show off his paces—particularly in the English tongue. English not having proved his strong point the unfortunate youth, prompted by the agent's knee administered to the seat of his pants, then stoutly proclaimed that on top of his other accomplishments he could daily carry a load 16 miles. This instantly disqualified him for I felt the distance rather beyond my own capacity to catch up with him should it become necessary.

Balram, Sax and I now decided that as the worst had apparently come to the worst, I should have to go without a cook/servant and we therefore broke off negotiations and drove down through the bazaar to the *Baria Naik*, or the government's official hirer of coolies. The signing on of coolies is simplicity itself. The *Baria Naik* sits in state outside a bazaar booth surrounded by squatting rows of hopeful applicants. Merchants, travelers, or expedition members anxious to hire coolies for a journey, approach the *Baria Naik* and announce their destination. This is shouted out and the coolies either shake their heads to signify assent, or spit on the ground to show they don't think much of the trip. One is permitted to pass down the ranks pinching and prodding like a butcher at a fat stock show, but this I refrained from doing, for it can be taken for granted that any coolie who announces himself ready to undertake a certain journey will prove tougher and stronger than his master and well up to his work. A good deal of formal haggling inevitably boils down to the fact that one will have to pay each man three shillings and sixpence—about half a dollar—a day, out of which the coolie must provide his own food and accommodation. Half the total is paid to the agent on departure and half upon a safe return. As the agent handles the money at both ends one feels this arrangement may be rather hard on the coolies, and in many countries would undoubtedly lead to a good deal of trade union trouble on the way. What usually happens is that the coolies run out of money in mid-journey and on the pretext that they will starve unless something is done about it, they ask for substantial advances on the second installment. This places them in a strong position when the final reckoning with the *Baria Naik* is made, but as the ensuing argument is enjoyed by all and the traveler is exonerated by both sides, far be it from him to interfere.

In my own case there was a preliminary formality to be gone through. After pondering the fact that I should be traveling entirely alone and was unfamiliar with the country, the *Baria Naik* announced that it would be better for all concerned if I obtained an official written authority for my journey. This would enable me to call upon the help of the headmen of the villages along the way, should I be in need of it. It would also safeguard the coolies, for once out of the valley they might not be able to return to it unless they were covered by some sort of document. At once my misgivings returned, for in most Eastern countries there is a vast amount of difference between a verbal assurance and the same assurance set forth in an official document appropriately signed and sealed. This, I felt, must be the long expected snag on which all my plans for my journey would shatter. Once more, this time very much cap in hand, I visited Mr. Dixhit and once more my fears were immediately allayed. Without the slightest hesitation Mr. Dixhit drafted me out a most imposing looking document which proved to be a "safe conduct" pass to visit "Namche Bazar *and the district beyond.*" Not wishing to appear too importunate I had merely asked for permission to visit Namche Bazar. This document was handed to me covered with all the signatures and official stamps that man could desire.

To Mr. Dixhit I also explained my troubles regarding the lack of a Sherpa and/or a good Nepalese personal servant. He at once suggested I visit the Sardar Sahib, who was in charge of that section of the Hospitality Department which dealt with foreign guests. As soon as I met the Sardar Sahib I could have kicked myself for not having thought of him before, for I was greeted with overwhelming courtesy and generosity. The Sardar Sahib knew exactly the right man for me, the only questions were when and where he should present himself. We settled on four o'clock the following afternoon in Balram Tandon's rooms in No. 5 guest house.

At Sax's suggestion we then called on the Forestry Department where a friend of his had the best available maps of eastern Nepal. These I was permitted to borrow so that I might make a rough sketch map of my own.

Things were at last moving well, the more so as, on our way back to the *Baria Naik*, we encountered Father Moran, the Jesuit missionary working in the valley, who gave me the practical advice to visit Dr. Toni Hagen, the Swiss geologist attached to the Nepalese government, before I set out on my trek. Few people knew the country like Hagen, and having accompanied the Swiss expedition of the previous year he was well acquainted with the route I was to travel.

The *Baria Naik* glowed when I presented my document and we got down to business. My first request was for a good Sirdar or porter "boss." If I had trouble on the road I could not deal with it, for I speak no Gurkhali. At once a swashbuckling bravo with a ferocious pair of mustachios was produced who, had he been able to express himself, would no doubt have claimed that there would have been no Mutiny on the *Bounty* had he been aboard. I have a weakness for fierce-looking men which has more than once betrayed me. For three years my chauffeur in Delhi had been a hawk-eyed Pathan with flowing black beard surmounted by a flowing pale-blue *puggree*. He was retained merely because he was decorative; he was quite the most expensively inaccurate driver I ever hope to meet. The Sirdar proved quite adequate until he hit the "beer belt" which coincides in Nepal with the Sherpa country between ten and fourteen thousand feet. Here his tremendous capacity for liquor rendered him worse than a dead loss, for instead of tightening his grip on the coolies he became an object of ridicule to them. Discipline once surrendered is seldom regained. But I confess that till the end there remained a soft spot in my heart for the Sirdar. However often his lapses from grace his mustachios never lost their somewhat pathetic air of aggressiveness. He was an honest man, and that says much. Before his engagement he was, of course, a paragon of efficiency. Together with a representative of the *Baria Naik*, he drove with me to the hotel to assess my equipment and calculate how many coolies would be necessary. The two men expertly broke down the gear into loads and tested and checked the weight of each. Without hesitation the Sirdar then announced I should need three men beside himself. As I had still provisions to buy I decided to take five. Money was no particular object and I wanted us to move comfortably and fast. The Sirdar and the *Baria Naik*'s factotum then departed with many protestations of good will and faithful service, and Sax, Balram and I drove on to visit Hagen who lives just beyond the hotel. Hagen, a strong, bearded fellow, was full of good advice and useful information. He told me, to the exact quantity, what provisions I should buy in the bazaar and also when and where I might obtain fresh food on the route and what prices I should pay for it. He then took my sketch map and divided it in daily stages—rather ambitiously as it turned out, for he was no doubt reckoning by his own endurance. He then counseled me to avoid drinking fresh water (Nepalese water, besides the normal hazards of the East, contains a high mica content which is injurious to the stomach and in some areas it is infested with the eggs of intestinal worms which are both disgusting and debilitating). Hagen also advised against camping in the villages at all costs. Coolies are sociable creatures, he said, and once left in a village overnight, they might take anything up to three or four hours to reassemble the next morning.

That night, Sax, who had been feeling ill all day, but had staunchly seen me over the worst obstacles, went down with a severe attack of malaria. From now on Balram took me over. Sax's last action was to present me with a couple of dozen envelopes, for sending dispatches, addressed in three languages to his wife at the Katmandu hospital. He had shrewdly foreseen that my runners might be intercepted—at a later stage those of Colonel Hunt actually were—but he did not think anyone would dare to appropriate an urgent letter sent to a hospital, which would have all the appearance of a pressing request for medical aid.

All our movements and actions at this time were impeded by the annual festival of Machendranath, the Rain-Bringing God, whose temple is at Pathan. Once a year the God is paraded through the streets of Katmandu, a process which is completed in easy stages and may take many days, for the carriage is fully 60 feet high and runs on four crude, solid wooden wheels about 10 feet in circumference. The ceremonial car is hung with greenery and resembles a decorated maypole and it is drawn by scores of volunteers, competing for the honor, who lay hold of a central shaft consisting of a single balk of timber possibly 25 feet long. Enraptured crowds throng about the car during its passage, which somewhat naturally brings all other traffic to a standstill. Culmination of the festival is the exhibition of first the god's cloak and then his person, represented by a roughhewn block of wood, dark red in color, to the assembled multitude on the great central maidan. Without hesitation all overhead wires which may hinder the passage of the car are disconnected until it has passed. Thus, during the festival, Katmandu suffers a succession of disconcerting power failures, and interruptions of the telephone service. It can, however, be said that the telephone in Katmandu has yet to come into its own as a beneficial modern invention. In the past the British Embassy line has been "cut," not by a single break in the wire, but by the removal of whole sections many hundreds of yards long. This technical hitch cannot be described as "theft" in the proper sense. Copper wire is highly valued in the Himalaya and can be put to a multitude of good uses, and it irks uncomprehending, thrifty and industrious Nepalese to see miles of it hanging about apparently serving no useful purpose.

That evening in the Rangana café I picked up a rumor of a sensational jewel robbery at the airport. A courier escorting a casket of jewels worth many thousands of pounds, which were apparently required for an impending state visit by the Dowager Maharani of a premier Indian State, had vanished shortly after they had been unloaded from the noon aircraft. This was an unusual occurrence enough—for organized crime on such a scale is totally unknown in Nepal—but the rumors also coupled the name of a mysterious Englishman with the disappearance. The trail had led to the Nepal Hotel. Although I had more than enough to keep my hands full at the time, as a newspaperman I could not possibly ignore this "story" and I set out for home forthwith. I went straight to Hutch's room to acquaint him of the headline news. He was still in bed with fever and with him was James Morris newly arrived in the country as "another member of the expedition." In a moment the mysterious jewel disappearance was cleared up and we all laughed heartily at a comedy of errors which could occur to anyone, anywhere, at any time. It appeared that when Morris was about to leave the airport one of the multifarious coolies assembled there, seeing a valise of obviously European manufacture standing on the tarmac had swung it into the boot of his taxi. At the Nepal Hotel Morris had been met by the usual procession of porters each of whom had seized a piece of baggage and followed him to his room where they had dumped their loads. As Morris was anxious to report at once to the embassy he had not given the luggage a second glance but had locked his door and set out. Hard on his heels to the hotel had come a police posse from the airport. Finding his door locked and not wishing to break it open without witnesses they had then followed him down to the embassy. Here, Morris, quite understandably, had indignantly denied possession of the dowager's jewels or anyone else's jewels for that matter. This could not satisfy the police, however, and finally it was decided that the whole party including Morris and Colonel Proud should return to the hotel. The locked door was duly opened and there, to the triumph of the police, and the utter amazement of Morris, the missing jewels were discovered. Happily, almost simultaneously, a second police posse arrived from the airport where further inquiries had elucidated exactly what must have occurred. The incident closed with laughter and apologies all round and thus Nepalese newspapers were deprived of what they might truly have described as Nepal's greatest jewel robbery of all time.

The next morning Balram and I set forth into the bazaar to begin the purchase of the more substantial provisions I was to take with me. There were a number of shops with a very fine selection of tinned goods, but I bought only enough to insure about three or four tins per week by way of variety. Flour, rice and particularly porridge were to be the main staples—with plenty of sugar, tea, coffee, cheese and tinned butter. My presence in the bazaar, which a few years before would have made of me an embarrassingly conspicuous object of curiosity, now passed almost unnoticed. The only unfriendliness towards the Western powers I ever witnessed in Katmandu occurred during the afternoon when it was announced that Stalin had died. On that occasion bands of youth who were members of one of a number of quasi-Communist parties had toured the streets in Jeeps calling out anti-Western slogans through loud-speakers and shouting for shops and businesses to close down for the day in mourning. No one took the slightest notice and after half an hour the demonstrators were dispersed. On Balram's advice I also bought an umbrella, a small tin trunk painted green and embellished with pink roses with which to carry my money, and a kukri. A kukri is one of the handiest implements imaginable in the wilderness and can be used for a thousand and one tasks. In certain circumstances it can also be a formidable weapon—but it is not true, as some war correspondents even in the last war would have us believe, that the Gurkhas "charge with flashing kukris." The trained Gurkha soldier—and there are few better—would no more think of preferring a kukri to a submachine gun in a charge than would a British infantryman.

We now set about the business of changing my paper money into silver coin. Coin is necessary, for the inhabitants in outlying areas still rightly or wrongly regard bank notes with suspicion, but the disadvantage to the traveler is that his privy purse immediately becomes almost a porter's load in itself. The Katmandu "Bourse" is an ornate building in the bazaar magnificently guarded by rows of gilded dragons, griffins, and other fabulous and ferocious animals. One squats on an open verandah and the coin is counted out to one in little heaps of five pieces each, before the admiring gaze of a couple of dozen or so idlers and beggars. The thought that it would have been an easy matter to lean over the balustrade and grab a handful of silver never appeared to occur to anyone—neither did Balram or I have the slightest anxiety in lugging our trunk full of coin through the narrow bazaar streets to the Himalaya Hotel, where we dumped it in the bedroom of the unfortunate Sax who was still shaking with high fever.

At four o'clock that afternoon Balrama and I returned to his guest house where we received the cook and general handyman offered to us by the government. Immediately he struck me as a man of such obviously excellent parts that he would be difficult to live up to—in fact the thought crossed my mind that he would probably expect me to dress for dinner on the trail. He was slender in build, rather darker in complexion than is normal in those parts, with a most attractive smile, and blended perfect manners with an air of dignified reserve, neatness, cleanliness and efficiency. With him he brought an equally dignified old man—who might well have been his father—who introduced him as "His Majesty's third cook." By this I think he meant that my servant—Narayan (or "Jeeves" as he was later inevitably named)—was normally cook at No. 2 guest house, and thus in the royal kitchens ranked third in precedence to the cook at the palace and the cook at the No. 1 guest house. I need scarcely add I was delighted to have him. Jeeves' fee was five shillings per day—find his own food and lodging.

Jeeves and his mentor now examined my stores and, in their anxiety to prove that they were used to providing for even the most demanding sahibs, they began to draw up a list of additional essential requirements of seemingly interminable length but finally ending with a modest request for "a small kitchen stove." As this list would have doubled the porter strength I slashed it remorselessly leaving my new acquisition in obvious doubt as to whether I had been sent to the right public school. It was, however, equally apparent that whatever was to befall me on the coming march of nearly four hundred miles there and back, I should not starve.

Balram, Jeeves and myself now returned once again to the *Baria Naik* for the final choice of coolies. In spite of the fact that the British and Japanese expeditions had already engaged nearly seven hundred between them, there was no lack of volunteers and I was able to weed out all those who admitted quite frankly that they had no idea of the way. This is not to say that all those who claimed to have made the journey before had really much idea of it. Lengthy arguments began, and my own sketch map, which was hardly better than a list of place names, did little more than add to the general confusion which the swashbuckling Sirdar finally quelled by talking louder and longer than anyone else.

Of the men eventually picked "No. 1" was an obvious choice. He was a big stalwart young fellow with a quiet manner and the obvious advantage that he had been to Namche Bazar twice in the previous year with the Swiss. "No. 2" was a short stubby man with immensely strong legs—every inch a weight-lifter and the inseparable companion of No. 1. He was to prove a tremendously hard worker. "No. 3" was a villainous-looking rascal with drooping tartar mustaches and an immense kukri stuck in his sash—his kindly disposition entirely belied his fierce appearance. "No. 4" was a cheerful lad with a hideously pock-marked face and good strong shoulders. "No. 5" apparently the local wit by the amusement he caused, had his head shaved completely except for a forelock and a topknot.

As these five all had the same name, or rather different combinations of the three same names, I was later to name them rather unimaginatively, "Diamonds," "Spades," "Clubs," "Hearts," and the "Joker," according to their various characteristics. In my suit "Diamonds" was trumps—an outstanding man in every way. "Hearts," in spite of his appearance fully earned his name by his repeated and successful wooing of the various young ladies we met along the way.

To these five I added two further men to help with the initial "lift" and to be sent back as couriers after three and five days' journey. Beyond that period I calculated I should soon be meeting Colonel Hunt's returning coolies who I could pay for carrying back further messages. The two new additions were a slim youth of about sixteen and an elderly man of about sixty. The Old Man's flesh was already hanging loosely over his muscles and he was plagued with a most appalling cough but he seemed so anxious for employment that I had not the heart to turn him away.

We were now up to seven men, or eight counting the Sirdar, but the Sirdar on hearing that Jeeves would not be carrying anything, decided that he should be excused also. It was—he now discovered—quite impossible for him to carry a load and keep running up and down the line marshaling the remaining coolies at the same time. There was some truth in this—although it was a complete change of front from his attitude of the previous day. An unseemly argument now ensued which Jeeves witnessed with evident distaste. As the Sirdar became truculent I announced I had decided to do without him—the *Baria Naik* replied that unless the Sirdar went, none of the coolies would go. It was then that Balram made the brilliant suggestion that the Sirdar should carry the money trunk. I was quick to catch Balram's train of thought and, praising the obvious integrity of the Sirdar, I proclaimed that he and no other should be given the honor of filling this position of trust. The unfortunate Sirdar fell for this flattery and later bitterly regretted having done so, for at each step he took on the trail the money chest clanked behind him giving him much the mournful aspect of a belled cat.

I now paid twenty days' wages in advance for everybody—excepting thc two couriers—and Balram ordered all to be present at the Himalaya Hotel at six the next morning.

Back for my last night at the hotel, I finished off my packing and wrote my farewell letters and my last dispatch. To say that I was cheerful would be an overstatement. Normally on setting out on such a journey my last evening would have been filled with most pleasurable anticipation. But I sorely needed a congenial companion; I had never attempted anything like this *alone* before. I was not at all confident of my own abilities. On the contrary, I felt fairly certain I should come to grief and make a laughingstock of myself. Above all I had no idea what on earth I should do when I got to Everest and what sort of reception I should be given by the expedition, except that it was already apparent that it was not likely to be a warm one.

That night I wrote: "While the adage 'he travels fastest who travels alone' may hold good in most parts of the world, a tenderfoot traveler in Nepal like myself would not wisely spurn experienced company if he could get it. In contrast to the inexorable progress of Colonel Hunt's party—supported as it is by three doctors among its thirteen Europeans, escorted by seven Ghurka soldiers and with seventeen Sherpas to act as guides and shepherds of three hundred and sixty odd coolies —I shall be setting off hopefully clutching a government safe conduct pass—for which I'm truly thankful—but mapless, with scarcely a word of any local language, with coolies who claim manfully to know the way but wilt under interrogation and protecting a large box of silver coin with an umbrella— which will also serve to ward off rain and leeches. We shall make no boasts until we reach Thyangboche monastery and no apologies if we are back within two days."

My qualms gave me a restless night, but no sooner had I risen at dawn and become actively engaged in the business of the day than a certain buoyancy and resolution returned to me which happily was to remain with me through the difficult weeks to come.

Balram had decided that I should start at 7 A.M., but he had ordered the coolies—who work on the principle that God made time and he made plenty of it—to be at the Himalaya Hotel an hour earlier. This ruse only partially succeeded, for when I drove up Joodha Street to the Himalaya the coolies had checked in their carrying baskets—from which it was easy to see that fresh garlic, the coolies' seasonal delicacy, was going to be a main staple of their diet—had waited half an hour, and then had drifted off into the bazaar. Jeeves had also reported "present" and then also disappeared.

Balram had procured a Land Rover and a Jeep for the first stages of the journey and as these were already waiting outside the door he counseled patience, and we adjourned for tea. One by one the coolies arrived again and with much shouting from the Sirdar the two vehicles were loaded to everyone's satisfaction. In addition to all my baggage they were to carry eight men each, grotesque overloading which not even the drivers thought amiss. All were now ready to start, a flatteringly large crowd had collected, Sax had risen from his sickbed and put his head out of an upper storey window, but there was still no Jeeves. Finally he arrived accompanied by two bazaar porters bearing a mound of vegetables sufficient to bloat an elephant. He was determined that I should lack for nothing, but the coolies complained, and as Jeeves carried nothing himself I upheld them and turned the new consignment over to the hotel kitchen. This shocked Jeeves, but I then learned that an additional cause for his delay had been the fact that he had remained behind to supervise the making of a number of cloth bags to hold rice, flour, sugar and other easily spilled provisions and I won back a little of his respect by complimenting him on this foresight.

With the arrival of Jeeves we perched ourselves on the mounds of luggage like currants on a couple of buns and set off. The first day's stage on all journeys of this nature is invariably an agonizing one. Apart from the speedy discovery of one's complete lack of physical training, there is irritation at the realization that one has, in spite of all precautions and checking, added a good deal of useless lumber to the baggage, and remorse that one has also forgotten a number of essential articles whose omission will sooner or later become painfully apparent. It is always as well to take the first day easily, to allow the coolies to work into their loads and to enable the march to settle down into a regular routine. But I was impatient. It was now the 26th of March. Colonel Hunt was already over two weeks on the road. Unless I could improve on his time it was already doubtful whether I should catch up with him before he left Thyangboche monastery and the last thing I wanted, at that time, was to be committed to chasing him up the mountain.

CHAPTER VI

I SET OFF

I SET my sights for that first day too high. It was two days later, when I was seated beside the twin rivers at Dolalghat, before I could bring myself to write about it. This dispatch I sent back to Katmandu with my first courier, the sixteen-year-old youth, who also carried the wreckage of my famous tent. The dispatch appeared in *The Daily Mail* of April 1. It ran:

"I am presenting these travel notes not because I am a person of any significance, but because the route I am following from Katmandu to Mount Everest is the standard route now taken by all Everest expeditions. A long way ahead of me—probably about to arrive at Namche Bazar—are Colonel Hunt's two parties. Behind me, possibly just starting from Katmandu is the third and last party of the British Everest expedition headed by Lieutenant Colonel J. O. M. Roberts and Mr. J. Morris who are escorting the expedition's oxygen equipment whose arrival in India was delayed. Very few Europeans—possibly three dozen at the most—have followed this route and the adventures and experiences which befall me will in greater or lesser degree be common to all of us. For instance for a great part of the way the ghostly outline of the snow-capped high Himalayas haunts the northern horizon. I can imagine experienced Himalaya climbers whiling away many weary hours marching by pointing out to each other possible routes up hitherto unclimbed peaks, and no doubt arguing fiercely whether or not they will 'go.'

"My own start was inauspicious enough ending short of the target and with a minor calamity. The tent which had been made before my eyes in Calcutta bazaar collapsed before my eyes in the village of Hukse, the poles going clean through the roof. I bore this mishap with fortitude, for I was convinced it would happen sooner or later and at least it gave the coolies their best laugh of the month. This I could not grudge them, as they have misfortunes enough of their own to contend with."

The exact manner in which the tent collapsed merits a few additional words of description. There was no level ground at Hukse. There was no ridge pole to the tent and getting it taut on a considerable slope was no light task. The coolies divided into two teams and seizing the main guy rope at each end began a tug of war. I saw at once what was going to happen and shouted to them to desist. These shouts they took for encouragement, in fact the louder I shouted the harder they pulled. Inevitably, there was a rending sound and the tent split right down the middle. Team "A" at the lower end went head over heels down the slope, the anchor man disappearing out of sight down a bank. Team "B" merely sat down with stunning force on their bottoms.

"I slept that night beneath a sacred pipal tree—an imprudent thing to do, many believe, for there is a common superstition in these parts that he who thus takes the goddess of the tree in vain wakes up in the morning to find his feet mischievously turned back to front. As I lay down I was so leg-weary that I would have welcomed this deformity, for at least it would have given me sufficient excuse to be carried back to Katmandu in a 'dandy' or litter.

"We left Katmandu ninety minutes late, for which I make no apologies, for he would be expert indeed who could start his first day on time . . . the delay did, however, insure timely delivery of two bottles of rum which had been promised (by Balram) but were threatening to miss the dead line—a welcome addition to a nonexistent cellar.

"I stole two days' marches on Colonel Hunt by jeeping the first two stages—an unwise move as it turned out, for while the first two marches are easy and give the legs time to condition themselves to unaccustomed work, the third stage which was described to me cheerfully (by Hagen) as "long but easy-going downhill," turned out not only to be extremely long and by no means all downhill.

"Across the floor of the great Nepal valley our vehicles roared between rice-paddy fields in a Japanese print landscape, the mountains being pale washes of mauve, while grotesquely shaped trees stood out against the mist in the foreground."

Between Bhatgaon and Banepa the road, by this time merely a rough track, rises steeply for about half a mile. The leading Land Rover, in which I was seated took this obstacle easily. The hapless Jeep, already battered almost out of shape, with damaged steering which caused it to take at least three shots at every hairpin bend, and with a badly leaking radiator, came to rest boiling furiously. This caused another long delay.

"Arrived at Banepa, our jumping-off point, we dismounted and set off up a gentle slope between terraces of ripening barley. The wind being aft of us, and I leading, we proceeded in a cloud of garlic—the coolies' seasonal delicacy of which we have a more than ample supply. This aroma, though unpleasant, gave no cause for anxiety as a reek of rum might have done.

"Clear brooks and tiny cataracts bordered by ferns and bright alpine flowers gave us refreshment as we climbed. It was not until we had reached the watershed and begun the long descent on the farther side, that the whole stupendous panorama of the Himalayas began to unfold itself, each turn of the trail round a new bluff presenting us with a fresh view to lift our hearts higher. But we had begun our march late and were walking in the midday sun which beat upon us so ferociously in the narrow nullahs of the lower slopes that soon our heads drooped and we had eyes only for the ground immediately in front of our feet. The heat across the paddy in the next valley was stifling and this brief stretch of level going was followed by a series of ascents and descents so fierce that I was soon wondering how I would continue to put one foot in front of the other. H. W. Tilman, that hardy Himalayan traveler counsels against drinking on the march, and this advice I had followed even to the extent of not taking a thermos or waterbottle with me, an omission which Jeeves had not ceased to inform my headporter (Diamonds) was a most reckless one. Tilman does concede that 'a pebble sucked in the mouth will do no harm unless swallowed.' I was in no fear of this for on the last agonizing slope to Hukse I could find no pebble smaller than a cricket ball. I had also resolved not to drink village well water, but this resolution soon went by the board." Seated on the rim of the well at Hukse, surrounded by curious villagers, I drained a great brass pot full of it. I do not advise anyone to follow my example; but a man who feels he is about to drop dead anyway for lack of water, will take a chance on a lingering death because of it.

"Faced with the prospect of staggering on into a possibly waterless waste I decided to camp the night at Hukse. Had I not known that the rigors of the first day's march afflict everyone and that I shall take four days or so to walk myself into condition I should have been in despair. And had I but known, as was revealed today, that another half hour's march would have brought me to the bottom of a delightful wooded gorge where water in abundance poured down from one inviting bathing pool to another I undoubtedly would have pushed on."

Physiologists may care to note that I was so exhausted that night I was unable to eat anything. Instead I drank a measured gallon of sweetened tea, but I was so dehydrated that I felt no compulsion to urinate before the following morning.

The main setback of the first day was, of course, the loss of the tent. My home for the next five weeks thus became the diminutive "pup tent" made by the American toy firm. This was no particular hardship, although I projected at both ends and could hardly turn round in my sleeping bag without rolling under the sides. But right at the start, my plan to trek up beyond Thyangboche monastery to the foot of Everest was thrown into doubt, for I no longer had any shelter to offer any Sherpas or coolies who might accompany me. However, at Hukse that seemed a problem for the remote future. The coolies had a weatherproof cow shed and plenty of soft dung to lie on, which seemed to please them, and at least as good accommodation could be expected every night till we reached Namche Bazar, and Namche seemed two thousand miles away instead of under two hundred.

It did not prove half as difficult to get going the next morning as I had anticipated. Jeeves brought more tea to my tent at six o'clock and later, although I still had no appetite, I managed to eat a plate of porridge and two boiled eggs, my first food for twenty-four hours. We were off by seven. From Hukse the track led pleasantly down hill, doubling back on itself through the trees and occasionally skirting neat little homesteads. We were soon down at the foot of the gorge and walking beside the river I have described, but to save time I decided to postpone a bath until our noon day halt, or at any rate until we were forced to turn away again from the water.

It was down in the gorge that an odd incident occurred. I had just clambered round some huge rocks and was following the path into a cleft in the cliffs when there was a cry and a small girl fell off the cliff right on to the track immediately in front of me. She had apparently been cutting fodder with a little bill-hook on the cliff side about 30 feet above my head when she had lost her footing and slithered down the intervening distance. Two older girls now appeared round the next rock and stood giggling uncertainly at the casualty who was moaning with her head in her lap and one leg buckled rather awkwardly beneath her. A broken leg was the last thing I wanted to be called upon to cope with, but it was quite obvious that unless I acted, no one else would. Accordingly I tried to lift her to straighten the limb, but still with her head buried she shook me off and moaned the louder. In desperation I took hold of her rather more firmly at which she looked first at the back of my hand and then up into my face with startled terror. Possibly I was the first white man she had ever seen—the effect was miraculous. With a piercing scream she bounded out of my arms and was off up the cliff like an antelope while the other two girls and the coolies howled with laughter and I gazed after her with unmitigated relief.

A farther ninety minutes of easy going brought us to the village of Dolalghat (in reality my target for the first day). Here two rivers meet to form one considerable stream flowing south. A good steel bridge for coolie or pack animal traffic leads from the right bank to an isthmus between the two rivers and a second similar bridge connects the isthmus with the farther side. At the head of the first bridge, beneath a pipal tree, a group of coolies were playing an elaborate game of pitch and toss. This struck Jeeves as a good place for a halt, as our own coolies were straggling, and accordingly he sat down on the bridge, borrowed a pipe from the local headman and gravely began to relate what I took to be the latest news from Katmandu. This pipe was a curious affair being shaped like a small earthenware porringer with a lid on it and emitting smoke through a short stem which could equally well serve as a handle. The pipe duly made the rounds and in politeness I took my turn at it, but the smoke so seared my lungs that I cheerfully dispensed cigarettes to everyone whereupon the pipe was hastily put away.

When the Old Man arrived with my washing kit in his basket I moved off down the river—with Jeeves in attendance—to find a good place for a bathe. This was none too easy, for the current was very swift, but eventually I found a tolerable pool, shaved, then stripped off my clothes and lay in the stream clutching a rock to prevent myself being washed away. It was one of the best bathes of my life, probably because I really needed it. The water was already too far from the snows to be too cold and for half an hour I floated there letting it soak into my body and melt the fatigue out of my system. Emerging from the water I felt for the first time on the trip that I was really enjoying myself.

We now all crossed over the two bridges to the farther bank and sitting on the sand, while Jeeves cooked some most excellent chicken cutlets, I wrote my first dispatch and saw my first courier off on his way back to Katmandu.

Three days later sitting beside the bridge below Charikot I wrote my second message. It describes my further adventures from Dolalghat and appeared in *The Daily Mail* on April 6.

"The trail from Katmandu to Everest runs roughly west to east, thus it cuts across the main drainage system of the Himalaya range which is a series of valleys, flanked by high mountains, running from north to south. Progress is therefore a switchback affair from one deep gorge up the next mountain and down into the next gorge. The physical effort involved is something like climbing up and down a structure many times higher than, say, the Empire State Building, three or four times a day. But at least there is variety in broken country and it is pleasing to walk from high summer in the valleys to early spring on the mountains and back again.

"I wrote my last dispatch at Dolalghat where there is excellent bathing to be had in either one of two rivers. But we had hardly so refreshed ourselves when a most violent sandstorm overwhelmed us smothering the food and the typewriter in sand. While a walking machine can absorb a certain amount of sand without deleterious effect, a writing machine most certainly cannot. From Dolalghat the trail winds steeply upwards with horrifying abruptness. This formidable feature was unmarked on my map, a fact which is scarcely surpising since I drew it myself with well-intentioned but somewhat inaccurate embellishments sketched in by friends. Two miles of stone steps (those who puff at the top of Saint Paul's please note) brought us to the village of Domre, still within the agricultural level, which here almost corresponds with the tree line, for every square yard of barely climbable slope is terraced and cultivated to its uppermost limit, giving a mountainside the appearance of having been scratched across with a fine-toothed comb."

At Domre the coolies decided to call it a day, they having found a cheerful, though obviously insalubrious, doss house which stands at what passes for a crossroads and sees much coming and going of porter traffic. But so intense is the cultivation here that we were hard put to it to find even a scrap of level ground on which to pitch the tiny one-man tent which is all that is now left to me. At length, under a flowering cherry tree, we discovered a strip of disused path which was, however, so narrow that had I stepped out of bed the wrong side next morning I should have rolled fifty feet.

"The next day Domre proved to be only one of many false horizons before we finally reached the pass separating this valley from the next. But one soon learns that no track is insurmountable in these parts owing to a most excellent local institution known as the *chautara*. These are stone benches, shaped like church pews, which are conveniently placed at the many heartbreaking points along the route for the solace and comfort of travelers. Here coolies can rest their loads while they rest their legs. They are erected by pious and public spirited men and in their more elaborate forms are shaded by both a banyan and a pipal tree—both trees being sacred and believed locally to be male and female of the same species. On stiffer sections *chautaras* sometimes occur in groups of three within an upward span of about 200 feet and one can imagine them labeled in ascending order: 'old men and boys,' 'average' and 'athletes.' While I was at first thankful to be able to totter to the old men's bench, I now make 'average' with ease and will soon be joining my coolies on the 'athletes'—no remarkable performance for unlike them I am under no fifty pound weight handicap.

"The first village over the pass afforded us some light entertainment—a graceful dancing girl in billowing flowered skirt pirouetting among the farmyard pigs, poultry, goats and sheep to rather offbeat waltz time thumped out by her mother on a three-toned drum. After a two mile walk over a mercifully level stretch of mountain heath, interspersed with rhododendron groves bearing raspberry-red blossoms, we met the first of Colonel Hunt's returning runners. He was a rather effeminate young man with black curls peeping from beneath a cap bearing an edelweiss device (Swiss expedition?). After groping in a capacious pair of cotton divided skirts, he produced a letter which he pressed on me urgently with the conscious air of a duty well performed. This letter, however, proved to be for Lieutenant Colonel J. O. M. Roberts who must now be somewhere behind me and, being a Gurkha officer, is no doubt hard on my heels. That night we arrived at the village of Langusha—still at a high altitude—which proved to be our first purely Buddhist community, judging from the many *chorten*, rows of prayer wheels and fluttering prayer banners. When we arrived the entire village was attending a religious ceremony on a neighboring hillside where the priests were apparently erecting two further prayer flags to the music of drums, clashing cymbals and an all male choir.

"Next day saw us again dropping down through rhododendron, buddleia and berberis, and occasional clusters of delicious wild strawberries, to the next gorge where hung cascades of pure white orchids. We followed this river to the valley head where stood another inviting *chautara* beneath a magnificent pipal. This most beautiful of trees has a heart-shaped leaf ending in a delicate spike which, as Beverley Nichols has already written, gives it the appearance of 'dripping green paint.' The ground beneath the pipal proved, however, to be infected with a particularly repulsive form of giant tick, fully capable of blowing itself out to the size of a large black grape before rolling lazily off one's back and sleeping the clock round till its next meal. Tea was therefore drunk standing up.

"The next climb began to prove too much for the coolies who are obviously beginning to wilt as my own powers increase. Thus half of them missed the next big laugh at my expense. I had tottered gratefully to a ramshackle *chautara* and had scarcely sat down upon it when I was twice prodded vigorously in the lower region of the back. Turning round with alacrity I was relieved to find the intruder was a large speckled lizard and not a snake as I had feared, for a tourniquet would have been most difficult to apply.

"We arrived that night on a pass overlooking my modest target, the village of Charikot, but still three miles distant from it. Farther the coolies refused to go, having discovered a congenial farmhouse with plenty of congenial female company. My consolation was a most magnificent view of the sun both setting and rising along the snow-capped high Himalayas and touching fire from the slopes as from a string of glorious opals. The coolies' triumph was also short-lived, for a most bitter wind sprung up on the pass and our dawn get-away was by far the speediest yet accomplished. But we had lost half a day laboriously won from Colonel Hunt's time and are now doing no better than level pegging. We have also lost our map. At first I thought it must have blown away in the sandstorm, but as it has the length of each day's march ambitiously marked upon it by an energetic Swiss geologist (Hagen) I now feel it is more likely that it has been judiciously tidied away to be held in safekeeping until we return to Katmandu."

The previous night we had been overtaken by a party of Sherpas also heading towards Namche Bazar. They were wild shaggy looking men of the unsophisticated class who have yet to make acquaintance with European expeditions and their friendly curiosity was almost embarrassing. Privacy being unknown in the Sherpa world, they peered amiably into the pup tent where I was lying in my sleeping bag reading by the light of a hurricane lamp and passed chuckling remarks upon my kit and general appearance. A cigarette all round sealed our friendship and finally they hitched themselves back into the straps of their carrying baskets and departed.

The next morning, after a lengthy walk along the flank of an escarpment, the track fell steeply down through a magnificent pine forest. Here among the trees we caught up with the Sherpas who were squatting round an immense cauldron of boiling rice. Once more I was struck with their remarkable similarity to Red Indians, in fact, the trees being what they were, it was easy to imagine the whole scene transposed to the backwoods of northern Canada. We made a short halt here and then pressed on down the track which had now once more become a cliff path. This eventually brought us out at the bridge below Charikot.

The man who travels with a dozen of his fellow countrymen supported by a train of nearly four hundred porters can view the loss of an odd load or two, either by accident or design, with equanimity—and with considerable fortitude if the lost load happens to contain the belongings of one of his companions. The man traveling alone, however, with his food and equipment slashed to a minimum, must regard each load as a vital part of the whole, the loss of which must inevitably be a cause of distress and possibly, in acute circumstances, of disaster. This is not an original thought but it was certainly uppermost in my mind as I approached the notorious Charikot bridge. This bridge merits two illustrations in the account of the Swiss expedition to Everest in the previous year. It consists of two slings of locally forged chain (in my opinion a recommendation for the locals who must certainly use it most) between which, at yard intervals, depend wire hoops which carry single lengths of footboard, none more than six inches wide. This makes it a strictly one way affair. The whole contraption, about 50 yards long, sags in a vast capital "U" about 60 feet above a turbulent river—at this time of the year mercifully low. Being no Blondin, particularly on the slack wire, this bridge had been foremost in my more unpleasant dreams ever since I saw the first pictures of it. Reality concedes nothing to the dream.

However, being anxious not to lose face before the coolies I launched myself upon it with jaunty confidence which was by no means reflected inwardly. There and then I nearly fell off, for the oscillations both up and down and sideways are not to be taken lightly. However, by planting one foot firmly in front of the other, while fervently praying that one of the loose slats would not spring up and smack me rudely on the nose before plunging me into the abyss, and restraining an impulse to run the last ten yards, I made a crossing in what proved to be the best time of the day. I need not have worried about the coolies. When I turned round the sight was both pathetic and comical. The inimitable Jeeves, in his clown's garb of balaclava with pompon, hooped jersey, striped underpants (he had discarded his trousers the day after leaving Katmandu), socks and gym shoes, stood miserably frozen to the bridge in the dead center of the stream. Behind him, Diamonds, who had apparently started out confidently enough, now stood nonplused by the situation. Behind him again squat, stubby Spades—a man with a very short reach—stood precariously maintaining a fingertip to fingertip balance on the chains with the agony of crucifixion on his features. It was not until Diamonds had relieved Jeeves of his umbrella and encouragement had been shouted from both banks, that Jeeves again began inching forward, his knocking knees adding a whole new series of intricate and interesting motions to the antics of the bridge. After this episode the remaining coolies elected to climb down the cliff, wade through the water and climb the far side with their loads. Shortly afterwards our Sherpa friends arrived and all without hesitation preferred water to air. It struck me that it would be interesting to inquire how many "failures" the British expedition had recorded among its vast train of coolies and I began to wonder how we would all fare on the way home if the river happened to be in spate as it might well be.

There are a number of such bridges on the way to Namche Bazar but none so formidable as the one at Charikot. I have never heard of such a bridge collapsing, but both coolies and Sherpas develop a diversity of performance upon them. In my own company, besides Jeeves, the Joker had a wretched head for heights. He would never cross a bridge if he could ford the river and if the water was too deep he relied on

Spades to carry his load across the bridge for him. On one ignominious occasion he had to be carried across a bridge himself. On the other hand, since these bridges are impassable for animals, I have watched a peasant carrying two live goats on his back across one of them and think nothing if it.

We had now reached the point where I was due to return my second courier to Katmandu and following a bath under the bridge I sat down to write my second dispatch. There had been some consultation among the coolies, and when I called for the courier Hearts stepped forward. This surprised me, for I was certain it had been clearly understood in Katmandu that the Old Man was signed on for the task. The coolies, however, backed Hearts to a man, and as if to prove the point the Sirdar produced a roll of rice paper on which the names of the coolies and their various functions had been inscribed by the *Baria Naik*. This was of no use to me—as the Sirdar probably well knew—for it was written in Gurkhali, and at length I reluctantly agreed to the change. I was sorry to lose Hearts as he was a strong-bodied, light-hearted fellow, more often than not with a merry song on his lips and always ready with a quip or two to cause blushes and giggles among the females we passed and hoots of laughter among the coolies. He was a good "morale" man. I had serious doubts about the physical capabilities of the Old Man, and I doubted whether he could stay the course. He was slower by far than the others and he only kept up with us by starting earlier in the morning and finishing later in the afternoon. He kept very much to himself and his dreadful cough, clearly a consumptive one, was getting no better. But the Old Man pleaded to be allowed to go on. It turned out that he had hidden resources of strength which were to astonish me. He never let me down; in fact as the weeks went by his performance actually improved. Some time afterwards I learned the truth of this incident from Jeeves. There had, indeed, been a change. The Old Man was in need of the extra money; Hearts was indifferent about the money and agreed to stand down—no doubt for a small commission. This seems a fitting place to add a few words about the coolie way of life in general. Most writers on travel in the Himalaya have their favorites among the local peoples be they Sherpas, Bhutias, Hunzas or what you will. Few find space to mention the humble coolie unless it be to abuse him for tardiness, drunkenness, lack of fortitude in times of stress, or some other failure or misdemeanor which does not happen to fit in with plans of a particular expedition. I do not claim to be an expert on coolies and many of my impressions may be wrong, but for lack of any other company I probably lived closer to them than do most Europeans and certainly I came to know each one of my own little party intimately. This can never be said of a larger expedition, for with increasing numbers coolies become impersonal ciphers to be reckoned by so many dozens, and to be communicated with solely through the Sirdar or porter boss. Yet the coolies of Nepal are a fascinating study, if only because they retain a pattern of behavior which can hardly have changed since prehistoric days. It must be remembered that until the first landau and the first Rolls Royce were carried over the mountains into the valley the use of the wheel as an aid to public transport was quite unknown. There are still no farm wagons or ox carts, even in the valley, where the roads are negotiable and the cheapest form of "taxi" remains one man carrying another on his back.

In the popular imagination coolies may well represent the lowest form of life in public service, but they are by no means necessarily poor men. Most of them own some land somewhere, or belong to families who own land, and when there is no work to do in the fields they hire themselves out to acquire "spending money," and believe it or not, for the company and excitement to be found on the road. Coolies are less easily obtained during the rainy season because they have pressing agricultural work to attend to and not always because, as is generally supposed, they find monsoon conditions unendurable.

The outstanding characteristic of a coolie is his absolute honesty. The load he carries is a sacred charge. (I am talking now of those to be obtained through the official agent in Katmandu. In the past, in outlying districts, some expeditions have been forced to conscript coolies from among the peasants of the villages through which they pass. Many of these men have probably been dragged from urgent farm tasks and it can scarcely be a matter for surprise that thefts and desertions subsequently occur.) To a professional, honesty is traditional and is no doubt based on the fact that when a mound of merchandise or equipment is broken down into sixty pound carrying units, with each coolie responsible for one of them, it is impossible to thieve and remain undetected when the loads come finally to be checked. In any case, if a coolie takes something from his basket he can only conceal it in his scanty clothing and this he no doubt finds less comfortable and convenient. It was not long before I became ashamed of my qualms about my box of silver. At first I kept close to it and slept with it beside the pillow in my tent. But one soon learns instinctively when one is with honest men and later I cared not a whit whether the silver was three miles ahead of me or three miles behind, as it more generally was, for the Sirdar was a great one for stopping off for a "refresher" at every other homestead we came to.

The standard by which all coolie work is done is the sixty pound load. This must be carried a fair day's journey for which the coolie receives three and a half rupees (Nepali)—say three shillings and sixpence. From this money he must find his own lodging (invariably free) and provide his own food (one shilling per day including a stoop or two of millet beer and cigarettes at 40 per one rupee). Youths not yet grown to full strength may hire themselves out as "half a coolie"—that is they contract to carry half a standard load at half the standard price. A few supermen (there was one with the Swiss expedition) hire themselves out as "two coolies" and carry a double load (120 lbs.) for double pay. It will thus be seen that at the end of a long trip a coolie has quite a reasonable sum of money to jingle in his jodhpurs and as his wife has been tending his little homestead in his absence he need not be at all as badly off as his lowly calling suggests he might be. How much money he cares to spend on his three chief vices: bhang (narcotic), chang (beer) and gambling is his own affair, and it is very often considerable.

Coolies are in the main raggedly dressed, to be sure, but who could be expected to subject his best suit to the rigorous wear and tear of the trail? What rags he does wear are kept as clean as circumstances permit, in fact in well-watered country the frequent pauses beside some stream for laundry purposes become embarrassing if one happens to be in a hurry. Coolies have a curious habit of exchanging garments on the march—probably as part of some complicated bargain involving beer, tobacco, sugar or rice. Nothing changes hands so quickly as a surprise addition to the communal wardrobe. A week or two out of Katmandu I wore the seat out of a pair of khaki drill trousers and threw them away. They were at once retrieved and appeared on five different pairs of legs in almost as many days. Finally they were cut down into shorts, the seat repaired with parts from the severed legs, and the garment did the rounds once again.

To the inexperienced traveler standing at the top of a pass surrounded by tattered scraps of triumphantly erected prayer flags, the trail as it stretches before him, meandering into the distance across escarpment after escarpment and sometimes visible for anything up to 8 miles, appears aimless, cheerless and devoid of any intelligent planning whatsoever. In fact, centuries of trial and error have contributed to its exact grading as regards rise and fall, while the discerning eye soon perceives that there is a track within the track, an endless succession of precise spots—denoted by the polishing of countless thousands of feet—where the traveler should place each step to insure the maximum convenience and the minimum effort throughout his journey. There are a variety of detours round specific obstacles and a selection of short cuts at each hairpin bend which can be regarded as "suggestions" any of which may be chosen by the traveler according as to how he assesses his physical ability at the moment. To the coolie, the track makes a very great deal of sense indeed. His requirements on the trail (in warm weather travel) may seem pathetically small, but to him they become all important. They are a convenient place to rest his load; water to rinse his mouth; a breath of cool air on his cheek and a place in the shade. All these four—plus a magnificent view—are generally to be found in the vicinity of the numerous *chautara* to which I have already referred. In those parts of the country where no *chautara* are found coolies carry wooden "T" pieces which serve much the same purpose as a shooting stick. In such circumstances, when he feels in need of a rest, a coolie merely hitches his "T" piece beneath his load and reclines backwards, thus taking the weight off his shoulders.

The winding trail is not without its decorations. On a barren hillside, the two wedded mango and pipal trees of the next *chautara* stand out like a beacon and become the coolies' humble target for the next half hour or so. Water, where it occurs from spring or brook, is generally funneled into a drinking basin through a finely carved stone spout. At a well-known watering place—generally of some historical or mythological significance—as many as seven carved spouts all gushing water may be found in line. Coolies are fastidious about drinking and will never put their lips directly to a spout. Instead they select a fresh leaf and place it over the underlip of the spout so that the water pours cleanly into their brass drinking bowls.

On a much used trail, the end of each recognized daily stage brings more substantial comfort in the form of a free lodging-house or *powah,* which may occur in a village or alone in the remote countryside. These are two-roomed, two storeyed houses of wood fronted by a verandah with carved balustrades. The upper floor is reserved for masters and that below for their men. Personally, I never availed myself of the privilege of the "masters" floor, preferring my tent, for I had a mortal—and possibly wholly unjustified—fear of my garments, or sleeping bag, becoming lice-infested. Where a journey stops short of, or exceeds, the daily stage, coolies find a ready welcome at isolated farmhouses or peasants' cottages. In economically stable areas they bring a little trade, and always they bring diversion and the news from faraway places to break the monotony of an otherwise lonely and eventless existence. They are always assured of either a verandah, or at least a cow byre in which to shelter.

Coolies are supremely efficient packers. I have always prided myself on my packing, be it anything from an airlines overnight bag to a balky mule, but I could never hold a candle to a coolie. Coolies memorize the exact location of everything they put in their baskets and any article can be produced on the instant. In setting up and striking camp they have all the proficiency of a well-drilled squad of soldiers or sailors performing at a military tattoo.

Coolies are seldom recruited into the Gurkha Regiments, but their paces are identical. They infinitely prefer mountain travel be it uphill or down. Uphill, an unencumbered European, in condition, can outstrip a laden coolie, although at the end of a long day the margin will probably not be as large as he may have thought on starting out. A level stretch of ground is the coolies' bane, and along it he can be easily outdistanced. (Colonel Proud now the Gurkha Recruiting Officer at Katmandu, tells me that new entries actually have to be *taught* to walk any distance on level ground, and that during the first three or four days' exercises pulled thigh muscles always cause numbers of men to fall out.) Downhill the race is the coolies' all the way. Beneath their sixty pound loads they literally drop down a precipitous slope, their legs twinkling as if they were pedaling a bicycle in low gear down a ski-jumping platform. I have often tried to keep up with them and, although carrying nothing, found it utterly impossible. Should a coolie slip with such a weight on his back, only Heaven could help him, but I have never heard of such an accident. In this connection a race which occurred in 1907, at Ranikhet, between 100 men of the 3rd Gurkhas and 100 men of the 60th Rifles is worth recalling. (Military students will know that the 60th form the élite of the King's Royal Rifle Corps. They may not know that it is Brigadier Sir John Hunt's Regiment.) The race was a "hill race" similar to that held annually at Grasmere in the Lake District, being straight uphill and back, from and to given points. Although inter-racial competitions were at that time forbidden in the Indian Army an exception was made in this case by Lord Kitchener the then Commander in Chief provided that it was staged as "a competition by time." I first heard the story of the race from Lieutenant-Colonel Hugh Rose of the 1st/3rd Gurkhas, but a good account of it is given by Landon (*Nepal,* vol. ii):

> So far as the climbing of the hill was concerned there was probably not much in it between the 60th Rifles and the 3rd Gurkhas. But, as General Woodyatt graphically described it to me, when it came to coming downhill the Rifles were simply not in it. The Gurkhas fell over the *khud* just as the raindrops collecting zigzag their way down a rain-beaten window. The result was that the first ninety-nine of the competitors belonged

to the 3rd Gurkhas! One is inclined to wonder what happened to the hundredth on his return to his own camp.

With this diversion we say farewell forever to Hearts—gay, young and strong and a faithful servant, for although I was not to know it—and had some qualms about it—his first action on reaching Katmandu was to go straight to Sax and hand over my latest dispatch.

The rest of us turned our attention to the next climb which was a long and very strenuous one which occupied the whole of that afternoon. The next night was a memorable one. We camped at a small village which stands on a saddle leading to the next valley and is surrounded on three sides by an extensive pine forest. There was no *powah* here for the coolies, but the weather was very warm and the sky cloudless and, of their own choice, they decided to bivouac beside the large central *chautara*. There was a small level field near by, whence a crop had just been taken and here we pitched the tent. As we were all tired we did not pay as much attention to the selection of the site as usual. As soon as I lay down stripped to the waist, and sweating, on my sleeping bag, I discovered that the tent lay directly across a main trunk route of ants and throughout the night I had to endure a constant procession of the creatures across my bare flesh.

In the early hours of the morning an animal, which I took to be a leopard, began calling close at hand on a course which was bringing it closer. This caterwauling I heard with mixed feelings but I clung—possibly pathetically—to my belief that a leopard, even at night, will not, if unprovoked, attack a human being, unless it be a man-eater. The presence of a man-eater in the vicinity is always widely advertised by the excitement of the local inhabitants. In the present case the villagers had gone about their tasks in a perfectly normal fashion and had not given us the slightest hint that anything was amiss. As it turned out the progress of the intruder was abruptly halted by a deafening report from the village. This could only have been that of an ancient muzzle-loader containing a generous portion of the community's spare hardware. An agitated clatter of doors and shutters and the clamor of many voices ensued. By morning this hubbub had died down to self-complacency, mutual congratulations, and much sage head wagging of the: "That was Alphonse; we always shoot at Alphonse," variety.

We were by now so well into the routine of the march that my diary records nothing for the next day or two except a meeting with Colonel Hunt's returning Gurkhas. Each of them had, as had most of us, a live fowl perched on his pack, which would serve as provisions farther along the road. The sergeant, who spoke some English, also inquired if I was Major Roberts, handing me a letter as he did so. This I returned and then questioned him as to the progress made by Colonel Hunt. To my astonishment he told me that the expedition had arrived at Thyangboche monastery a week before (March 26). This greatly added to my anxiety for it would have meant that Hunt had cut two days off his schedule and that far from gaining on him I was actually falling behind.

That afternoon we came to the gorge of the Chumti River and, after crossing a couple of chain bridges rather firmer than that at Charikot, we entered the village of Palam. Here once more we could find no patch of level ground which afforded any privacy, until the police finally took pity on us and let us into the compound of a disused mill whose ancient machinery now looked long past repair. The fact that three or four high walls now separated us from the village street proved no obstacle for the villagers and soon crowds of curious spectators were either perched along the tops of the walls in rows or clinging in bunches to the neighboring trees in order to get a better view of us. This well suited the coolies, who had suddenly become men of importance, but it was acutely embarrassing for me for I could not perform even an elementary task without being greeted with gasps of surprise or swelling peals of laughter. Palam did, however, afford us an opportunity to replenish supplies and even buy a new glass for one of the two hurricane lanterns which had been broken earlier on.

Very early the next morning Jeeves woke me with the news that another of Hunt's runners had arrived, was pausing for refreshment and was willing to take another dispatch for me if I could have it ready in twenty minutes. Seated unwashed and sleepy-eyed on a rock I tapped out the following:

"Colonel Hunt leading the British Everest expedition, reached his 'low level' base at Thyangboche monastery at the foot of Everest last Thursday, I was told by returning runners this morning. He had made an extremely rapid march from Katmandu, considering the size of his coolie train, and cut his schedule by two days.

"The weather has remained clear and sunny this week and it is to be expected that the expedition's climbing parties have been making good use of it by acclimatizing themselves on the surrounding peaks. No climbing is to be done on Everest itself until the expedition moves up to its rear base proper in about two weeks' time.

"My own party is now rather more than halfway to the monastery, and, if still going well, we should arrive in about a week.

"We have crossed the last of the back-breaking lateral ranges we shall meet for a day or two and are now moving up the deep gorge of the Chumti River with magnificent pine and fir forests on either hand." (Wishful thinking this based on inaccurate information. Halfway through that morning we were again slogging up the next range.) "We have left behind the neat red brick and thatch cottages which lack only a central chimney to look in place in the English countryside. Now we are passing through villages where tiny houses, with deep eaves and boulders on the roofs to keep the shingles in place, might well be located in Switzerland.

"Here at the village of Palam we are able to replenish stores, for the first time, in the small bazaar center where the shopkeepers on both sides of the narrow, cobbled streets pass away the time by tapping on drums to tunes from antiquated accordions.

"The farther we penetrate the more unsophisticated and friendly the inhabitants become. Indeed it is embarrassing, for they finger our clothes and equipment in wonderment and follow us in droves wherever we go."

As I have suggested, the information I was given at Palam regarding the next stages of the trail were entirely false. We did, indeed, start up the fairly broad, comparatively level, bed of the Chumti crossing and recrossing the river in orderly fashion as if we were heading right to its source. But we had hardly been going two hours when the river forked, a minor tributary coming in from the right. There was a considerable bluff in between, and beyond that towering mountains rising to dizzy heights. Here Diamonds leaned his basket against a rock, unhitched himself from it, stretched himself and then fluttering his hand in an upward spiral emitted a sound which I had come to almost dread. Put into words I can only describe it as: "Shih-shih-shih-eee-eee-eee" and it was only used for the worst ascents. If Diamonds had been able to speak English he would probably have contented himself with saying: "A one in two gradient for about two days!"

Jeeves and I conversed in broken Hindustani and broken English and he actually had one or two semi-slang phrases such as: "Let's go, Sahib, please!" But I had no common language with the coolies although they picked up a few odd words from me such as "camp," "matches," "cigarette," or "tea," which they used among themselves in preference to their own language as it was a sure means of raising a laugh.

The next ascent which started up the bluff and then swung up to the right, above the tributary, did, in fact, turn out to be one of the worst of the whole journey. By nightfall we were only a little more than halfway up it and we camped on a tiny platform of land hanging over the valley and next to a chalet-shaped peasant's cottage. The next day saw us traveling through dense forest—ever upwards—until the pines and firs thinned and we came out once more into rhododendron thickets in full bloom and this time dazzlingly set off by patches of snow between the trunks and stems. This was the first time we had encountered snow.

The top of the pass was, as usual, indicated by piles of stones set carefully one on the other and by fagots bearing scraps of prayer flags, but this time the view was particularly rewarding. Immediately beneath us were vivid acres of rhododendron, then came a belt of conifers and beyond stretched an immense pastoral basin dotted with cattle and washed with a sheen of pale blue primulas. The lower lip of the basin curved over and down into the next dark valley and once more ridge upon ridge was visible rising again to the gleaming snows. Halfway across the basin, sometime after we had reached springy turf of the pasture, stood two small stupas side by side and encircled by a stone-lined trench. There was a *powah* of sorts here, and we therefore decided to stop the night. As the whole basin inclined downwards it was again difficult to find a level place to pitch the tent and rather inadvisedly we finally erected it across the trail. This led to the loss of my hurricane lamp. As usual I had been reading at night in the tent and on extinguishing it had placed it outside the flap by my head. It thus remained in the dead center of the track throughout the night and I imagine that some traveler in the early morning hours found it an irresistible temptation and walked off with it. The loss infuriated Jeeves who wasted much time the next morning by visiting every peasant hut within sight, laying down the law about stolen property, to no avail whatsoever. The lamp had vanished and there was no reading at night from then on.

The morning's march was an easy one, being entirely downhill and it brought us to the foot of another gorge where a considerable torrent—the Bhote Kosi—was spanned by a flimsy bridge of poles laid haphazardly from rock to rock. We paused on the near side and I had an icy bath while lunch was prepared. I was sunning myself on a large rock when suddenly a barrel-shaped animal standing about two feet at the shoulder came lolloping up the farther bank right in front of me. Because I remained motionless and the roar of the water deadened any other sound it was entirely oblivious of my presence and I had a prolonged view of it from a range of not more than 25 yards. It was marked like a Siamese cat, with gray coat merging to black limbs, snout and tail. The snout was very elongated and the tail bushy. I have since tried to identify it, even going to the length of examining the drawers full of skins in the cavernous cellars of the British Natural History Museum, but I have failed to do so unless it be a Ratell, or Honey Badger. I am prepared to accept this identification rather than be accused of trying to foist a new species of mammal on the world, but I have to confess that I, myself, am not particularly satisfied, especially as regards the snout and the tail.

That night, after traversing an immense cliff and coming to another grassy upland smothered over its whole extent by the same blue primulas, we came to the small township of Junbesi. This was our first Sherpa community. A large prayer mill (the big beautifully painted prayer drum revolving incessantly, it being geared to a water wheel beneath it and the whole enclosed in a structure resembling a commodious beehive), stood at the entrance to the town and passing this we were led straight to a small monastery. Here, we were invited to spend the night, but as the cloisters of the central quadrangle were already fully occupied by numerous families and their still more numerous livestock, my own accommodation proved a problem. The abbot, being at a loss, kindly suggested I use the temple itself but this I felt—in spite of the invitation—I could not do without giving offense. I therefore instructed Jeeves to lay my air mattress and sleeping bag on the broad stone step immediately in front of the temple door. I had not the slightest compunction about sleeping without the shelter of the tent but what I had not bargained for was that, throughout my preparations for bed and—I suspect—until long after I was asleep, I should be surrounded by a crowd so dense and pressing that the foremost ranks were constantly being pushed almost on top of me. As almost every Sherpa remark begins, ends, and is punctuated by, weighty and deliberate expectoration this was even less pleasant than it sounds. The coolies, however, in a large barn-like building had possibly their best night of the trip for cheerful fires were lit, company was flattering and beer flowed freely. It was here for the first time that I met Sherpas wearing an odd article or two of European clothing, the proud badges denoting service with previous expeditions. We were now obviously approaching climbing country. But we were by no means finished with monastery life—in fact it was only just beginning. The next night saw us at Tashingtok monastery high up on a wooded mountainside and commanding—as do most Buddhist establishments of the kind—another stupendous alpine view. It is a long low building of white stone with ample, finely carved wooden eaves and window frames which from a distance give it something of the appearance of a luxury hotel in a Swiss winter sports resort. As we approached, groups of monks in yellow garments were sitting in circles on the lawn outside the monastery practicing chants which they read from parchment hymnals bound with two boards. This activity ceased on our arrival and once more we were the center of kindly, but overwhelming attention. There was ample space for the tent here, but I withdrew to a nearby rock to type out my next message. In one way it was a fatal thing to do, for the intricacies of a typewriter were a general source of amazement. The abbot, himself, at once sat down beside me, placing his hand on my knee and leaning closely over my shoulder watched the formation of every word I wrote. Soon I was so hemmed in on all sides I could scarcely move my arms.

Composition under such circumstances was difficult, but I had seen enough of the trail by this time to realize that while it provided quite tolerable going in fine weather, it would prove the very devil during the rainy season. I therefore took as my text a remark by Raymond Lambert who, after picking leeches from his ears, is alleged to have said he would rather climb Everest itself as far as comfort was concerned, than be forced to do the approach march again during the monsoon.

I wrote:

"Namche Bazar, jumping-off point for Everest expeditions, can be reached by four different routes from India. That from Darjeeling, used frequently by Sherpas, is very difficult and sudden breaks in the weather have cost many lives. Two routes lead up roughly south to north from Jainagar and Jogbani, both on the India frontier. The Jainagar route is long, while that from Jogbani, though attractively short on paper, can be deceptive. When Eric Shipton led the British Reconnaissance Expedition up this route in 1951 he had hoped to reach Namche Bazar in fifteen days. Instead, monsoon conditions, washed-out bridges and coolie troubles caused him to take nearly one month. This leaves the route from Katmandu, which, because of a number of advantages, is likely to be that chosen by all future Everest expeditions. In the first place it provides an ample pool of coolies at the Katmandu end. It is comparatively well-bridged and though long—it can be anything from 150 to 170 miles whichever deviation you care to take—it presents no difficulties to athletes such as Everest climbers are expected to be. The average man, however, may wilt at finding that sometimes he is expected to spend a long full day's climbing to surmount a single pass. But this route, in fine weather, has delightful compensations. Rushing torrents and deep wooded gorges, free of any mechanical devices save ancient water wheels turning stones which grind the corn, remind one of nineteenth century prints of the Black Forest or the Tyrol.

"One climbs upward through clusters of orchids, later through patches of violets and wild strawberries and thickets of golden raspberries and finally over a carpet of pale blue primulas between groves of rhododendrons now gorgeously dressed in deep red, cerise, cream white and sulphur-yellow blossoms. Always away to the left are the majestic snow clad high Himalayas all too frequently at this time of year hidden in haze. The company one meets along this trade route which meanders on beyond Namche Bazar into Tibet is excellent. One is constantly stopping to pass the time of day with craftsmen and peasants carrying stacks of homemade rice paper or large wicker baskets of clucking and crowing poultry down to Katmandu. One is constantly overtaking, or being overtaken by, parties of Sherpas or Tibetans making their lightly laden way homewards, their business in the great valley successfully completed. We have been greeted with friendliness and hospitality in every village we have come to—an openheartedness somewhat tempered by the conduct of the village mastiffs who are the shaggiest and fiercest dogs I have ever encountered. These, however, can be subdued by a salvo of well-directed stones of which, happily, there is always an ample supply to hand.

"There is, though, an ugly reverse side to this picture and this will be shown when the monsoon arrives. Colonel Hunt's expedition will experience the worst of it [owing to a most abnormal season they just managed to escape it] for the attempt on Everest will not be concluded until after the rains have arrived. By that time hundreds of feet of dry firm boulders which now form convenient "ladders" up some of the stiffer sections will be roaring watercourses. Miles of upward winding paths now baked clay, will be greasy mud where one slips back a step for every two gained. Worst of all, dense vegetation which clothes most of the route will be infested by leeches. To a man struggling up a greasy slope in streaming rain, panting and perspiring, nothing can be more depressing than leeches. Out here, in a badly infested area, leeches occur not in twos and threes but in hundreds of thousands. They drop on your hair and down your neck from the trees—attach themselves to your clothing and slip inside your shirt as you brush past bushes—cling to your boots and work their way through the eyeholes as you tread on sodden leaves.

"Most people evolve their own defenses against leeches. Tobacco leaves stuffed in the uppers of boots, and salt, are two well-tried remedies. But one cannot use salt next to the skin and pickling the trousers in brine ceases to be effective as soon as one has waded through two or three watercourses.

"There are two good points about the leech. The bite is painless, the first one notices of it being a telltale red patch on the shirt, or the squelch of blood in one's boots. Secondly, although the leech injects some substance into its bite to make the blood run more freely—and thus more difficult to staunch—the tiny wound will not turn septic of itself. A healthy man can also stand a very large number of bites without feeling ill-effects—on a previous expedition I, myself, counted up to one hundred in a single morning. The torture is purely a mental one and if Edgar Allan Poe did not write a story about leeches I feel he ought to have done so.

"Footnote: An example of the friendliness one meets along this route is the fact that I have been writing this dispatch surrounded in closest proximity by the abbot and ten shaven monks of this monastery and fifteen women and children. A tablecloth would cover the lot of us."

No one who has endured leeches over any length of time—as I had previously done—would, I think, aver that the above description is exaggeration or sensationalism in any way.

I might have added an extra footnote to the effect that throughout the writing of this message the abbot followed every word in rapt attention although it was entirely incomprehensible to him. He was particularly surprised at the efficacy of carbon paper, and when I presented him with a few sheets he received them with delight. Early the next morning he called for me and escorted me on a tour of the monastery pausing every few minutes for lengthy explanations and descriptions of which I, in my turn, understood not a word, although I should dearly like to have done so. We parted the best of friends.

Another long march at last brought us over the final lateral range and to the bed of the Dudh Kosi gorge. We crossed the river and turned north up the true left bank in the direction of Everest. It was now clear to me that I should, after all, reach Namche Bazar, and for the first time I began seriously to think of a more ambitious target, the mountain itself, or rather as high up it as I could get. For me, that meant the top of the Khumbu glacier, for I had no illusions that I should ever be able to get up the Icefall unaided. My plan was to leave the coolies at Namche Bazar and to recruit, if possible, two or three Sherpas there for the "lift" beyond to the mountain. It was now that the loss of the large tent began to weigh more heavily on me. I no longer had anything to offer the Sherpas in the way of shelter. When I finally caught up with the expedition I wanted my own little party at least to look moderately competent. Mountaineers are critical people and should I turn up with a tent for myself and a couple of Sherpas half dead from exposure because I had not given them adequate shelter, they would have every right to criticize. In any case all European travelers in the Himalaya are morally bound to do their best for their men, to keep up the high standard which has been set and to insure that those who follow after shall be given the same service as they themselves enjoyed.

At the time, because I had seen so much equipment from past expeditions about, I thought there was a small chance that a discarded tent might still be found at Namche.

The track up the left bank of the Dudh Kosi is not an easy one and sometimes climbs two or three thousand feet above the river. (Dudh Kosi can be literally translated "Milk River" owing to the fact that the opaque water is churned into white foam along many miles of what is virtually an endless cataract.) The scenery on either side of the gorge now began rapidly to eclipse anything we had experienced hitherto. The slopes along which we were passing remained thickly wooded, conifers alternating with rhododendron trees whose blazing blossoms were now even more vividly offset by wax-white magnolia flowers. When weather conditions permitted, and they were not obscured by the crests of the gorge, mountain peaks of almost sublime grandeur appeared on either hand buttressed by fluted columns of ice. Green, incredibly plump, monal pheasants scuttled in the undergrowth one of which, to everyone's astonishment, I secured for the pot by knocking it over with a stone. In contrast to these exotic birds, the whole of the length of the gorge we were dogged by the persistent calling of cuckoos.

So exhilarating did I find this scenery that I gave myself up entirely to the pleasure of it. It was thus some time before I discovered that this Sherpa district of Sola Khumbu held other pleasures of more direct appeal to men of the Sirdar's appetites. We were, in fact, in the middle of the "beer belt." At first, when we passed a Sherpa small-holding, the Sirdar would merely excuse himself for a few moments on the pretext of buying an extra chicken or a cap full of eggs and he would rejoin after half an hour or so generally without eggs or a chicken but with a self-contented expression on his face and a new swagger to his mustachios. Soon, however, the Sirdar's pauses became more frequent and of longer duration and what had passed for secret drinking became blatantly overt and his hiccups, curses and snatches of song as he reeled along in the rear became as much an accompaniment to our progress as the fluting notes of the cuckoo. It was not long before only the abstemious Jeeves, Diamonds and the Old Man stood firm against temptation; Spades and Clubs succumbed readily and it was not long before the Joker followed their example. Daily we thus became straggled out over a considerable length of trail and I began to fear that a night would come when the tippling rear guard would fail to catch up with us. In fairness be it said this never did happen. The length of the day's march remained the same; it merely took longer to complete, and I was now in a desperate hurry to push on.

On the evening of April 8 Jeeves suddenly announced we should arrive at Namche Bazar on the following day. We had just made our way down from a considerable height to a stone bridge where we crossed the Dudh Kosi to enter the village of Panga. Here we were met by a shaggy, vociferous Sherpa wearing homespun clothes and a felt and fur Tibetan cap who explained at some considerable length and for some reasons of his own—possibly a local epidemic—that no accommodation was available in the village. Showing every willingness to be of service he then led us on up the right bank of the river until we came to an immense overhanging rock which resembled a robber's cave. Our voluble friend then gave an endless series of instructions which resulted in my tent being pitched beside the water—well below flood level I noticed with some concern—and the coolies building a huge fire at the mouth of the cave which was enthusiastically kept burning all night. It was not for some days later that I discovered the reason for this precaution. I was in a hurry to be off the next morning, and we made an early enough start, but we had hardly gone half a mile when our talkative friend of the night before hailed us from the porch of a nearby cottage with what was obviously an invitation for a pre-breakfast "refresher." The coolies responded to a man, leaving Jeeves and me standing on the track. After twenty minutes it became obvious that the session was likely to be a long one and I decided to push on alone, knowing that Namche Bazar could scarcely be more than half a day's march away. Two hours of easy going beside the river brought us to the foot of the last two thousand foot climb to the Sherpa capital. This is a severe ascent which in the more frightening sections is assisted by what Mr. Eric Shipton has the mountaineer's nerve to term "an interesting series of log platforms."

Being no mountaineer, those platforms will remain another nightmare not easily forgotten, especially when negotiated in a high wind. They may have shrunk to about 18 inches since Mr. Shipton's day but the nearly sheer drop of many hundreds of feet beneath them remains the same.

At the top of the cliff I came upon a solitary Sherpa sitting on a rock beneath a pine tree. He greeted me as if he had long expected me, and fell in beside me as I struck off along the ridge towards Namche, keeping up a lively conversation of which I understood nothing. Jeeves had remained halfway up the cliff to spur on the coolies.

CHAPTER VII

NAMCHE BAZAR, THE SHERPA CAPITAL

IT WAS THUS that I came to Namche Bazar, attended, although I did not know it at the time, by what passed for a plain-clothes policeman. Namche Bazar, capital of Sola Khumbu district, is a town of about sixty houses arranged in a hemicycle in terraces round a cup-like depression in a mountain top. The houses are spacious and give a general impression of affluence and well-being, for they are made of solid blocks of white stone with carved wooden lattices across the windows.

Almost every house has its lengthy prayer banner fluttering from a pole beside it, while a mountain stream which roughly cuts the town in two is straddled by a series of prayer mills each in its beehive-like housing.

The town is the last station on the trade route over the 19,000 foot high Nanga La Pass into Tibet which undoubtedly accounts for the large number of plain-clothes police, for in a wheel-less community such as this the only traffic offense which could possibly be committed is riding a yak to the danger of the public.

My own escort led me at once to the police chief who

received me courteously enough and who then led me to the headman upon whom he intended I should be billeted. My qualms, I fear, at once returned and in my anxiety not to give offense I made myself out to be a rabid fresh air fiend who never slept in a house anywhere, at any time, if he could possibly avoid it. This was a pretty thin case and acutely embarrassed Jeeves who had now rejoined me, and it was made no more plausible by the fact that to pitch a tent anywhere on the almost precipitous slopes of Namche Bazar would be fully as difficult as trying to set one up on a steep staircase. I was now surrounded by a considerable crowd of Sherpas all of them pathetically anxious to please a visitor and clamorous with suggestions and advice. The ultimate consensus of opinion was that as I was unaccustomed to sleeping in houses I had best be accommodated in the cloistered courtyard of the temple, where I should be surrounded by the benefits of civilization and yet have the wide blue sky above me while I slept. As I felt it would be churlish to continue in obstinacy I agreed—although memories of Junbesi crowded in upon me—and the whole procession of us climbed up the mountainside to the temple. Here I found the cloisters enclosed a space about as big as a badminton court which was already occupied by the local school, the community soup kitchen and a queue of the devout waiting to churn the immense and gaily decorated prayer wheel. An attempt to change my khaki drill trousers for a pair of woolen ones—for it had turned very cold—convinced me that to camp in the court would be to risk being trampled to death, and I speedily evacuated it and was fortunate to find a tiny square of level ground on a nearby potato patch and this, with the temple cloisters providing shelter for the coolies, became my headquarters.

The police chief who had remained with me throughout was still anxious to clear my papers and accordingly, when the tent was set up, we scrambled back to the temple where at last I was able to exchange whole sentences in my own language with the schoolmaster, a charming and cultured Sherpa by name Tshiring Dorje. This excellent fellow translated my letter from Katmandu to the police chief's satisfaction and then invited me to inspect his school. An English composition class was in progress and with some astonishment I read the lesson for the day. It went like this:

"What animals did you see at the zoo?"

"We saw a lovely zebra."

Anything more out of place than a zebra in this remote community which can never hope to see one can scarcely be imagined, but when I reflected that my own monopoly of knowledge of the animal is tempered by the fact that any of the shorn, patch-breeched, cheerfully grubby children could give me a detailed description of the Abominable Snowman whose habitat this district is, I decided that honors were no more than even.

I had taken fourteen days and two hours to reach Namche Bazar from Katmandu which, subject to confirmation, I believe is a European record. The feat was nothing to boast about, for it would be foolish to make a race of such a journey, but I took a modest pride in the achievement for it had been accomplished without a map and with a scratch lot of coolies from the bazaar who, however, had turned into as cheerful and willing a team as any man could wish for. They had done the whole journey barefoot and it was with relief that they learned they were not expected to go farther—relief, I may say, which was strengthened by the fact that as the sun began to sink snow began to fall heavily.

I now had to organize my own further progress and I was at a loss where to begin, when suddenly a tall Sherpa dressed from head to foot in Swiss climbing clothes appeared outside the tent accompanied by Schoolmaster Dorje. The newcomer spoke some English and introduced himself as Sherpa Gyalsen. He explained that he was not accompanying the present Everest expedition as he had overtaxed his strength during the two Swiss attempts of the previous year. To emphasize this he pounded his chest, coughed vigorously and spat emphatically on the ground. Gyalsen announced that he was quite prepared to organize a small excursion up to Everest—that is to the top of the Khumbu glacier and the foot of the Icefall—and would lead it himself providing he was not expected to carry anything. I settled for this arrangement over hastily, I am afraid, for there was a pallor in his complexion which should have warned me that his health was not so far recovered as he, himself, thought it was. We settled that he should be paid five rupees (Nepauli) per day and that I should provide a further three and a half rupees each for two Sherpa coolies. (I use the word coolie here advisedly, for there is a social distinction between the humble low altitude (about 19,000 feet) carriers and the booted, cramponed and expedition-clothed high altitude Sherpa porters.) We were to start the following morning and take provisions for one week. As regards the tent, there were stone huts which could be used until halfway up the Khumbu glacier. If I wished to go farther and was prepared to carry something myself, one coolie would be sufficient to help me lift a single night's camp to the top of the glacier, and both of us could share the small tent. In the interests of the "story" I agreed to this arrangement—there was, obviously, no alternative.

Namche Bazar seems a fitting place from which to introduce a tribute to the gallant Sherpa porters who do the donkey work of carrying camping gear and food for the climbers to the highest possible altitude. As I wrote in *The Daily Mail* (May 19, 1953):

"Nowadays they have become so much a part of the Himalayan mountaineering picture that a major expedition without them would be unthinkable.

"The assets they offer are exceptional lung power, strength, stamina, sure-footedness, cheerfulness and courage. But to keep a tribute in proportion it is only fair to add that they are temperamental, prone to forming intense likes and dislikes (which accounts for some outstanding successes and not a few seemingly inexplicable failures), individualistic, insensitive, do not take kindly to regimented discipline and possess a keenly developed business sense which can prove an embarrassment to the unwary.

"Very few Sherpas are ever likely to reach the standard of technical perfection of a first-class Alpine guide. Prominent exceptions are, of course, Tenzing Norkey, and little Ange Tharkay, whose fine work with the French Annapurna expeditions has now earned him a free trip to Paris. Both these men have great records of courage and endurance stretching as far back as the early thirties. They are supermen in any climbing company.

"The thirty-five Sherpas now with Colonel Hunt are probably as fine a team as it is possible to collect. They are all handpicked—so carefully selected, in fact, that certain men warmly commended by last year's Everest expedition have been considered not quite up to our standard and have failed to find a place with us.

"The Sherpas are a mountain-dwelling caste inhabiting the remote district of Sola Khumbu, in easternmost Nepal. So isolated is their country that they are almost beyond central government control. Isolation breeds individualism and independence of action, and the Sherpas are used to moving to and fro across the Tibetan frontier. In appearance, customs and costume they are indistinguishable from their neighboring Tibetans.

"They prefer to trade across the 19,000 feet Nangpa La (Pass) to the north rather than undertake the tiresome and lengthy journey south to India or west to Katmandu.

"Because of the changed political situation in Tibet, a police check point has now been established at the tiny 12,000 feet high Sherpa capital of Namche Bazar, and it is a strange sight to see two slender police radio masts raised amid the forest of poles bearing prayer banners. But controlling a Himalayan frontier is not only a disheartening task, it is well-nigh impossible for plainsmen.

"It was Everest pioneers who first discovered the potentialities of Sherpas as high altitude carriers. Early writers expressed astonishment that it had never occurred to the Sherpas to climb their own mountains, and it apparently did not occur to the writers that a practical man who has to earn his living the hard way will seldom go up a mountain if he can find a convenient way round it. However, under patient tutelage of men of outstanding character such as Generals Bruce and Norton, the Sherpas gradually learned the necessary discipline and advanced climbing technique. More important, General Norton managed to convince them that there was a blue riband to be won in carrying a load farther and higher than anyone else.

"Today climbing has 'caught on' in the Sherpa community, and each village has its local hero, clad in climbing boots, quilted windproof suit, balaclava, and goggles—souvenir presents from past expeditions—his face smeared with sunburn cream, dazzling his companions in much the same way as an immaculately clad skiing instructor in an Alpine village still dazzles his poorer peasant cousins.

"In the little school at Namche Bazar, where English is now a compulsory subject in order to prepare pupils for expedition work, if you asked any of the eager urchins what they want to be when they grow up, they would answer to a boy: 'A man like Tenzing!'

"Nowadays Sherpas consider themselves an élite corps. They demand and get 5 rupees per day—more than double prewar rate—while 'tigers' (the title won by Sherpas who have carried loads to 25,800 feet) expect bonuses of anything up to £15 for a single lift between the highest camps.

"Sherpas and their money are usually soon parted, again with the exception of men of exemplary character such as Ange Tharkay, who has now saved enough to open a tourist and travel agency in Darjeeling.

"Sherpas are now also apt to claim that it is beneath their dignity to carry a load on a long approach march to a mountain. They use the climbers' argument that they must husband their resources for the mountain itself. Expeditions which accept this are usually chagrined to find, when the march begins, that the Sherpas are indeed carrying a load. It is not expedition equipment, but merchandise which the Sherpa has bought for himself or for trade among his fellows.

"Veteran British climbers are inclined to deplore the present trend. They point out, with some truth, that climbers of other nations have deliberately and recklessly inflated the bonus rate to get more out of their men and have added lavish presents of expensive equipment which few British expeditions can afford to give away. [The manner in which American troops—with customary liberality—splashed dollars about in Darjeeling when on leave during the past war, also contributed to raising the expected daily rate.]

"Against this must be set the grim and mounting roll of death and disablement which the Sherpas are suffering. Few fates are worse for an able-bodied man than to be totally incapacitated in a primitive community where there is no pensions system. His very presence is an incentive to others to enhance their value. Many people would consider the devotion of a good Sherpa, if it can be won, to be totally beyond price.

"Mountaineering knows no more tragic and heroic tale than the death of Sherpa Gaylay during the disastrous 1934 German expedition to Nanga Parbat which cost four German and six Sherpa lives. When Dr. Merkl, the last German survivor of a party which became trapped during descent down the mountain could go no farther and collapsed in an ice cave, Gaylay remained with him although it meant certain death.

"Gaylay did not give his life to save Merkl's—that was impossible. He deliberately chose to die with his leader rather than save his own life, as he still could have done."

With the above in mind we can consider the case of Pasang, under-sirdar (chief assistant) to Tenzing with the British expedition. By a coincidence Pasang quit the British at Thyangboche on the day I arrived at Namche Bazar (April 9), and that night he came to my tent, he having walked down from the monastery in the afternoon. He was on his way to the village of Tame where he intended to spend some days with relatives before setting out for Darjeeling by way of Katmandu. If I planned to be back at Namche Bazar within a week he wished to join forces with me: "for company, not for money. May be I help you, may be you help me." I was a little dubious about entering into this arrangement for I felt that the fact that I had signed up a disgruntled Sherpa the moment he had been sacked from, or had deserted, the British expedition, might be misinterpreted and I also had doubts whether a man who had left an expedition in the field might not cause trouble among my own little party. As it turned out I need have had no fears about Pasang. He proved a loyal and excellent companion and he can, I think, be written down as the perfect example of the complete unpredictability of Sherpas, their temperamental nature and their proneness to forming likes and dislikes, which results in a constitutional inability to afford different masters equal service. Pasang, still only twenty-two, had the highest possible references from the Swiss. Dr. Chevalley, leader of the second Swiss expedition of 1952, had written that had not Tenzing been so outstanding, he would have had no hesitation in appointing Pasang in his stead. Exactly what Pasang's trouble was I never found out, for he was discretion itself concerning his relations with the British. He may have been jealous of Tenzing, but I suspect the root of the matter was that he had lost his heart to the Swiss and did not feel happy away from them. I lost track of him after we reached Katmandu but I heard a rumor that after arriving back at Darjeeling he immediately signed up with a Swiss expedition which was attempting Dhaulagiri in northwestern Nepal. The fact that he could not get on with the Everest expedition, but worked exceedingly well with me signifies nothing, for I was merely the convenience which afforded him entertainment and diversion on the dreary march back to the capital.

It is true that up to this stage Colonel Hunt had had his Sherpa troubles—I frankly disbelieve that any expedition, however well organized, can avoid them—but they by no means amounted to a "revolt" as has been suggested by some people who were in no position to judge. The stable incident in Katmandu had been an unfortunate beginning. There was a complaint that Sherpa stores were not issued until the expedition reached Namche Bazar. (I feel this was a wise precaution for taking into account the Sherpas irresistible itch for trade and barter, a number of articles essential on the mountain might easily have been disposed of before Everest was reached.) There was a complaint that when the stores were finally handed out they were issued "on loan," rather than as "gifts" as had previously been standard practice. (It was Colonel Hunt's intention to turn the "loans" into "gifts" *after* the completion of the attempt. He wished to retain some control over the stores during the actual climb, for if men fell out, as they invariably do, there might not be a sufficient reserve of gear to equip substitutes adequately.) There were the usual complaints about carrying loads on the approach march—about the fair weight of a standard load and, allegedly, about the fact that, during the early stages, the Sherpas were expected to eat local food rather than share that of the Europeans. This last complaint I find difficult to accept—although it has appeared in print—for there can be few Sherpas, indeed, who prefer Western food to their own. None of these complaints singly—or all of them together—can I think have so upset Pasang as to cause him to throw up a profitable commission in disgust. To my mind he had what are now known fashionably as "mental troubles."

The next morning began in leisurely fashion as Thyangboche monastery, our target for the night, was barely three hours' march away. Dorje, with a group of small, sniveling, scholars arrived for breakfast and I delighted them all by showing them a picture of themselves in Eric Shipton's book *Mount Everest Reconnaissance 1951*.

I then visited the coolies and found them very comfortably installed in a room of their own beside the temple. At their request I gave them all a substantial advance of pay although I was fully aware what the result would be. However, I reckoned that a week would give them ample time to sleep off what promised to be a cracking collective hang-over. As a reward for good service I bought them a sheep carcass which at least insured there would not be too much drinking on empty stomachs. Jeeves had made his customary neat job of packing my own provisions and, faithful servant that he was, seemed genuinely concerned that he was no longer to accompany us and, I think, a little jealous of Gyalsen who was to take his place.

Soon after, Gyalsen himself arrived, accompanied by the two shaggy work horses who were to carry our gear. These were Nawang Tensing (no relation of "Tiger" Tenzing) and Kirkia, a loyal, amiable, gorilla-like man who was to combine considerable resource with prodigious endurance. Unlike Gyalsen, who as I have said was dressed from head to heel by the best wintersports outfitters in Switzerland by courtesy of the two Swiss expeditions of the previous year, the two new recruits wore rust colored homespun cloaks, kilts and breeches and Tibetan felt boots. Both affected pigtails which they braided over their woolen caps to keep in place the headbands with which they supported their loads. Instead of carrying baskets they used contraptions like school easels the loads being wedged between the back and front frames. I was appalled to notice that before any of my own equipment had been added, each was already carrying what most men would consider a very substantial load. Had I been a man of the caliber of a Shipton or a Tilman, I should probably have gone through these loads and ruthlessly discarded all non-essentials of which, I need hardly add, there was a considerable quantity. Kirkia, for example, was later to produce a cumbersome leather bellows big enough to have served a blacksmith but so much useless lumber as far as we were concerned. As it was, I did not feel I had the necessary experience to interfere and I thus watched gloomily while my own equipment was divided between the two and perched precariously on the already filled frames. It did not seem to me that we could possibly get far and that we should take a long time over doing it. Dorje, who tested each load, announced that they were both well over 100 lbs. which evoked roars of laughter rather than sympathy from the inevitable crowd of sightseers. An obstinate pride, however, seemed to infect both Nawang and Kirkia and rather than confess themselves beaten in front of an audience they hitched themselves into the loads, heaved themselves grunting to their feet, nearly fell flat on their faces, recovered and finally staggered off up the trail followed, at funereal pace by Gyalsen and myself.

The track led us high up along the right bank of the Dudh Kosi and progress was fully as slow as I had expected. To my concern, however, it was not Nawang and Kirkia who held us up but Gyalsen who paused every 50 yards or so, and bent himself over his staff while he shook with dreadful spasms of coughing. Thus at this early stage it became problematical whether he would stay the course. As regards the time factor there was no particular need for alarm. It was now Friday and I had been told by Pasang that Colonel Hunt did not intend to move his base camp to the head of the Khumbu glacier until the following Monday.

A long descent now brought us down into the gorge at the point where the Dudh Kosi is joined from the east by the rushing torrent of the Imja Khola. Here, beside a small mill, I stopped to shave and wash my feet, while the Sherpas cooked lunch. We were now faced with the long 2000 foot ascent to Thyangboche monastery itself. Our pace now became so pitifully tardy that at length I pulled a book from one of the packs and progressed sedately upwards reading as I climbed in true monkish fashion (except that the book was some of the more risqué stories of Guy de Maupassant).

The Buddhist monastery of Thyangboche is about 12 miles south of Everest and stands on a 12,000 foot high saddle which cuts right across the valley of the Imja River, leaving only a narrow and profound gorge in the extreme left corner, facing north, through which the torrent may pass. It may be said that the saddle divides two worlds. To the south the mountains are comfortably tree-clad, alight with gorgeous rhododendron blossoms and magnolia flowers and alive with brilliant butterflies and birds—to which may be added the homely cuckoo. A mile to the north begins the bleak harsh moorland where only men of the hardiest stock can survive, let alone make an annual living, where a sudden worsening of the weather can convert the countryside into a nightmare land.

CHAPTER VIII

ADVANCE TO EVEREST AND RETREAT

THYANGBOCHE monastery is a group of white buildings surmounted by stubby gilded finials and with the customary carved window woodwork. Although by this time I had seen many superb views I can think of no more perfect site for the followers of a religion which includes the contemplation of mountains as one of its main tenets. All round rise gigantic peaks serene, remote, inviolable and guarded by majestic ramparts of rock and ice. Spiritually the monastery is linked with the larger establishment at Rongbuk on the northern and Tibetan side of Everest, and frequent visits are made between the two over the Nangpa La. Both monasteries are dedicated to contemplation of sacred Chomolungma (the Everest massive). In this respect the monks of Thyangboche are the less fortunate, for from the south only the summit pyramid of Everest—a grim black triangle streaked with white—is visible, the bulk of the mountain being almost totally obscured by the Lhotse-Nuptse Range, a vast curtain of snow, rock and ice nowhere below 25,000 feet in the whole of its 5 mile length.

During the last stages of my climb I had been wondering

how I should present myself to the expedition and what my reception would be, but at Thyangboche, where I had confidently expected to meet Colonel Hunt, we received our first shock. The tents were there all right, ranged round a central flag post flying the Union Jack on one of the two upland meadows used by the monks for grazing yak. But they were deserted except for Thandu the Sherpa cook. (Here I might add that we certainly showed the flag during the expedition. Each piece of equipment was boldly lettered "British Mount Everest Expedition, 1953." The Japanese attempting Manaslu contented themselves by stenciling their gear with the capitals "J.H.E.," standing for "Japanese Himalayan Expedition.")

An unsatisfactory interrogation of Thandu—over a mug of tea which he provided—elicited the information that "all the climbers have left for Everest tomorrow." Making allowance for his imperfect English I took "tomorrow" to mean "yesterday." This surprised me, for it did not agree with what Pasang had told me, nor with the plans Colonel Hunt had outlined in Katmandu—namely that he would not move up to Everest until the second or third week in April. It was now only April 10. However, as there had apparently been a change of plan there was nothing to do but set off in pursuit. It was too late to make farther progress that day and after inquiry at the monastery a small guest house was put at our disposal. This I turned over to the Sherpas and had the tent pitched beside it. (At night I regretted this decision for it snowed heavily and turned bitterly cold and I lay awake sleepless and shivering.) The arrangement suited the Sherpas admirably and they retired to the first floor where they lit a huge fire and made themselves thoroughly comfortable. All Sherpa houses are built on the same plan. The ground floor is reserved for stores and cattle, an inside ladder leading up to the living quarters—generally a single room spread with rugs, surrounded with shelves carrying cooking pots and jars of chang and rakshi rice-spirit and with a fireplace at one end. There is sometimes a cooking alcove and always a latrine at the end of a screened corridor down which ashes and pine needles can be thrown.

The labors of Nawang and Kirkia had so distressed me that, against their protests, I was determined to engage another coolie if possible. By happy coincidence Nawang's brother Da Tensing, an equally uncouth youth, arrived by chance at the monastery that evening and was at once engaged to everyone's satisfaction. It was as well we had him, for otherwise our journey would have come to an abrupt end on the following day.

From Thyangboche the track leads pleasantly down through woods of juniper, fir, rhododendron, and a species of birch more gold than silver. Most of the trees carried beards of pale green moss on their branches. Fat pheasants scratched unconcernedly in the thickets, for while Sherpas though Buddhists, are meat-eaters, and indeed have few scruples, there is a ban on the taking of wild life in the vicinity of the monastery. The trees remained with us for one mile only and until we had crossed the cataract of the Imja River to the farther right-hand bank.

We had now reached the bleak upland heath country of yellowed turf blotched with brown patches of withered scrub juniper. The track now followed the river, being sometimes close to the water and sometimes veering upwards and down again to by-pass some rocky outcrop. At every few hundred yards *chortens*, or rows of tablets bearing Buddhist prayers had been erected while every convenient boulder bore engraved religious texts. Where these had been newly cut on moss-grown rock they appeared as if etched on brown velvet.

A few miles brought us to the village of Pangbochi, the highest permanently settled Sherpa community—a dismal collection of cottages which, like the walls which enclose the tiny pastures, are built of roughly shaped rocks with nothing to plug the interstices. Shingles, or bamboo mats are used for roofing materials.

A Sherpa community can own as many as three different villages each at a different altitude, moving from one to another, according to the season and condition of the grazing.

Shortly after Pangbochi the Imja River is joined by a small shallow stream known as the Chola, and into this valley we turned. It contains the grazing villages of Phariche and Phalong Karpa, then only partly inhabited, and some miles up on the right-hand side, it receives the snout of the Khumbu glacier, which was to lead us to Everest.

The valley is broad and rises gently, and if one ignores its enclosing horizon of peaks of 20,000 feet or more, is not unlike many to be found in Wales.

We were fairly into the valley, when suddenly, without warning, a most violent snowstorm descended upon us. Those who have experienced a blizzard in a Welsh valley at, say, 2,000 feet can possibly imagine the fury of a similar occurrence at 15,000.

For some minutes we plodded on through what was literally a howling waste until we finally blundered into a disused yak shed. Here, while snow whistled in through innumerable chinks in the walls and spiraled down through two large holes in the roof, we managed to light a fire.

I was miserably wondering how long we were likely to be snowed in and how this would affect our one week's supply of food, when equally suddenly the sky again cleared. It was the sort of thing that happens at high altitudes and which can obviously be a lethal hazard on a mountain.

Half an hour later, in brilliant sunshine, I had peeled off my shirt and was enjoying a much needed, although icy, wash and shave. That day was memorable for I sampled my first deep draught of yak's milk. It is rich and creamy and, in my opinion, surpasses cow's milk, an astonishing performance on the part of the yak when one views the wretched pickings she is expected to graze on. (Yak's milk should not be confused with "lama's milk," the name given by previous travelers to the fragrant, clove-scented rice-spirit, brewed by the happy monks of Thyangboche.)

My lasting impression of life at high altitudes—at which I count anything over 15,000 feet—is that it is lived within far closer limits. Storms are fiercer, the cold more sapping, and one's endurance, strength and ability to overcome natural obstacles far less. Consequently one has to allow a far wider safety margin if one wishes to avoid trouble.

The snowstorm which overcame us in the Chola Valley, although brief, put paid to "Tiger" Gyalsen. For some miles past he had been coughing like a barking deer. More snow fell that night, but when I scrambled out of the tent in the morning the sky was again clear. Inside the stone hut I found Gyalsen lying in his Swiss eiderdown sleeping bag almost on top of the fire, sweating profusely and alternately gasping and coughing. At first I thought I should never get him to his feet but he did, at last, rouse himself and by stages of a few hundred yards at a time, managed to drag himself up to the snout of the Khumbu glacier. Here, where the terrain rose abruptly, he collapsed.

Some hundreds of feet up the snout there are two empty huts known rather flatteringly as the village of Tula. To these we managed to haul Gyalsen—an effort which nearly finished me for as I had no load most of the weight came on my shoulders. Our meeting with the British expedition, which I had imagined would be merely a social occasion, had now suddenly become a matter of urgency, for to go back in search of medical aid would have meant retracing one's steps to Katmandu, a return journey of nearly four weeks.

Accordingly, I left Gyalsen with Nawang Tensing, half our food, and, what was more important, half our firewood—for with two fires going our operational time limit was cut to two and a half days instead of five—and set off up the glacier with the two remaining Sherpas Da Tensing and Kirkia.

So frequent had been the delays that we made only another mile and a half up the glacier that afternoon. We reached what might be called "Base Camp minus one," another extremely draughty stone hut beside the lateral moraine. This—the Lubja Camp—was unfortunately also deserted, although some burst cartons were evidence of recent occupation by the British, as were some empty soup packets with German lettering evidence of an earlier occupation by the Swiss. That night I abandoned the tent—the temperature fell to five degrees above zero—and slept in the hut with the Sherpas, sharing the soft mattress of yak dung and a few fleas that they may well have brought with them. The latter they bore with a good-humored philosophy I found it quite impossible to match.

The next morning Da Tensing also went sick, complaining of stomach pains. This hardly surprised me, as two-thirds of his load was made up of food for himself and he had been eating enormously. But his defection further complicated our plans for the day, or rather simplified them, for with only one Sherpa left out of four not much choice remained for us. Accordingly I abandoned the plan of moving the camp a farther day's march up the glacier because Kirkia could not possibly lift all the necessary gear and equipment himself and I had learned, from my previous day's experience, that having marched continuously with no pause for acclimatization, I should be in no condition to help him when we approached 18,000 feet.

We therefore decided that Kirkia and I should make a quick dash for the British expedition camp and return to our present base that night. It seemed easy. The Khumbu glacier itself cannot be more than six miles long. Looking up the glacier from left to right, the peaks of Pumori (23,200 feet) and Lingtren, the snow saddle called the Lho La, the North Peak behind it, the northwest shoulder of Everest leading up from it, the huge bulk of Nuptse (25,700 feet) rising from the right-hand side of the glacier and almost entirely blocking out Everest, all seemed near enough to touch. I reckoned that, at the outside, we should not have more than eight or nine miles to cover in the day. I felt so confident that I took only one bar of chocolate with me as provision for the two of us. Experienced mountaineers, of which I am not one, will no doubt smile at this presumption, and rightly so.

All went well at the start. For three-quarters of an hour we made good progress up the turf along the left-hand side of the glacier. Then a rock face forced us on to the moraine and at times on to the glacier itself. This meant scrambling up and sliding down what seemed a never ending series of banks of rocks, boulders, and ridges of shattered and splintered glacier debris. Every few hundred yards small cairns had been built to mark the route and although one pressed forward to each in order to put a fresh mark of forward progress behind one, it was disconcerting to find when checking one's advance with, say, the massive flank of Nuptse, that one appeared to be making no headway at all.

Kirkia, born to these altitudes, made light work of it, strolling along, hands folded behind him, in his odd shambling gait. I floundered in the rear, my heart thumping as never before, occasionally starting small landslides and sometimes going down with them. Midday was already passed when we reached the first true Base Camp—sometimes called the Lake Camp after the small sheet of glacier water it stands beside. This time it was a real shock to find another camp deserted, though there were plenty of signs of very recent occupation.

Fresh boot tracks led off towards the glacier head, and there seemed nothing to do but to follow them. The going over the glacier now became rougher still, and at times involved the crossing of sheets of water on floes of rotten ice. To add to the sense of urgency, which was unnecessary in view of the anxiety with which I was now viewing the speeding hands of my watch, evil-looking clouds began piling up behind us.

Mountaineering books are full of warnings against pressing an attack too long, and it is, of course, true that every additional half hour spent in advancing must mean anything up to one hour's further delay in arriving back at one's departure point. It was deathly still on the glacier. The only sign of life I saw there was a single robin, and the only sound was the distant rumble of avalanches.

To add to my exasperation, although we were now definitely approaching the glacier head, there was no sign of the British camp, nor was there any of the Icefall. The apparent nonexistence of the Icefall approached from this angle, is due to an odd optical illusion on a gigantic scale, for one has to remember that the fall is 2,000 feet high and 300 yards across. But until one is almost on top of it a buttress of Nuptse, on the southern side, appears to be a continuation of the Lho La Saddle on the northern side, and completely hides it from view.

This last stretch of the glacier is steeply pinnacled, reproducing a fantastic and beautiful moon-landscape reduced to a scale of about 50 feet and composed of pyramids and spires of pale green, blue, and pure white ice. It was here, in a fold of ground which gave it protection from the wind, that at last we found the British camp. The discovery was made by Kirkia. Two minutes before I had been on the point of turning for home, a heartbreaking decision to make, for it would have meant accepting defeat by a few hundred yards after having walked nearly 200 miles—defeat in the last few minutes of a journey that had lasted nineteen days. However puny my own effort may be compared with the colossal task of climbing Everest, it is a good example of the stark fact that any high altitude endeavor can fail by as little as only a few feet unless the build-up behind it is sufficient and carefully planned. In my case I had unwittingly cut things as fine as they possibly could be cut. To have allowed a proper safety margin I should have turned back short of the camp. That would have meant going right back to Namche Bazar to re-organize and re-equip—a lapse of about eight days before I should have once more been in a position to tackle the last 200 yards. It would be seldom that a full-scale expedition tackling a major Himalayan target would get such a second chance in one season. The camp we had come to was not the expedition's main base, as I had imagined it would be, but four tiny lightweight tents, two scarlet and two yellow, of a forward reconnaissance party which was making a preliminary exploration of the Icefall. What had happened was that the expedition after leaving Thyangboche, had split into a number of small parties which were then dispersed at various points round the surrounding mountains, before converging on the Icefall.

For some minutes I sat on a bank of scree too breathless to go farther and watched some Sherpas erect a rock wall round their kitchen quarters. Still too out of breath to hail him, I watched George Lowe, the New Zealand climber, emerge from a tent, walk over to an ice block and then return into the tent without noticing me. By the time another figure appeared among the ice pinnacles—that of Dr. Pugh the expedition physiologist—I had regained sufficient strength to introduce myself. After recovering from his surprise—which I believe was quite genuine—Pugh greeted me in very kindly fashion. Pugh's task, as I have already indicated, was the vital one of working out the expedition's acclimatization program, which had to be followed rigorously if the climbers were to have any hope of operating successfully at 28,000 feet. In a minor way I therefore became an object of interest for interrogation for in nineteen days, without any acclimatization whatsoever, I had walked up to over 18,000 feet. Of special training I had had none (I added the gratuitous and slightly inaccurate information that I did most of my training in night clubs). Yet I did not suffer from altitude sickness, nor from headache and if I was tired and breathless, I should have been breathless and tired (though obviously to a lesser degree) if I had just finished climbing over the same rough country we had just traversed, had it been at sea level. I am not extolling my own strength and stamina—I should be foolish to do so at my present age of forty-three—I am merely pointing out that altitude has different effects on different men and it is, in fact, seldom that two men of apparently equal physique and constitution react in an identical manner to lack of oxygen. Why this should be so is the sort of question that interests Dr. Pugh. (The fact that night-club habitués become accustomed to a deficiency of oxygen in the atmosphere cannot be considered a valid argument!)

It was now teatime and Pugh led me to the tent where I met George Lowe and cameraman Tom Stobart. Both were wearing the fashionable "Everest" beards. Pugh, himself, was scratching a stubbly chin having just abandoned a resolution to shave daily in view of the combination of icy shaving water and fierce glacier sunburn. I had shaved again that morning and this, coupled with a silk scarf and neatly brushed hair, made me look more out of place than I had intended. I had not wanted to give the impression that I considered myself a climber—a "social climber" perhaps, but certainly not an "Everester." I learned afterwards that my spruce appearance caused me to be accused jocularly of "one upmanship."

For half an hour I sat in the tent and drank mug after mug of steaming tea. From Lowe I learned that the season so far had been unusually warm. Warmth renders snow "sick" and ice rotten and greatly increases the avalanche danger. But even as we were speaking we could see the minute figures of Hillary, Band and Westmacott high up the Icefall where they had made very considerable progress on their first attempt.

George Lowe told me that while the Icefall may look awe-inspiring in fact almost terrifying, from where we were standing, as indeed it does, one only gets a true and complete picture of its difficulties when one is actually climbing it. This, however, was entirely beyond me. At any moment a move of the main mass of ice may splinter and devastate a huge area of itself as if by an earthquake, inevitably wiping out any party which might happen to be on that particular section at the time. My colleague James Morris who later climbed the fall on an expedition "rope" described it as like "a squashed meringue" with men reduced to the size of insects crawling across it. It should be pointed out, however, that this apt description applies only to the Icefall and not to the mountain itself, for Everest, in its most familiar aspect is not a snow and ice mountain. The massive summit pyramid looks like nothing so much as a vast lump of sleet-smitten coal. Tom Stobart I found enraptured at the prospects for his film (later to become that magnificent work of art *The Conquest of Everest*). Even at this early stage he told me: "There's so much beauty about it's difficult to know what to leave out."

The afternoon was now advancing rapidly and no further time could be lost if I was to return to my own camp by nightfall. I took some hurried photographs of the camp while the climbers sheltered in the tent having now been warned that there must be no more posing for "outsiders." To my distress, by a mischance, the party, in a hurry to pack at Thyangboche monastery, had left out of its kit the medicine which we desperately needed for Gyalsen. Kirkia and I thus set off down the glacier empty-handed with barely three hours' daylight left to us to reach our own base, whence we had needed over five hours on the journey up.

In mountains it is generally a matter of chagrin how height laboriously won is so easily lost. But descending from a high altitude one feels nothing but an indescribable sense of elation and relief.

We almost ran down the glacier, experiencing only one check where an ice floe had drifted away from its bank, leaving a gap of water impossible to bridge. Here, Kirkia wanted to wade across with me on his back, but this I refused to allow for there was still a chance that a sudden storm would cause us to be benighted on the glacier, in which case he could scarcely escape frostbite. At length we managed a detour through the ice pinnacles, which was really ice-ax work, and delayed us fifteen minutes. We reached home, however, in three hours and twenty minutes, just as dark was falling.

In the day Kirkia and I had accomplished what is normally considered four days' stages for laden porters at that altitude. Kirkia had worn the bottom right off his pair of Tibetan boots, and for the last half hour had been walking barefoot. Next morning we both woke up three parts snow blind.

Playing hide-and-seek round Everest with highly mobile mountaineering parties is a thankless task. When the game suddenly changes to blind man's buff it becomes a hopeless one. For some minutes as I lay in my sleeping bag in the stone hut I could not see a thing. I knew at once that I was snow blind, although I had noticed nothing the day before. I also knew that the condition is temporary, and my feeling was therefore one of annoyance rather than anxiety. The complaint is acutely painful—painful to open the eyes and painful to close them again; but provided one does not aggravate the condition by a further dose of glacier glare, the effects soon wear off. I cursed myself for having after all forgotten to buy sun glasses. I had reminded myself often enough in Katmandu, only finally to leave the capital without them. Omissions and mischances plague the best regulated expeditions. The British expedition had forgotten to pack enough matches for its smokers—there were very few in the party. Of the two field teams I was to meet, both, although attended by eminent doctors who also happen to be prominent climbers, had forgotten to take medical kits with them. As for mischances, the expedition's Sherpa mess-men in an unwonted fit of house-orderliness were responsible for throwing all the expedition's spare flashlight bulbs away.

A grunt from the other end of the hut, followed by a pantomime communication, informed me that Kirkia, too, was as good as blind. Kirkia, that ambling alp, was really more culpable than myself, for he had had sun goggles with him, but the day before he had left them in the hut before starting. The reflected glare from a glacier at such altitudes is terrific and I was soon to find that it would burn the skin off the backs of my hands until they were raw.

My one thought was to get off the glacier before the sun climbed high, but in this we were frustrated by Da Tensing, No. 3 Sherpa coolie. Da Tensing was determined to celebrate his recovery from stomach-ache, which had incapacitated him the day before, by cooking and eating an enormous meal. I hate to grudge a poor man his food, but three hours for breakfast is, I think, excessive for anyone.

While the seemingly interminable process of baking, stewing and boiling went on I stumbled round the hut with a scarf tied round my face like a masked bandit, declaiming in muffled tones one of the few tags I remember from Kipling:

> And the end of the fight is a tombstone white
> With the name of the late deceased,
> And the epitaph drear "A fool lies here
> Who tried to hustle the East."

This irony was entirely lost on Da Tensing, who, however,

managed a mournful look of reproach while continuing to shovel huge pats of butter into himself with his fingers, pausing occasionally to wipe his mouth with the end of his pigtail.

When at last we did set out the sun was brilliant, and while Da Tensing and Kirkia, once more safely behind his goggles, made swift progress, I tottered and stumbled behind, petulantly, I fear, but fully conscious I deserved what I was getting.

My chief anxiety was for Gyalsen, left in the hut at Tula, a very sick man. It would not have surprised me to find Gyalsen dead. It certainly did surprise me to find him not only up and about, but apparently fully recovered and preparing to join us up the glacier. This power of recuperation astonished me. I was later to discover that he certainly had no need to sham sickness. With my slight medical knowledge I had thought that he must be suffering from pneumonia. In point of fact I was told by Major Wylie who signed on the British expedition porters, that he had been rejected from that company because his medical record showed that he was in an advanced state of tuberculosis and had already lost one lung.

The four Sherpas, being once more gathered together, decided that the occasion merited a celebration, and out again came the cooking pots and pans.

Two hours later, when it became obvious that we were not going to get much farther that day—a matter of no concern to the Sherpas, who, being paid by the day, are always willing to make two days' work out of one—I decided that something drastic must be done.

I therefore announced that that afternoon we would walk over the ridge that leads down from the Lhotse-Nuptse range, to the village of Dingboche in the Imja Valley to the east. This meant climbing back to 17,000 feet, but I considered it might be good for certain digestions if it might be bad for my eyes.

It proved a happy decision—although greeted by a little

demur and one or two groans—for soon a thick blanket of cloud obscured the sun, while there being no snow on the ridge meant rest for the eyes on great stretches of green-brown turf.

Finally, on the heights above the Imja Valley, we were rewarded by the sight of another four of the British expedition's gaily-colored tents pitched in the village of Dingboche itself.

Dingboche, being possibly the highest Sherpa grazing village, had not then been reoccupied, it being too early in the season, and it was not long before my Sherpas had found themselves a convenient hay-filled barn and a cottage without a roof, which served as a good windbreak within which to pitch my tent. After we were comfortably settled in, Gyalsen and I walked over to the British party which consisted of Tom Bourdillon and Dr. Charles Evans (who were to make the first assault on the summit), Alan Gregory, Major Wylie and "Tiger" Tenzing. All were deeply sun-tanned and bearded—with the exception of Tenzing who like most Sherpas could probably not grow a beard if he tried.

This party had been probing up the Imja Valley towards the great peak of Makalu (27,800 ft.) but had been paying most attention to the south face of Lhotse (27,900 feet) from whose northern face the South Col leads on to the final pyramid of Everest.

It was an embarrassing meeting for both sides, for while not even Britons can usually bring themselves to cut each other dead in the wilderness, the regulations about denying expedition information to "strangers" were more rigidly held here than on the Icefall. In addition, Gregory, responsible for most of the expedition's still photography, was obviously not going to surrender his prerogative easily to a competitor. Therefore, after a fruitless request for medicine, for there was none—I was assured it would be available at Thyangboche—I retired outside the camp perimeter and took a number of long-range pictures of the camp, whereupon the members vanished into the decent obscurity of their tents.

What annoyed me particularly was that, owing to the delays of the morning, I had missed a meeting with Colonel Hunt. Earlier in the day the Colonel's party had crossed from the Dingboche camp towards the Icefall on the very path which I had used in the afternoon. If my own party had been able to keep to any sort of a timetable I could not have failed to have met him. Now the chance was gone and in his absence, and without his permission, the rest of the expedition could hardly be blamed for refusing to speak "off the record." The Dingboche party were due back at Thyangboche monastery the following day. This was my own intention, as my food supplies were almost exhausted, and we arrived almost simultaneously at noon. There was now every sign of animation at the monastery camp—preliminary acclimatization excursions were over, the time had come to move the Base Camp up to the Icefall and the general air of expectancy and resolution was reminiscent of the "this is it" feeling one remembered before a big show in the last war. Once again I regretted bitterly that I was merely an "intruder" with not even the smallest possible part to play in the events to come. My own small effort was over. It had been interesting for me because there had been a certain air of originality about it—or rather it could be considered a "throw back" to the days of cleft-stick journalism. In the mountaineering sense it could not be rated very highly for Everest is so colossal that one can walk up to 18,000 feet on the south and, I believe, to over 21,000 on the northern, by way of the east Rongbuk glacier, without encountering any serious obstacle. It is above those heights that the appalling difficulties begin and many would argue that I, myself, had never actually been *"on"* the mountain.

When my dispatches from what I could truly call "the foot of Everest" if no higher, arrived in London, my newspaper

The Daily Mail expressed some jubilation in editorial comment (May 8, 1953), but they were careful to keep the comment in its proper proportion:

> Izzard's adventure is not, after all, the full Everest climb. It is just another example of a good reporter's determination to cover his assignment at all hazards. Nothing like these dispatches has come from Everest before.
>
> No one, however, will claim that they record anything like the ordeals which await the climbers themselves—least of all Izzard, whose modest account of his experiences is not the least of their recommendations.
>
> The mountaineers, under the leadership of Colonel Hunt, will meet rigors which are to be found nowhere else on earth. To go up to 19,000 ft. (they flattered me here) needs a good constitution. To climb to 29,000 ft. in bitter cold and tearing gales—that is work for heroes.
>
> The final assault is expected to be made at the end of next week—and once again our hopes and our good wishes will be with that small band of lonely figures who will be climbing far upwards on the roof of the world.
>
> This year's expedition is better equipped than any before. The weather conditions are promising and the newest approach is thought to be not quite so difficult as that which used to be followed.
>
> Some experts rate the chances of success as higher than usual, while others think they are about even. It would be a mighty achievement if, after 30 years of striving, the British flag could be planted on that demonic summit.
>
> There would be no material gain, no territory won or treasure garnered—nothing except the joy of achievement and the knowledge that man's unconquerable spirit had accepted another challenge and had again conquered.
>
> If it is done it will be a triumph not only for Colonel Hunt and his party but for all those who have gone before—all who have struggled and suffered and died so that their experience could be given to those who came after.

> What a grand thing it would be if this stupendous feat could be brought off in this year of all years. It would be a fine gift from men of our blood to the Queen at her Coronation.

This last sentence was a nice piece of anticipation and the whole leading article, I hope, absolves me from any charges of presumption.

Although the hustle and bustle at Thyangboche was considerable, Charles Evans and Major Wylie found time to broach some stores and give me all the medicine I required for Gyalsen. Wylie called for Gyalsen himself and added the most implicit instructions in Gurkhali which one could only hope he followed. It was the general opinion that far from climbing around on the slopes of Everest, he should be in a sanatorium.

I now decided to push on to Namche Bazar in order to reorganize my return to Katmandu as speedily as possible. The afternoon still held sufficient daylight and for the last time, on top of the Thyangboche saddle, I turned my eyes towards the black pyramid of Everest trailing its plume of snow above the Lhotse-Nuptse curtain, and I confess I shuddered. At Namche the Katmandu coolies awaited me with delight and took over the pitching of my tent on the same patch of ground as I had previously used. I had been away exactly one week and as far as I could gather they had spent this time in feasting and general rejoicing. Taking over the money box from the sirdar I paid off the four Sherpas and thus ended our odd little adventure together. Of the four men Gyalsen had obviously been outstanding in his time, and stricken and ill as he now was—no doubt because of his faithful service to previous expeditions—it would be unkind to criticize him. Kirkia I had found a delightful character—one could not but admire his rugged endurance and unfailing willingness and good temper. I had not seen so much of Nawang Tensing, but he struck me as a reliable man of about average performance. Brother Da Tensing was just a nuisance.

I was just settling down for the evening when I heard that Major J. O. M. Roberts heading the expedition's rear party had just arrived from Namche and was quartered in a house lower down in the town. I at once went down to see him and found him camping out on a verandah where, as he speaks fluent Gurkhali, he was commanding a good deal more attention than myself. We spent a very pleasant hour in conversation. Roberts' main party of seventy-seven coolies and James Morris was still climbing up the Dudh Kosi Valley. Roberts had found the going too slow and had come on ahead to hear the latest news of the expedition. This, in part, I was able to give him and he, in his turn, related such events as had happened in Katmandu since my departure.

That night I went to bed healthily and happily tired, having been making double marches for the past three days. There was one further interruption. Pasang arrived from his village and announced he was ready to accompany me the next day to Katmandu.

CHAPTER IX

THAT ABOMINABLE SNOWMAN

THERE WAS one task still left to me at Namche Bazar—a quick investigation of the tales regarding the Abominable Snowman. When I had passed through a week before I had mentioned the subject to Schoolmaster Tshiring Dorje and had been told by him that a man who had seen one at close quarters was living in the town and could give me an accurate description. As I lay in my sleeping bag with snow falling gently on the roof of the tent, and drifting beneath its shrunken sides, I determined that in the morning I should meet this man.

The next day was again clear. The warmth of the rising sun soon caused the thin layer of snow to vanish, but long before this had occurred I was once more surrounded by a chorus of small boys inching ever nearer, watching every motion as I drew upon my cigarette, tensed for the scramble which would ensue as soon as I threw away the diminished butt.

I was struggling for the necessary elbow room within which to eat my breakfast when Roberts appeared to say farewell before pushing on to the monastery. This was a civility which

I deeply appreciated for the detour involved a climb of several hundred feet in altitude out of his way. Roberts, being the newest attraction in the village, had not been allowed to sleep long and being less accustomed than I was by this time to a gallery of grinning faces round the bed, had called it a night and risen from his verandah rather before the lark. I half thought of asking Roberts to act as interpreter during the forthcoming interrogation but decided not to do so in case some clue should be turned up which would be within the powers of the expedition, but not within my own to pursue.

As soon as Roberts had left, Dorje (which is translated "Thunderbolt") appeared, walking majestically up the path from the monastery, the center of another horde of small boys who clung timidly to the jacket which he had bound about his waist to act as skirt. The mere mention of *yeti* (the Sherpa word for Abominable Snowman) was sufficient to cast a gloom over the morning which visibly affected Dorje and particularly our small audience. Dorje, in his role of Man of Letters, appeared dubious whether *yeti* constituted the sort of subject he might be expected to know something about and yet not appear ridiculous. Eventually, he volunteered diffidently that there are Greater and Lesser Snowmen. On pressing, he affirmed that *yeti* occurred "there" (pointing vaguely towards Thyangboche monastery and beyond to Sikkim—and "there" (pointing roughly north towards the 19,000 foot Nangpa La Pass and the Menlung Basin). These were apparently the haunts of Snowman Major. He then pointed down the Dudh Kosi valley and alleged that Snowman Minor was frequently seen in the woods surrounding the village of Panga, one day's march away. This was of interest, for it provided a possible explanation of the conduct of the voluble and gesticulating Sherpa who had met us outside Panga on our journey up, had led us through the village to our robber cave quarters in the Dudh Kosi gorge and had helped us build the immense conflagration which had been kept burning all night and was guaranteed to singe the hide off anything at a range of 25 yards. This deduction seemed to receive the support of some of the coolies who had now wandered up and began nodding emphatically. Encouraged by acclaim from an unexpected quarter, Dorje now led us down into the village in search of the local *yeti* expert. This search was none too energetically pursued, however, and after a good deal of time had been wasted it was announced that the star witness had apparently left the village on a journey of indeterminate length. This fact may appear suspicious but I was neither abashed nor disheartened, for the dossier on the Snowman already contains any number of sworn statements by Sherpa eyewitnesses following interrogation by reliable Europeans or Indians.

This is, I think, a fitting point to examine part of this dossier.

Snowman literature contains no more entertaining contribution than Appendix B ("Anthropology or Zoology with particular reference to the 'Abominable Snowman'"), to H. W. Tilman's book *Mount Everest 1938*. After setting up the Aunt Sallies of boulder, bear, monkey or man as possible authors of the strange unexplained footprints which have been seen so frequently across the whole length of the Himalaya, Mr. Tilman demolishes each in turn, and concludes by counseling us, until the Snowman exposes himself as either a hoax or something already within our knowledge, to give him the benefit of the doubt. At the time he was writing (1947) Mr. Tilman's admirable essay on the Snowman could be regarded as positively the last word on the subject, being an expert summary of all evidence until then available.

In the six years which have now elapsed, a number of other champions have, however, entered the field and Mr. Tilman himself has returned to the charge. I submit that no fresh evidence which has been brought to light in any way denies the Abominable Snowman his identity as a distinct animal in his own right—in fact indications seem stronger than ever that we are dealing with "Animal X" an unknown variety, or possibly species, a dangerous beast of marked ferocity, who has little to commend him other than his rather endearing name.

Let us now examine the post-1947 evidence particularly as it affects Nepal. As preface we can do worse than quote from Mr. O. Polunin's contribution in an Appendix ("The Natural History of the Langtang Valley") to Mr. Tilman's book *Nepal Himalaya* (1952: C. Univ. Press). Mr. Polunin, a distinguished naturalist writes:

> From time to time during the last 150 years, interesting details of the plants and animals of the high alpine regions of Nepal have come to light when collections made by native collectors have been sent back to Europe. Our knowledge of the adjoining countries of Sikkim and Kumaon have helped us to build up a broad picture of the flora and fauna of Nepal, but probably more than 500 square miles of the steepest country in the world lies waiting for detailed investigation by trained naturalists.
>
> Within this area many hundreds of species of plants, insects and other small animals may remain unknown to the scientific world. In addition our knowledge of the distribution of plants and animals, from east to west, and from west to east, along the Great Himalayan Range will continue to be full of gaps until Nepal has been fully explored. Nepal lies roughly at the junction of two lines of migration where plants and animals from Kashmir and Afghanistan meet those from Burma and China. No plants, as far as is known, have invaded the high Himalaya from the plains of India, and few have come south from Tibet.
>
> At the meeting place of two previously isolated groups the biologist expects interesting things to happen; hybrids may be formed and new species evolved.

I should add at once that at no place in his illuminating appendix does Mr. Polunin have the temerity to mention the Abominable Snowman. He merely sets the stage for us; scarcely penetrated Nepal (at least by Europeans) meeting place of two lines of migration where, in consequence, strange things may happen.

In his own text (*Nepal Himalaya*) Mr. Tilman records two further incidents relating to the Snowman. The first concerns a meeting (in 1949) with herdsmen in the Langtang Himal, about 80 miles west of Everest.

> In the course of conversation these herdsmen confirmed the existence, or rather the recent presence, of the Abominable Snowman in the Langtang, pointing out a cave which had been his favorite haunt. Six years previously these beasts (whose existence is surely no longer a matter for conjecture) had been constant visitors but had apparently migrated elsewhere. The small kind, the size of a child, they called "chumi," while the big fellow went by the name of "yilmu." Since sceptics like to affirm that the tracks made by these creatures are in reality bear tracks, it is worth mentioning that the herdsmen were able to show us some fresh bear tracks. It is noteworthy, too, that although bear tracks were fairly common in the Langtang we saw no tracks on snow, which confirms the natural supposition that it is a rare occurrence for a bear to go above the snowline. In the absence of rigid proof to the contrary, it is, therefore, safe to assume that if tracks are seen in snow they are not those of a bear.

In his subsequent journey to the vicinity of Everest (1950) Mr. Tilman relates how the Snowman cropped up again—this time at the Sherpa grazing village of Phalong Karpa at the snout of the Khumbu glacier.

> As we sat in the secure circle of the fire, our backs to the stonewall of the hut, the talk turned naturally to the Abominable Snowman. As one might expect they are found in these

parts in numbers, especially around Namche Bazar in the depths of winter when the cold drives them lower. Danu (a Sherpa) affirmed that the previous year (1949) a friend of his named Lakhpa Tensing had had his face so severely mauled by one, on the Nangpa La, that he died. By running downhill, which is of course, the only way a man can run at these heights, one can usually get away from these creatures whose long hair, falling over their eyes, hampers them, but the unfortunate Lakhpa had apparently tripped and lying half stunned by the fall became an easy prey.

Champions of the Snowman—among whom I number myself—are however indebted to Mr. Eric Shipton's Mount Everest Reconnaissance Expedition of 1951 for the clearest proof yet provided of his existence. Mr. Shipton, after reconnoitering the Icefall between the Khumbu glacier and the Western Cwm, turned his attention to the country to the west of Everest. It was on a glacier of the Menlung Basin, at about 19,000 feet, that his party came upon, and photographed, the remarkable series of footprints which have aroused so much comment.

In his book *The Mount Everest Reconnaissance 1951* Mr. Shipton describes finding the prints and adds:

> We did not follow them further than was convenient, a mile or so, for we were carrying heavy loads at the time, and besides we had reached a particularly interesting stage in the exploration of the basin. I have in the past found many sets of these curious footprints and have tried to follow them, but have always lost them on the moraine or rocks at the side of the glacier. These particular ones seemed very fresh, probably not more than twenty-four hours old. . . . Sen Tensing (a Sherba) who had no doubt whatever that the creatures (for therc had been at least two) that had made the tracks were *Yetis* or wild men, told me that two years before, he and a number of other Sherpas had seen one of them at a distance of about 25 yards at Thyangboche. He described it as half man

and half beast, standing about five feet six inches, with a tall pointed head, its body covered with reddish brown hair, but with a hairless face. When we reached Katmandu at the end of November, I had him cross-examined in Nepali (I conversed with him in Hindustani). He left no doubt as to his sincerity. Whatever it was that he had seen, he was convinced that it was neither a bear nor a monkey, with both of which animals he was, of course, very familiar. Of the various theories that have been advanced to account for these tracks, the only one which is any way plausible is that they were made by a langur monkey, and even this is very far from convincing, as I believe those who have suggested it would be the first to admit.

I understand that the proponents of the langur—and it would have to be a giant variety behaving as no monkey normally does—are no longer very happy with their theory.

Mr. Shipton's discovery is also referred to by Mr. W. H. Murray in his book *The Story of Everest*. Mr. Murray, himself a member of the reconnaissance party writes: "Some of the prints were particularly clear and must have been left within the last twenty-four hours. Pad marks and toe marks could be distinctly seen within the footprints, which were twelve inches long, and where the creature had jumped the smaller crevasses the scrabble marks of its nails could be seen on the far side." Mr. Murray, who traveled the same route three days after Mr. Shipton, adds that he and his companion Mr. T. Bourdillon "followed the tracks for the better part of two miles (the animal had chosen the best possible route), until on our second day, we too had to take to the moraine."

Having made a major contribution to the Abominable Snowman's dossier Mr. Shipton and Mr. Murray appear to have been content to let the case for the defense rest. Not so Dr. G. N. Dutt an Indian Geologist who also accompanied Mr. Shipton. Dr. Dutt has done some research work of his own and has dug up some instances which may have escaped Mr. Tilman. Dr. Dutt published his findings in *The Times of*

India (May 17, 1953). After recalling that the first Everest expeditions had also come across *yeti* footprints when approaching the mountain by the northern route, Dr. Dutt claims that the earliest published account appears in *Altai Himalaya* (Roerich) in which the author describes how a Major of the British Army saw a tall man, almost naked, standing and leaning on a high bow.[1]

Nicholas Roerich was a Russian painter and mystic. He designed the original *mise en scène* for Stravinski's *Sacre du Printemps.* He left Russia after the revolution and following a brief sojourn in America (there is a museum of his paintings in New York) retired to the Himalaya finally settling, with his family, in the Kulu valley of northern Punjab. *Altai Himalaya* is an account of an extensive journey through Central Asia in the form of "jottings from the saddle." Paragraphs are often unrelated. That concerning the Abominable Snowman is sandwiched between a homily on the punctuality of the English and an anecdote of a "sadhu's" railway journey without a ticket. It runs:

> It all began with the unknown traces found by the Everest Expedition [1922?]. Then in the *Statesman* [presumably of Calcutta], an English Major related how during one of the expeditions into the region of the Himalayas, he encountered a strange mountain inhabitant. At sunrise, amidst the frosty snows, the Major walked away from the camp and climbed the neighboring rocks. Glancing at the nearby rocks, the Major to his astonishment beheld a tall man almost naked, standing, leaning on a high bow. The mountain inhabitant did not look at the Major, his attention being completely attracted by something unseen behind the curve of the slope. And suddenly the man bent, strained himself, and by madly dangerous leaps rushed from the rocks and disappeared. When the Major told

[1] It may be mentioned that Colonel L. A. Waddel in his book *Among the Himalayas* (pub. 1898) describes how he came across the animal's tracks on a snowfield in northeast Sikkim in 1889.

his people about the meeting they smiled and said: "Sahib has seen a 'snow' man. They are watching the guarded places."

Earnest seekers after truth regarding the Abominable Snowman would I think, do well to leave Roerich out of their researches. As a mystic he was much given to symbolism and could "see" the outline of men and gods in rock faces or headlands and painted them as such.

Dr. Dutt continues:

> Another story goes back to the time Sir Charles Bell was Indian Political Officer in Sikkim, a feudatory state north of Darjeeling. Some workmen of the Posts and Telegraph Department were reported missing while they were at work near the Jelap La (Pass). Immediately afterwards the British troops stationed nearby were summoned to search for their bodies and also to account for their mysterious disappearance. A few hours' search resulted in the discovery of a Snowman, who was apparently responsible for the death of the missing persons. It was an easy target for the rifles. The body was alleged to have been twelve feet tall, with shaggy hair and toes pointing backwards.

Dr. Dutt then describes how, having the necessary languages at his command, he was able to interrogate Ange Tharkay, the Sherpa Sirdar of the 1951 reconnaissance. (Ange Tharkay, an older man than Tenzing Norkey, now runs his own tourist and travel agency in Darjeeling. In his heyday he was regarded as at least Tenzing's equal by Himalayan climbers.) According to Dr. Dutt, Ange Tharkay, after giving a general description of a Snowman, added a plausible and never failing method of avoiding death when face to face with the creature. "In such a predicament [said Ange Tharkay] one should not lose courage but collect pieces of stones, wood—in fact, anything handy—and throw them one by one at the Snowman. The creature would then collect them with both hands outstretched as if they were prized valuables. As soon as the hands of the Snowman are thus full, the person must scamper to a place of safety."

Dr. Dutt also carried on his investigation at Thyangboche monastery where: "a Tibetan monk told me that he had seen a "Shukpa" (*Yeti*) at the bank of the Imja Khola at dusk. The creature was drinking water there. The monk took fright and fled to his village." This appears to be a distinct visitation, not to be confused with the commonly recounted story of the appearance of a Snowman on a field beside the monastery when a festival was in progress attended by some scores of Sherpas and visiting lamas from Rongbuk monastery. There are innumerable witnesses to this incident which may be the same as that told by Sen Tensing to Mr. Shipton. If this is so the date of the occurrence would be 1949.

Dr. Dutt's most graphic story relates to a fight between a Sherpa strong man and a Snowman. He writes:

> A man of Monjo, a village in the valley of the Dudh Kosi, told me a story relating to his father who was a man of great strength and courage. He was told by the elderly people of the village that there was a meadow of soft grass and junipers about 6,000 feet up on the southern slopes of the 22,340 foot Kangteka peak, and that if the Snowmen were not there, it would have been ideal pasture land for the yaks. Once, grass grew scarce in the vicinity of the village and, consequently, the milk supply of the yaks decreased considerably. The spirit of adventure of the strong man prompted him to go in search of pastures new. He collected all the yaks of the village and went up. Having left them to graze, he took the opportunity to search for the Snowmen who were supposed to haunt the place.
>
> Two black shadows fell across his path suddenly from one of the overhanging cliffs. Looking up he saw one of them vanish quickly and the other one advance. In a few minutes he found himself struggling with a monster. After a bloody duel, the villager extricated himself from the clutches of the creature with

a superhuman effort. When he returned his fellow villagers found him swaying with giddiness and blood oozing from his eyes and nostrils. He fell into a swoon and was revived with a strong dose of *rakhsi*—Nepalese wine. Incoherently he muttered about his almost fatal encounter with the Snowman.

Thinking that the Snowman had died, the villagers went to the scene of the struggle early next morning. The crushed grass, the dislodged stones and the ground in general bore testimony of the previous night's struggle; the Snowman was, however, not found. The villagers concluded that the body of the Snowman must have been carried away by one of its companions.

Dr. Dutt concludes with an eerie story of his own.

Almost all the residents of the high-altitude pastoral villages believe in the existence of the *Shukpa* (*Yeti*). The men were afraid to remain alone in their potato fields, especially when evening approached. The lowest altitude they were found to descend was around 13,000 feet here, but I found footprints as high up as 20,000 feet. The imprints on snow could definitely be identified as the footprints of an animal walking on two legs but, however indistinct they were, the dwellers of the snows did not appear to be walking with toes reversed.

At the time I was exploring the Cho Oyu (26,750 ft.) region on October 12, 1951, I camped by the side of a lake at the foot of the Kyojumba glacier. Next morning, I went up the slope between two rocky promontories, leaving the main glacier on my right. The col in front was about 1,500 feet high. Since there was no track, all I could do was scramble between rugged boulders, some as large as 50 feet across. It was 10 A.M. The sun had begun to melt the snow on the rocky slopes. Melting snow and dislodged rocks made the track treacherous. Although something told me that my movements were watched, I was so preoccupied with finding a safe route up that I did not pay any attention to the foreboding. Finally, I reached the top of the col enjoying the view. Cho Oyu faced me directly and only Pumori and its smaller satellites prevented me from seeing gigantic Everest.

I did not stay long here to enjoy the landscape because the wind and glare were telling on my nerves. All the time I was on snow I was following large queer footsteps which ran in the opposite direction. As I was alone, the discovery of the footprints urged me to return quickly.

Back at the col, I took a minute's rest, wiped the sweat off my goggles and almost involuntarily looked up. I fancied I saw a creature watching me from the ridge to the left. By the time I put on my glasses, it was out of sight. All that I was able to see in that short interval was that it had grizzly brown hair on its head. When I told this to my porters afterwards, they severely reprimanded me for going up alone.

Was it merc hallucination? It is true my eyes had been aching at the time I saw it, but all the time I was up the rocky slopes I had a feeling that someone was watching my movements. Suddenly I realized—and as I did so a shudder went through me—*those footsteps went up towards the west ridge.*

Many of us, and not only the hypersensitive, have felt the sense of a "presence" at high and desolate altitudes and can sympathize with Dr. Dutt. Nine times out of ten this "presence" is felt to be malevolent rather than benevolent although an outstanding exception is the experience of Frank Smythe during the failure of the final attempt on Everest made by the 1933 expedition. Returning to rejoin Shipton at Camp VI, after his forlorn solo effort to reach the top, Smythe records that he felt an overwhelming sense of being accompanied by a companion whose function it was to watch over his safety. So strong was the feeling that when he sat down on a rock to eat some food and being in the dream state which overcomes exhausted men at high altitude, he divided the food in half and turned to offer a portion to his "friend." It almost startled him to find no one there.

But whether or not Dr. Dutt was suffering from hallucinations and was deceived in what he saw, nothing can wash out the footsteps he discovered and Dr. Dutt is the sort of man who can be relied upon to recognize a footprint when he sees one.

If we ruthlessly discard Dr. Dutt's brief glimpse, unbelievers certainly have a telling point when they challenge that no completely reliable witness—certainly no European—has actually *seen* a Snowman in recent times. The latest recorded viewing by a European that I can find was by Mr. A. N. Tombazi who relates in his book *Account of a Photographic Expedition to the Southern Slopes of Kangchenjunga* that in 1925 he sighted what *may* have been an Abominable Snowman at a distance of two to three hundred yards while camped under Mount Kabru at a height of 15,000 feet. It may be pointed out that this location is not many miles from the Zemu Gap (Sikkim) where in 1937 Colonel Sir John Hunt discovered one of the first sets of authentic footprints. Our case for the Snowman, therefore, relies chiefly upon the tradition and the tracks.

Traditions are tricky things to trace down. The tradition of a Snowman is certainly widespread. Mr. Ronald Kaulback when exploring across the Tibeto-Burma frontier records it as far east as the Upper Salween—where he also came upon the tracks in a region where there were neither bears nor monkeys. In 1948 when I was myself on trek in the Himalayan foothills of northern Assam the tribesmen there spoke confidently of "naked men of the snows" who dwell in the higher mountains to the north. We have seen that the tradition is particularly strong both in Sikkim and around Namche Bazar in eastern Nepal. It occurs again farther west in Nepal and taking the Himalayas as a whole is to be found as far west as the Karakorams.

Local names naturally vary according to the language or dialect spoken in any particular district, but it may be noted that whatever the local name, throughout the whole length of the Himalaya—rather more than 1,500 miles—where across vast stretches lateral communication is next to impossible, all names mean roughly the same thing in English. *Shukpa* and *Yeti* can both I think be safely translated as the "wild (in the sense of untamed) men of the snows." I understand the alternative Tibetan name *Metch Kangmi* which originally gave rise to the rather joyous translation of "Abominable Snowman" has not been rendered quite accurately. *Kangmi* certainly means "Snowman" but *Metch*, to a pedant, more closely denotes "unkept" or "unwashed," to a repulsive degree. We are, I think, indebted to Mr. Tilman for the happy Latin classification, *"Homo niveus odiosus"* (this should not be beyond the Lower Fourth Form).

One must make allowances for the observations of frightened and imaginative men when attempting to describe the appearance of an Abominable Snowman. He has more than once been described as up to twelve feet tall—he is probably nearer six. He is invariably described as covered all over in reddish hair except for the face, but the hair of the head is long and falling over the eyes hampers vision. The feet—by accurate measurement— are between 12 and 14 inches long and broad in proportion (the shoe would certainly fit no known monkey). The more imaginative Sherpas believe that the feet of the Snowmen are turned back to front to enable them to walk uphill more easily. Rather pleasing flattery this, for to the music-hall mind it emphasizes that the best way to elude one would be to run downhill in which case the Snowman would presumably stand every chance of stubbing his toe and turning a back somersault. So much for tradition.

Our own case rests chiefly on the track. One must concede that doubtless there is a perfectly logical explanation for numbers of tracks which have been reported from time to time, did one but know all the relative circumstances. But this does not alter the fact that numbers of other tracks have been reported for which no logical explanation is conceivable, and reported by men who not only know what they are talking about, but whose integrity is unquestioned. Surely, as Mr. Tilman writes in his essay: "If fingerprints can hang a man as they frequently do, footprints may be allowed to establish the existence of one."

The question we have to answer is who or what made the prints? The possibilities, as outlined before are boulder, bear, monkey or man and, one hastens to add "animal X," a hitherto unknown species.

Thanks to Mr. Shipton's remarkable photograph we can throw away the boulder for boulders do not have five toes, although it may be said that a boulder falling from a height and bouncing down a glacier can make a very realistic series of tracks. I discovered one such halfway up the Khumbu glacier, to the great perturbation of Sherpa Kirkia who, snuffling like a bloodhound, immediately set off on the scent and refused to relax until he had found the spot where the offending rock had come to rest. I later learned that the Swiss expedition of the previous year claimed that while negotiating the Khumbu glacier, which was then shrouded in heavy mist, they passed through a herd, flock, school or whatever it is of our friends but without being able to make any positive identification. (*Everest 1952:* Andre Roch.) Kirkia had accompanied the Swiss and the main cause of his anxiety when with me, was the fact that the spot where the pair of us had discovered our false trail coincided almost exactly with the position where the Swiss subsequently came upon genuine tracks of one *"abominable homme des neiges."*

As for the bear, almost all Himalayan travelers can tell a bear's print at a glance, for they are common at lower altitudes. This would be certainly true of such men as Colonel Hunt and Messrs. Shipton and Tilman—particularly so of the last two for at the close of one expedition—which I personally would consider rather too lightly provisioned—they were forced in order to sustain life to become rivals with the local bear population for the district's few available bamboo shoots.

And although Mr. Bertram Mills has shown us that bears can be taught to ride tricycles they do not normally walk on two feet. This fact, I consider, also rules out the monkey if nothing else does. I am open to correction, but to my knowledge the only monkey or ape which walks naturally on two legs is the gibbon and the gibbon only leaves tropical forests for excursions to such places as the London Zoo.

The theory that the tracks were made by a man is a little more difficult to disprove. It is known that in Tibet, where there is no capital punishment, criminal offenders are exiled from their communities and could possibly have taken to a caveman—or one might say Snowman—existence in the mountains. If this be so it is remarkable that all seem to have size fourteen feet and seem to exist on nothing at all unless it be an odd Sherpa or two, a rather indigestible diet for any man. It is also known that Hindu ascetics can sometimes be met on pilgrimages to the snows. Mr. Tilman again in his same essay, recounts a charming story of a Captain Henniker, Royal Engineers, who in 1930, on the summit of a 17,000 foot pass in Ladakh, met a man completely naked except for a loincloth. "It was bitterly cold and snowing gently at the time. When he expressed some natural astonishment he met with the reply, given in perfect English, 'Good morning, sir, and a Happy Christmas to you' [it was actually July]. The hardy traveler was an MA of an English University (Cambridge one suspects) and was on a pilgrimage for the good of his soul." This delightful little anecdote is included purely for its entertainment value, for although 17,000 foot in Ladakh is inhospitable enough, even in midsummer, it cannot match the utter desolation and complete apparent pointlessness of the places where *yeti* prints are most often found. Mr. Tilman, himself, hastens to spike Captain Henniker's guns with his own forceful confutation of the *homo sapiens* theory.

> We mountaineers may be wrong in thinking that a liking for the high snows is peculiar to us but I should be astonished to find a native, Tibetan or any other, however guilty, ascetic, or careless about washing who shared our taste for such places. There are ascetics to be found living not far below the snout of the Rongbuk glacier, but they remain immured in their caves, tended by their admirers and never in my experience mortify the flesh still further by a promenade up the glacier.

We are therefore left with animal "X"—an unknown variety or species.

That it has not yet—or rather recently, for the earlier trails are now too cold to follow—been seen by a European is not entirely surprising. European mountaineers in the Himalaya are still far from frequent and they go there more often than not with the single-minded purpose of placing their feet on the summit of a particular peak. Sad though it be for the interests of science, nothing will divert them from this main objective. Then, when one remembers the vast network of unexplored, forest-clad mountains and valleys where the Snowman can roam at will, it can scarcely be wondered at that he keeps out of the path of the very occasional small party which happens to come his way—quite apart from the fact that, like any number of other animals, he may be a creature almost entirely of nocturnal habits.

Few of us who have gone into this matter of the Snowman's credentials will not agree with Colonel Hunt when he says that sufficient reliable evidence now exists to warrant the organization of an expedition founded on a proper scientific basis and charged with the sole objective of proving or disproving his existence. Until that moment comes our Abominable friend will continue to shamble on his mysterious errands, credited by some, discredited by others, but with this to be said about him—there is now vastly more evidence to prove that he does exist, than there is to prove that he does not.

CHAPTER X

RETURN TO KATMANDU

Our search for the Namche Snowman expert had brought us down to one of the lower terraces of houses. We were, in fact, standing—possibly rather injudiciously—beside the house which had been used as quarters by Eric Shipton's 1951 reconnaissance expedition and which was now serving as the Security Police radio station. Two or three Sikh radio operators passed us, their immaculately groomed appearance in marked contrast to our group of ragged and shabby Sherpas. We were now joined by both the Headman and the Namche Police Chief, both of them wearing slightly worried expressions.

As there was little point in dragging back up the slope to the temple I sent a message for the coolies to bring their loads down. This they did, arriving however, without the Sirdar. After a lengthy interval another clamorous search produced a very drunk Sirdar—it was 8 A.M.—supported on the arm of a slightly flushed Pasang, who however still had enough wits about him to navigate for the pair of them. At the time the thought crossed my mind that Pasang with his self-imposed terms of contract—"me no money; maybe you help me a little maybe I help you"—might be more a hindrance than a help on the journey home. But these suspicions turned out to be totally unjustified. In loyal service and all round proficiency, for he had no caste inhibitions, he almost outshone the faithful Jeeves. Pasang, equipped from balaclava to boots by the Swiss expeditions of last year was completely self-contained. Sometimes he would forge ahead of us and sometimes lag behind, but he was always there when needed. Occasionally he would tire of carrying his own Alpine rucksack and hire local help for the day. If, more often than not, his daily help turned out to be a comely young maiden, it was no concern of mine, for not being on the pay roll he could make his own arrangements and pay for them in cash or kindly attentions, whichever proved the more acceptable.

The party being now complete, we all crossed the stream with its rows of beehive shrines within which the falling water, churning the prayer wheels like grindstones insured incessant invocation of the gods that be. A short climb brought us to the track leading to the Dudh Kosi gorge and here Dorje, the Headman and the Police Chief halted and went into close consultation. I had had an uneasy feeling that they had something on their minds but I was put off guard when Dorje, breaking up the conference, requested politely that I take their photographs. I was only too anxious to comply and accordingly lined them up before some boulders inscribed with Buddhist slogans, with the village in the background, and tried with various antics to relax three rather frozen yet slightly agonized expressions meant to convey dignity. As usual, Jeeves insisted on being in the picture, but as I was tiring of photographing him in every conceivable situation, I placed him on the wing where, unknown to him, he was conveniently left outside. Composition was not aided by the "noises off" provided by the Sirdar who with strings of curses, an explosive belch or two and an occasional, raucous snatch of song, came stumbling up the path behind us. Sherpas like their revelry as much, or more, than most men, but even with Sherpas there is a proper time and place for everything, and obviously the painful process of posing for photographs did not constitute an occasion where unseeming interruptions could be lightly tolerated.

Photography completed, there was another hurried consultation which ended with Dorje approaching me in rather embarrassed fashion:

"The Police Chief has just one question to ask you. Your papers say you were coming to join the expedition. Why did you not do so?" This was rather a facer, for I had never known what the papers did say, either in their original form, or in Dorje's translation. After Jeeves had faded into the background, as he invariably did when brushes with the law threatened, I hit on the happy explanation that the two words "join" and "meet" can mean either the same thing or have two different meanings. I had gone beyond Namche Bazar to "meet" the expedition and having done so I was now returning home.

"Was I returning direct to Katmandu?"

"Most decidedly."

This explanation seemed satisfactory, if a little puzzling, for the Police Chief and Dorje, and after exchanging addresses we said our farewells.

I learned later that news of my "sudden change of plan"—in fact, I had naturally had no intention at all of misleading anyone—was very smartly flashed through to Katmandu. This action was of considerable benefit to me, for the news was communicated to Saksena and by him to London, where it was received with some relief, for I had been "lost," as far as the office was concerned, for rather more than ten days. It was now April 16.

That morning I felt fitter and happier than at any time during the trip, although I was reluctantly turning my back on Everest. At any rate I had "been and seen." I had some sort of story to tell. If, back in Katmandu, I had known how easy it was to be, I might have laid in more provisions and budgeted for more silver coin. So equipped I might possibly have pitched camp at the top of the Khumbu glacier and held out there many days. But had I done so I should have been an embarrassment to the expedition and should have seen nothing more than a triumphant procession of climbers disappearing out of my sight up the Icefall to regions where, alone as I was, I could not possibly follow them.

As it was, I had a story which at least was original and, if I got back to Katmandu in double-quick time, would still retain some air of topicality about it. Here I made two sad miscalculations. I had not then realized how very fast, and how very far in a day, a good Sherpa runner can travel, carrying no more than a knapsack. I had also imagined—quite vainly—that a week's rest would find the coolies restored and willing and anxious to put their best feet forward. It was not so, and probably never is so. I have now learned that a week's carouse with money to burn and no authoritative hand to stay the consumption of rakshi at one rupee a bottle and an ocean of chang to be had for the same price, is enough to upset the rhythm of any march. It was certainly so in this case. At least three or four days elapsed before the tempo of our retreat in any way matched that which had developed during our advance. Coolies are not to be hurried. It is no good offering double pay for a double day's march. A coolie argues with devastating logic that when paid by the day and where the ultimate reward is the same, there is no sense in exerting oneself to the extent of crowding two days' work into one. If there is extra money to be gained, the easiest way to earn it is to make two days' work out of one—or to take, say, sixteen days over a march normally considered to be fourteen.

The sensible thing to have done would have been to sit down quietly at Namche Bazar, write my message in comfort and send it off ahead of me by runner. I might then have followed at leisure.

The route from Namche Bazar to the bed of the Dudh Kosi gorge is one of the few sections on the trail to Katmandu where the none too experienced traveler can feel a sensation of height amounting almost to giddiness. Other sections of the trail run high indeed, but nearly always bushes, boulders or trees reassuringly buttress the "off" side.

On the patch below Namche—which drops about two thousand feet in three miles—and is none too broad at the best of times—there are a number of places where the cliff drops sheer for several hundred feet. As I have mentioned before the more spectacular of these are crossed by narrow platforms of pine boughs braced round such obstructions as immense boiler-plate boulders too solid for hawing or cutting. These must be crossed for the simple reason that there is no possibility of detour. Jeeves and I, as had become customary, had rapidly outstripped the carriers, and when we arrived at the most perilous place of all I called another halt for picture taking. I was in such good form that morning that the dizzy height worried me not at all and I hitched myself up the rock on the near side of the cliff to await the coolies. These arrived rather flustered and a good picture obviously required certain reorganization. This was by no means accepted with good grace, Diamonds, Spades and the Joker all looking at me reproachfully to emphasize the fact that marching and counter-marching to and fro across a two foot wide and none too stable gangway, with Eternity beckoning about 400 feet below, was rather much to expect from men handicapped with 50 pound loads on their backs. However, we all reached the river side in safety, not excluding the Sirdar who was still inebriated enough to be blissfully ignorant of where he was going or what he was doing.

Down in the gorge it was once more almost oppressively warm. Summer had come with astonishing rapidity in the nine days since we had first passed that way. The cuckoo's incessant voice had already broken, the rhododendron flowers were now tarnished with decay and there was already a hint of budding wild roses. We had been threading our way through the huge boulders of the riverbank for about half an hour when I suddenly caught the sound of voices round the cliff immediately in front of us. A moment later I came face to face with James Morris, heading a "motley army of men and boys, the matron and the maid" who carried their loads marked "High pressure oxygen: handle carefully" with a gay abandon which, Morris confessed later, had made him shiver at the thought of each new day's march. A pause by the wayside for comparison of notes being indicated, we each selected a convenient rock and settled down, while Diamonds lit a fire and boiled a kettle and Jeeves unpacked a parcel of homemade biscuits baked at Namche Bazar.

For half an hour the conversation was general in character; the movements of the expedition as far as I knew them, the hardships of the trail, the rigors of the daily bath, and the behavior of coolies. Morris, with some disgust attributed his own rather haphazard progress to the defections of his sirdar who as a toss-pot, once he had hit the "beer line," had apparently developed a capacity superior if anything to my own. Mercifully fate decreed that the two should not meet, for when Morris' sirdar staggered past us in full song (he had been drunk for four days) mine had passed out behind a boulder, snoring loudly enough to bring down an avalanche had there been snow about.

There then occurred one of those incidents which will amuse the newspaper world if no one else. Up to this point I had always regarded Morris as a member of the expedition and had, in fact, frequently referred to him in my dispatches as "Mr. James Morris who is escorting the Expedition's oxygen equipment up to Thyangboche monastery." While we were gulping mugs of tea and munching biscuits it struck me that Morris might not have heard of the expedition's ban on "pirate" photographs. Morris, squatting informally on his rock, looked as if he might be taken for the asking and accordingly, in what I hoped were disarming tones, I introduced the question:

"Would you mind if I took your picture?"

Morris, in equally disarming tones, replied: "Not a bit, do you mind if I take yours?"

For a moment the joke was entirely one-sided, but we had hardly lowered our cameras after exchanging shots when Morris said: "Do you know I think we had better drop this; I am *The Times* correspondent." At that we both laughed heartily. *The Times,* it may be noted, seldom puts its correspondents' names to their dispatches, but did I not have a memory like a sieve I might have recalled that we had actually met before—twelve months previously, at dusk in a dormitory of the British Army Press Camp at Moascar in the Suez Canal Zone. Morris had been covering the Zone troubles; I had stopped off on my way back from Port Said to Cairo. It was a brief meeting, I doubt if we even shook hands, but my only excuse for not recognizing him again is that it never occurred to me to associate the Suez Canal with the Dudh Kosi gorge.

The disclosure started us off on a new trend of talk—the Press "shop" which pressmen will talk endlessly, any time, anywhere to their own vast entertainment and no doubt to the intense boredom of those without the circle. I learned, with intense gloom I confess, that the expedition had guaranteed Morris, as the favored *Times* Correspondent, what amounted to "safe conduct" up the Icefall, if it could be opened, and that he was on his way to establish headquarters in the Western Cwm. I blenched at the thought of what a skilled pen and a Leica camera could do to the opposition from such an elevation, and at the time I would gladly have surrendered a couple of frostbitten toes to the surgeon's scissors to have had the same privilege.

For the first time it now occurred to me that Morris was only two days' march from Thyangboche, and that if he cared to write a dispatch there, I should only have, at the most, four days' start over any runner he might care to send down to Katmandu, in which case he might well overtake me. Keeping my anxieties to myself, I therefore decided to push on with all speed. Morris and I parted on the best of terms and although I was bitterly disappointed at the turn of events, I can say with truth that I later read with as much enjoyment as anybody the brilliant dispatches he was able to write among surroundings and in conditions which must have been as daunting and depressing as could well be found in peacetime.

My own plan for speedy progress met with a setback straight away when Jeeves, as the morning drew on, missed the path and led me off on a track which was wretchedly overgrown, always precipitous and sometimes—where it had been swept away by landslides—nonexistent. We had crossed to the right bank of the river and should, in the normal course, have recrossed again to the left, but pride forbade Jeeves the admission of an error and his chosen short cut—if such it could be called—lost us a good two hours of marching time.

By pure chance this at times desperate scramble brought us back to the main trail exactly at the "robber's cave" just above Panga. The lucky stroke at once caused Jeeves to assume a supercilious air as if he had known all along where we were going. This notwithstanding the fact that the coolies who had been lagging badly behind us had now arrived at this point fully an hour before us. Much as I had come to love Jeeves, his refreshing cleanliness and tidiness, his superb cooking, his general probity and scrupulous honesty, there were times when I could have kicked him.

Diamonds, however, already had a fire going and while lunch was cooking I sat down to wait for it on a rock by the river. For half an hour I was entertained by a small species of dipper which kept popping off a small nearly submerged boulder into the foamy ginger beer colored water and after disappearing for some seconds re-emerging in almost the same spot. It remains a mystery to me how such a small bird can maintain itself in a current which would certainly have swept me off my feet.

Lunch was followed by the inevitable question: "Sahib camp here?" This I firmly refused to do and reluctantly carrying baskets were once more shouldered. A mile farther on, at Panga, the question regarding the camp was repeated with somewhat more urgency, but I again refused to the especial sorrow of the Sirdar who had now recovered sufficiently to relish the prospect of another debauch. I was soon to regret my decision for, having crossed again to the left bank, one of the lengthiest and steepest ascents of the whole journey begins. The bare essentials of a comfortable camp are water and firewood and these are most readily found in the vicinity of a village or farmhouse. We climbed for another hour without sighting either, and while there was plenty of wood about, the river, which would have supplied water was now far below us. Nor was there any flat ground at hand where a single man could stretch out, let alone pitch a tent. As I was now giving the orders the coolies were perfectly content to leave further arrangements to me and—as they no doubt hoped—it was not long before I began to feel that I had overreached myself. By good fortune, however, a turn round the next cliff brought us to a deep cleft in the side of the gorge. This carried a small waterfall and beside it stood a huge overhanging rock. This had obviously already offered third-class accommodation for other parties and was all right for the coolies. The tent was a different matter. We were now joined by Pasang, who had been missing all day, trailed by a buxom young Sherpa woman who was privileged to carry all his belongings besides her own. Pasang, after a good look round, pointed to a vast turnip-shaped boulder in mid-torrent surmounted by a few inches of soil and thick wiry scrub. He then borrowed the kukri from Clubs, climbed the rock, trimmed off the scrub and somehow managed to get the tent up. It was a wild setting and the usual evening thunderstorm now broke over us, peal succeeding peal and echoing and re-echoing round the gorge so that the din became incessant and unending. While the coolies remained dry under their rock I spent an uncomfortable night on my eyrie fervently hoping that a scrub spike would not puncture the air mattress and that if it did I would not roll under the tent and off the rock.

The trail continued upwards the whole of the next day and when in midafternoon we finally surmounted the pass and came to a few huts standing on a grassy alp, which had been one of our previous camps, I was as willing as anyone to rest there. With something of a shock I realized this was the site whence it had taken us only a day and a half to reach Namche Bazar. On the return journey, which was to be a record-breaker, we had required two full days. There was some comfort in the thought that the next day would be all downhill, and during it, as it turned out, we accomplished nearly two days' march—quite our best effort up to that time. I remember that day particularly because of a curious incident which occurred in the early morning. I was swinging down the hill, a magnificent view of range after range of mountains before me, when rounding a corner I came on a large herd of yak being driven up the slope towards me. The path was too narrow, and the sides too steep, to move quickly and before I could get out of the way the yaks spread in all directions in plunging disorder. There was a farmhouse hard by and one cow with a calf at foot got stuck halfway across the fence which surrounded it. After a few rather futile efforts to assist in the round up, I got out the camera to photograph the stranded yak. This animal was rather understandably agitated and I was having some difficulty in approaching her when I was suddenly interrupted by a melodious female voice speaking perfect English with a slight American accent: "I should be careful of that yak if I were you, she may be dangerous." Nothing could have surprised me more for hitherto the only Sherpas I had met who could make any pretense at all of speaking English were Pasang and Schoolmaster Dorje. I turned to find a handsome, unusually tall Sherpa woman laughing merrily at my discomfiture. After gazing at me quizzically for a moment she said: "Come, I will give you a better picture." Seizing two yak calves by the scruff of their necks and tucking one under each arm, she knelt down and smiled up at me. With her hair falling in two long braids over her beautifully embroidered cerise-pink apron she made a pretty picture indeed. Sitting down on the turf beside her I then asked—with somewhat natural curiosity—how she came to speak English. It was a fairly simple story. During the war she had been in service with an American family in Calcutta. When they had left for home she had returned to the farm in the hills. Her name, as I learned from a gold bracelet she had received as a farewell present was "Anidede." Our next exchange, resulting in a misunderstanding, set the seal on a happy morning. Fingering her apron, with due apologies, I said: "Is this Nepalese, it is very beautiful, I would like to buy something Nepalese for my wife." At this Anidede flung her head back, showing a fine set of teeth, and burst into peals of laughter. At last she said: "What. You want to buy yourself a Nepalese wife?" In vain I protested that I was married already and had five children in the bargain. The joke stuck. Pasang, who had then come up with the coolies, must needs translate it to them and baskets and all they rolled on the ground howling with mirth. There was thereafter no respite for me throughout the journey home. Whenever we passed a woman, however wrinkled or toothless she might be, someone would nudge another and say: "Sahib, wife," and the chortling would break out afresh. Even Jeeves would occasionally permit himself a polite snicker. Congenial relations having been established, Pasang was all for camping there and then and had it been evening I should have readily agreed. But I was madly impatient to get on and I gave the order to move. Looking back I am sorry that I did so, for of all the Sherpas I met, Anidede, talking on Sherpa lore and life, would obviously have been the one most worthwhile listening to. We did not, however, part without a stoop of *chang* all round, and the Sirdar, remembering his proper functions, completed a none-too-severely contested bargain for three hens and a cap full of eggs.

Two hours' slog down hill—a prolonged descent can become quite as tiresome as an ascent—brought us to another little homestead beside a stream which poured from the top of a high rock into a perfect bathing pool. Fed by a subsidiary conduit a grindstone whirred softly in its own little house. The trail crossed the lower end of the pool across a single slab of rock, making the place rather public, but as there was no one about when I arrived, and as I had not had a proper bath since before we reached Namche Bazar, I decided to make use of it. Jeeves and Diamonds halted to cook lunch while the rest of the party moved on up the trail with what occurred to me at once as rather a suspicious display of energy. I shaved rapidly, washed two or three pairs of socks and then, after a hurried look round the apparently deserted countryside, slipped out of my clothes and into the pool. It was quite the iciest bath I can recall and to cap it all, hardly had I surfaced, gasping for dear life, when a party of about ten women appeared on the bridge. They gazed at me in astonishment and then, giggling in the best of good humor, settled down to watch. In vain I splashed water in their direction and shouted to them to go away. Nothing would induce them in a situation like this to admit they understood me. The giggles increased. Both Jeeves and Diamonds ungallantly stood idly by vastly enjoying my predicament. To me it was obvious that if I stayed in the water much longer I should have a heart attack. One does not die of exposure in such circumstances and finally, swallowing my pride, and accompanied by excited exclamations I made a dash for the bank.

This incident, harmless enough, was followed by one rather more sordid. The three of us spent some time by the pool and two hours must have gone by before we caught up with the coolies. We found them sitting on the steps of a stupa in a small village surrounded by a jocose group of Sherpas. The Sirdar, Spades and the Joker were all helplessly drunk, while sounds of a very good party indeed continued to issue from the open doorway of a nearby house. Worse still, beside the Sirdar lay the battered remains of the tin box containing the silver coin. This last sight shipped Jeeves into a fury and for a full ten minutes before the assembled multitude he lashed the unfortunate Sirdar with his tongue. The latter, speechless and uncomprehending, merely stared stupidly in front of him. As Pasang later explained, the Sirdar had not deliberately broken open the box. He had drunk his fill and in trying to hitch the box up again on to his back it had slipped out of the sling. This had so unbalanced the Sirdar that he had sat down heavily—on the box—the resulting damage being argument enough against the purchase of mass-produced tin trunks. Jeeves, however, was not to be stayed in his wrath and before the Sirdar's eyes he spread a cloth on the ground, poured the contents on to it and counted and recounted every silver piece in turn. Nothing was missing. Jeeves then made a very ostentatious entry in his notebook and producing another cloth bag poured the silver into it. He then bound the bag with cord and completed the job by sealing the knots with my sealing wax. The bag then went back into the box which was roped in its turn and then pitched at the Sirdar with such force that he promptly sat down again. The whole process, although it had a sobering effect all round, ultimately became a nuisance, for from then on we could not make even a trivial purchase without unroping, unsealing, uncording, recording, resealing and reroping until even Jeeves tired of it and sought the first suitable opportunity when coin was no longer required, to change the remainder back into notes which he turned over to me.

After this incident, which had chastened everybody, we had no difficulty in dictating terms for the rest of the day, and with good going downhill and on the flat we covered a very reasonable mileage.

The next morning saw us make our last crossing of the Dudh Kosi and high up among the trees on the far bank we came to a hut with a magnificent Tibetan mastiff tethered to a pole outside the door. This was a very fierce animal of a fierce breed and any moment I expected either the rope to break or the pole to be rooted out of the ground. As soon as he saw us the mastiff set up a tremendous deep-throated baying which soon brought the owner, who proved to be an ex-Gurkha soldier with some English, to the door of the hut. As soon as he saw me he produced a litter of fine puppies and told me I could pay any price I liked for them. Although tempted, I refused for the breed is difficult to tame, and in any case I doubted whether one would survive the terrific pre-monsoon heat of the Indian plains before I could get it to a cooler climate. I am now sorry that I did not try, for I am told the breed is now dying out in Britain, where it was never firmly established, for lack of a bitch.

The Tibetan mastiff is a cousin of the Pyrenean Mountain Dog and the chow, but it is larger and has a thicker and shaggier coat. It is difficult to see what useful purpose a mastiff can serve as a guard dog in Sola Khumbu for theft and crimes of violence there are scarcely known. Very possibly they are used to protect herds and flocks against leopards and other wild animals. The breed occurs right through Tibet, especially in the south, where they can sometimes be seen chained to either side of the entrance to a monastery. My friend Mr. Charles Stonor tells me that when traveling along the border between Assam and Bhutan he came across them frequently. They were there used exclusively for guarding herds of yaks, cattle etc., against tigers and perhaps other enemies, being left out all night with the herds. In those parts it is claimed that two or three will join forces and tackle a tiger. Mr. Stonor says the ones he saw were actually not at all fierce or bad tempered—no doubt their disposition depending on what purpose they were trained for.

Our next march brought us back to Junbesi which we reached in the early afternoon. I, myself, could not remember whether there was suitable camping ground for some miles beyond us and I decided to stop for the night—thus giving the coolies ample time to wash their clothes which were sorely in need of it. This time I followed Morris' advice and had the tent pitched down by the river beside a roofed bridge which is like many to be seen in the Alps. Although I appreciated the pressing attentions of the good folk of Junbesi, nothing would induce me to spend another night in the temple court there.

At Namche Bazar the tent did at least afford a flimsy screen to shield me from the multitude. To lie on paving stones in a public place and settle down to sleep surrounded by a jostling throng of the curious and inquisitive takes considerable composure and although I had achieved it once I was not anxious to repeat the performance. The new site was not entirely to the liking of the rest of the party. Pasang had friends in Junbesi and was therefore well accommodated, but all the coolies could find were some rather shallow caves in the bank of the river which faced the prevailing wind. Just after dusk another heavy thunderstorm broke and taking pity on them I packed the coolies off into the village, whither they sped with alacrity. I then bedded down alone in the tent trusting that the river would not rise rapidly in the night and sweep me off under the bridge and downstream. In spite of my misgivings that they might make another night of it, the coolies all arrived back at the camp surprisingly early the next morning, and in the best of spirits. We were now due for another long ascent, first across the high grassy alp which on our journey up had been a carpet of pale blue primulas and was now again bare of them and then, after fording two streams, up the long incline which finally leads to the pastoral basin in the hills where stand the two stupas of Chyangma. The second ascent begins very steeply up some terraced agricultural land where the little farmhouses were smothered in carmine, pink and pale yellow wild roses. Here we were able to replenish our vegetable supplies, a welcome addition being some tender and delicious green peas. Terraced country is, I think, the most arduous of all to travel, if approached directly, for with deadly monotony one is faced after each 10 or 12 yards of level going, by a vertical 10 or 12 foot bank which has to be climbed. A mile or two of this brings the strongest traveler to his knees and I was not surprised to find the coolies making hard work of it. Above the terraces, Jeeves and I at the head of a wearily struggling column, entered a patch of almost tropical jungle which caught the full force of the noon sun. Here, for the first and only time we were assailed by Dim Dam flies. The Dim Dam generally occurs at lower altitudes. Like a miniature house fly in appearance, it raises a tiny blood blister which becomes maddeningly irritating, and both Jeeves and I had one thought—to get out of the woodland as fast as our tired legs would carry us. We were just emerging at the foot of the basin when we were confronted by two highly excited peasants who thrashed the air with their staves and pointed back up the way they had come. After a rapid conversation, Jeeves unsheathed the kukri which he was carrying for some purpose of his own, and the three of them tore off up the trail. Thinking that at least a tribal war had broken out, I followed as best I could. Three hundred yards on, the trees thinned and I came out beside a broad shallow brook. Here at least twenty men were grouped on the far side each brandishing a weapon or implement of some sort. Two or three with their skirts hitched round their loins, were standing in the water beating the surface rather circumspectly with sticks at a point where the roots of a large tree overhung the bank. By the aid of pantomime I was informed that the cause of the disturbance was a large snake of a very venomous variety. To simple country folk, both in Nepal and India, all snakes are poisonous but some are more poisonous than others. There is however no mistaking the general agitation with which the discovery of a really dangerous one is received and the stouter hearts in the vicinity unite at once to destroy it. This particular snake had been sighted about 2 miles away and had been chased across open grassland until it had taken refuge under the tree. It may seem remarkable for a large snake to be making a hurried and lengthy journey across country in broad daylight, but I understand that such journeys are not, in reality, infrequent and are best explained by the mating urge. This particular snake refused to be lured from the tree and, as it was quite obvious no one was going to climb under the roots and get it, Jeeves and I pressed on. A long steady pull across the basin and up the far side brought us back to the two stupas, the obvious spot to pause for lunch. It was some time before the coolies caught up with us and for some time we had been able to watch their progress through the glasses, first as they paused in turn before the holed snake, no doubt to give gratuitous advice and encouragement, and then as they wound up the downland which separated us. Upon arrival a movement started to settle down for the night, for it was a recognized camping stage, but this time the move was firmly squashed by Jeeves who was not going to risk a further loss such as another hurricane lamp. It was now discovered that we were nearly out of sugar but Pasang volunteered to find some in a village which, he said, was near by, but must have been at least three miles away for we could see that distance at least in any direction. The rest of us plugged on up towards the pass which we reached at sunset. As everyone wanted to be out of the wind we added another good mile down the far side for good measure. It had been a long day for everyone and particularly so for Pasang who had added a half a dozen miles or so to the performance of the rest of us and yet appeared fresher than anyone at the end of it. Two other equally lengthy marches followed so that on the evening of the sixth day I was delighted to find us camped in the Chumti gorge only a few miles above Palam.

I would have liked to keep up this progress, but it was not to be. To begin with the Chumti River provides possibly the best bathing and dhobi facilities of the whole route, the water being neither too cold nor too swift. Next morning I chose the best of many magnificent pools and wallowed in it with such obvious enjoyment that I was finally joined (for the first and only time throughout the entire trip) by Jeeves, Diamonds, Spades, the Joker and Pasang, all stripped down to their loincloths. The Old Man, Clubs, and the Sirdar refused to be tempted and frowned at us with obvious disapproval as if the coolies, at least, were guilty of the height of bad form. The bath proved so invigorating to the rest of us that very light work indeed was made of the remaining distance into Palam. Here there were a number of purchases to make—rice for the coolies, tea, sugar, eggs and chickens for me and, above all, cigarettes for everyone. Having given away about five for each one I smoked, I had now run through my own and from then on had to be content with Bus brand, the coolies' solace, at forty for a shilling. No one would willingly smoke a Bus, or even the slightly better Motor (at about thirty a shilling) if he could buy an Abdullah, but an addict will smoke anything he can get and in far away places he buys a Bus and thinks it luxury. Our modest shopping requirements again collected a considerable crowd about us and what with yelping dogs, screaming children, scurrying chickens and general commotion, one might have thought as we progressed up the narrow cobbled main street, that the circus had come to town. Crossing the bridge to Palam (south) we turned off into the walled police paddock where the gates were barred to all but privileged spectators, of whom there were enough in all conscience. Lunch became quite a festive occasion, both chang and rakshi being produced in quantity, while for dessert the foraging Jeeves triumphantly provided a bunch of small and rather wooden bananas. When the time came to move on, none of the coolies, with the notable exception of the Sirdar, could be found. This development I may say I deserved, for having noticed that no one for some days had had anything left to smoke I had dispensed a "cigarette bakshish" of five rupees per man, on entering the town. To the coolie mind five rupees can mean either two hundred cigarettes, or forty cigarettes and four bottles of rakshi and no Gallup Poll is necessary to decide which is the more attractive alternative. Feeling that all might not yet be lost, I sent the Sirdar back into the town to rout out the truants. The first sweep produced Pasang, now minus the Sirdar. Pasang, with a convenient lapse of fluency in his English, explained first that no rice was available and then, when this was indignantly denied by a townsman, that the rice was of too poor quality, that the price was too expensive and that there could be no hope of concluding a successful bargain before the next morning. Jeeves, who had found a companion from Katmandu, (a quiet likable lad) in the crowd, seconded this statement. In vain I suggested that I pay the difference between the standard rate for the rice and the enhanced price. Pasang took the stand that whatever I liked to pay, and he advised against it, the best counsel he could offer was to stop over the night. At this point the Sirdar, still sober, arrived with the Old Man, also sober, and Diamonds, Spades and the Joker all very drunk and embarrassingly affectionate. There was no sign of Clubs. Pasang now renewed the argument, pointing out that the coolies during the past three days had gone magnificently—as indeed they had—and that if I gave them the half day off they would go all the better for the remainder of the trip. Upon this being translated all the coolies nodded vigorously and swore that instead of the customary eight days to Katmandu, they would take six, five, or even four if the Sahib really desired it. The sight of the lionhearted Diamonds now in the opposite camp after weeks of stupendous effort, decided me, and I struck a bargain for a half day against a six-day trip, and this, to their lasting credit, the coolies kept. The one condition was that we move the camp at least a mile from the town and this was readily agreed to. Clubs was produced from his lair and we all set off in good spirits crossing the next bridge and pitching camp on a meadow beside the river. Jeeves' friend now suggested that he, myself and Pasang should join him for some refreshment at his house and this I at once agreed to for few things are more depressing to a well-regulated mind than to be stone cold sober when a party is progressing about one in full swing and swig. Jeeves' friend lived in a neat little house with a pleasant view over the river. We climbed to a spotlessly clean room on the first storey and squatted in a circle on the baked mud floor. Our friend's wife then produced an immense earthenware jar of rakshi and a brass bowl which passed round the circle with considerable dispatch but always with complete decorum and dignity. Rakshi, or rice wine, as brewed in Nepal, tastes exactly like Japanese sake except that it is drunk cold instead of warm. Conversation flowed as freely as the rakshi, the air became blue with tobacco smoke and some hours must have passed before Pasang suggested that as, by now, the coolies had probably exhausted all their money, it would be a good idea to go in search for them. Jeeves received this suggestion with some reserve, but feeling that it might be better to get the coolies back to the camp where they would have a chance of sleeping off their hang-overs, rather than leave them scattered throughout the night in various unknown haunts about the town and then waste time by having to round them up in the morning, I agreed. Pasang, who knew where the "local" was to be found—and had probably pointed it out in the first place—led the way. We went right back through the town to the point where we had entered it and I could not help noticing for the first time that there were a number of dead rats about—praying fervently that this might not mean an outbreak of bubonic plague. At length we came to a ramshackle house at the extreme end of the town. We groped our way up a narrow unlit staircase to the first floor—as usual the ground floor serving as a shop or store—and came to what served as the saloon bar. This was a fair-sized room with a low ceiling and lit by a small guttering oil lamp. Once more both walls and floor were of brown baked mud, again swept spotlessly clean. Diamonds, Spades, Clubs and the Joker sat cross-legged on the floor with, facing them, an ancient crone beside whom stood an immense jar of rakshi which I judged to be at least a twelve bottle Jeroboam. I had rather expected a scene of wild debauch and I was pleasantly surprised. It was, in fact, the best behaved drinking bout I have ever attended. After welcoming exchanges, room was made for us on the floor and once more a little brass bowl began to circulate briskly to be refilled each time it returned round the circle to the crone. Besides dispensing liquor this aged female prepared for us an immense omelette, cooked over a small charcoal burner—an excellent omelette which we ate with our fingers as it too passed the round. We were well into our third Jeroboam when the party broke up by mutual consent and after paying a ridiculously small bill we clambered down the stairs into the street. By now the moon had risen and rather than trek back through the village, as neither Spades nor Clubs were too steady on their feet, although otherwise models of deportment, we climbed down into the ravine, crossed the river by stepping stones—the cause of some amusement this, though nobody fell in—and reached the camp by a long detour down the right bank. Here the Sirdar, who was atoning for past lapses by remaining cold sober—he may well have been anxious that I would give him an unfavorable report in Katmandu—had had the presence of mind to stop a passing fisherman and buy a string of fish resembling trout. Cooked in butter they were delicious and although it was nearly midnight I made an excellent supper from six of them. Balancing the immense amount of liquor consumed against the fact that there were no broken glasses, no arguments or brawls, no disturbance of neighbors and nobody put to bed with or without their boots on, one may claim it was a highly successful party—so much so that we can gloss over the fact that there were no glasses to break and no footwear except the tennis shoes sported by Pasang, Jeeves and myself. The general effect on the party was electrifying. We were once more a cheerful team and from then on no march was too long and no start too early. Most of the coolies were, in fact, already on the road the next morning before I had finished breakfast and when Jeeves came to me with his inevitable "Let's go, Sahib, please," the camp was deserted.

I remember that next day for three encounters. We had just rounded the first bluff and were turning away from the river when we sighted another of the strange creatures which I had first seen beside the Bhote Kosi River. It had apparently been scavenging in a small lateral nullah and on being alarmed set off at an effortlessly fast pace straight up the mountainside. I followed it through the glasses for a considerable time as it dodged between bushes and trees, and can only confirm the description I gave of it previously—about 2 feet high at the shoulder, narrow pointed muzzle, bushy tail, shaggy hair covering the barrel and legs and markings similar to those of a Siamese cat, gray body and black or dark brown points. I had imagined it to be a fairly common, easily recognized animal, as it was most unlikely I should be given two clear views of a rarity in broad daylight, but I remain puzzled. Whatever its vices may be, it gave me the impression (which may be entirely illusory) of a lovable, happy disposition. There was no stealth about it; its gamboling, lolloping movements were a joy to watch.

We climbed over the next ridge and there, on a single tree of medium height standing by the track, sat a strikingly beautiful bird, the size of a canary but bright red in color. It was such a pretty sight that I stopped the coolies and we watched it—they rather bewildered—for some minutes before it finally left its perch and sped off down into the valley.

That evening saw us traveling along the face of another vast precipice with the cliff of the right-hand side soaring sheer for hundreds of feet above us. A turn into a great rift in the rock face disclosed an immense wild bees' nest plastered to the cliff about 200 feet above our heads. We were examining this through the glasses when there was a sudden rush of air above us and a superb eagle diving down from fully 2000 feet, arrested its flight in the canyon by an imperceptible movement of its wings and planing up again, disappeared at a point high up in the cliff. This eyrie was not hard to find, for it was marked by the chalk-white splashes of innumerable droppings, and the glasses then revealed two of the magnificent birds, both fully grown and standing shoulder to shoulder, the last rays of the sun glinting on their golden plumage. This was a noble sight which only those who have seen an eagle in its full pride and strength in its natural surroundings and at comparatively short range, can fully appreciate. A thought of purely academic interest occurred to me that it would be a comparatively easy matter to reach the nest, which was about 50 feet below the cliff top. Exactly above it stands a single, well grown pine tree and any climber with a nerve for heights would find no difficulty in roping down to it. I hasten to add that nothing on earth would induce me to attempt such an escapade.

At noon the next day we arrived at the small village where at night, on our journey up, we had been disturbed by the calling leopard. Here we ate a hurried lunch and as the coolies were once more involved in bargaining for rice—a process which is never hurried in any circumstances—I set off alone. Once more the path led off down into a ravine, but here the undergrowth was much thicker and the path wound round numerous spurs and rocky outcrops. I had gone about a mile, and had reached about as desolate a spot as I could do, when I caught the pungent, unmistakable odor of cat—I mean a big cat, nothing smaller than a leopard. When one is armed only with a walking stick this is not a pleasant experience. I still hold to the belief—and I hope no one disillusions me—that a normal leopard will not usually attack a human being in daylight if it is not provoked—but I had read enough of Jim Corbett's books on man-eating tigers and leopards not to feel entirely comfortable. The scent came in waves, neither stronger nor weaker and as the trail offered scores of most excellent ambush points both before and behind me, I halted at a complete loss what to do next. For some minutes I stood there irresolutely calling myself a cautious idiot while yet counseling myself to caution. There was no movement, and no sound except the buzzing of insects and occasional bird-calls. The latter I thought would tell Corbett all he wanted, but they were no use to Izzard. Happily, after an unworthy interval, I caught the sound of another band of travelers climbing up the path towards me. The clatter and clamor they made was sufficient to dissipate both the scent and my fears and closed an altogether undignified episode.

The floor of this ravine carries another deep-flowing river of milky water spanned by a steel bridge constructed some years ago by a Scotch firm for foot passengers only. It is severely kinked at one end probably by a tree trunk carried down in time of flood and had I thought of it at the time I should probably have done many people a good turn by photographing the damage. As it was, all I was thinking of was another bath and this, after stripping on a great round boulder at the water's edge, I thoroughly enjoyed. That afternoon the sun was particularly strong and for some miles I continued walking without the silk scarf which I normally bound round my head as protection. Down by the river Jeeves had caught up with me and he now forged ahead. His progress was such that I began to fear that the coolies would protest, and rightly so, that we were going far beyond a normal day's march. But this time there was no stopping Jeeves. At each bend I expected to catch up with him, but on rounding it, if I ever saw him at all, it was just as he was rounding the next. Jeeves obviously had his own target for the night.

The trail now plunged downwards abruptly towards the bottom of another immensely steep gorge. I was now beginning to feel very tired indeed—not the breathlessness which comes from imperfect training but muscular exhaustion typified by rubbery knees and a growing inability to place one leg before the other. I continued increasingly to curse Jeeves. Once again I was within the trees which grew rapidly denser as the path descended. Turn of the rough rock-strewn trail succeeded turn, seemingly interminably, and the sun was fast disappearing beyond the cliffs above us before I caught the sound of water. A few minutes later I came out of the forest on to a small alp and quite unexpectedly—for I had forgotten the sequence of landmarks—found myself at the head of the bridge below Charikot. On a small *chautara* on the far side of the gorge sat Jeeves, legs crossed casually, and a more than self-satisfied expression on his face. Whether he had negotiated the bridge or climbed down the cliff and up the farther side I could not tell, and I had the delicacy not to ask. To my rather heated: "Coolies no come so far," Jeeves merely remarked with supreme assurance: "Coolies coming, Sahib." As usual Jeeves was right.

For scenery and amenities we might have chosen a far worse camping ground. Just above the famous bridge the river swung round in a wide curve washing the fringe of a pleasant stretch of lawn above which stood, like an open-fronted sports' pavilion, a substantial coolies' shelter of brick and timber. All that remained to do was climb down the cliff and cross the river—by stepping stones as I did—for I was too tired to take off my shoes and socks and trousers, or by fording waist deep as did the Joker and Clubs. While the coolies prepared camp I strolled up and down the river deciding which of many fine bathing pools I should use the next morning. It was after I had returned to the camp and was sitting on a rock beside the tent waiting for supper, that I suddenly began to feel ill. A few minutes before I had merely felt exhausted, but tiredness is not sickness, in fact throughout that day and for many days before I can truthfully say that I had seldom felt fitter in my life. But there was no doubt now that I was in trouble. The first symptom was a headache so violent that I almost groaned with pain. Simultaneously I felt my temperature rising in fever higher than I had ever known before. Wretchedly I worked my way into my sleeping bag and lay there alternately burning with fever and shaking with chills so intense I began to fear my bones would leave their sockets. For sometime I felt both appallingly lonely and very frightened. When he is in robust health a man of my disposition can find his own company—if he has none other—very tolerable. There is this to be said for traveling alone: if you have complaints to make you must address them to yourself and you are thus assured of a fairly sympathetic hearing. But sickness changes this state of affairs entirely. The man who falls sick in the wilderness with no better counsel to turn to than his own, can be a very lonely man indeed—and if, as in my case, he has no idea what ails him, he can be very frightened. It was some time before I could master my fears and collect my thoughts. Having little medical knowledge it had not taken me long to persuade myself that I had fallen victim to one of the uglier diseases to be found in that area. It is a formidable list: cholera, typhus, bubonic plague (the dead rats of Palam were vividly before me), polio, smallpox, malaria—and if malaria, it could be the dread "awal" fever of the Terai which can kill in a night. To counteract any or all of these afflictions (most of which in modern times can be halted if—a redundant "if" in my case—one can be rushed to a good hospital) I had Paludrine, aspirin and sulpha tablets—the last named to be taken only in case of pneumonia which was the one illness I was convinced I had not got. As I had no abdominal pains, no stiff neck, no rash, and no swelling under the arm I made the oversimple diagnosis that I had malaria—I had had it before but never so violently and never in quite the same manner as this. However, having convinced myself, without further ado I took an enormous dose of Paludrine tablets, how large I am not prepared to say in case some one tries to equal or exceed it. This having been done, and the dose having been kept down, I felt momentarily better and tearing a leaf from my diary I made a brief note of my position. This included a summary of my movements (not forgetting the Palam incident) and my symptoms together with a list of all inoculations and vaccinations I had undergone before entering the country. This slightly melodramatic memo was intended for reading by anyone who could understand English should they happen to find me after I had lost consciousness. I was suddenly aware that the chances of any English speaker passing that way were only one in many thousands, but I postponed the extreme and probably useless step of sending for help to Katmandu. For one thing none of the coolies and not even Pasang was in condition to go much farther that night. For another, I argued to myself that a runner would take at least four to five days to reach the hospital. Even if a doctor were available—and God knows they have work enough of their own to do—he would calculate it would take him another five days to reach me; ten days in all, by which time he would very properly decide I must be either dead or cured.

As my diary entry began to tail off in a rather absurd scrawl

I completed it, sank back comfortably in the bag and awaited the next development. Almost at once a blissful feeling of lightheadedness overcame me. Gone were all my trepidations of two hours before. I smiled rather ruefully to myself that I had attempted so much, alone, but I was past any feeling of regret whatsoever. I had done nothing brilliant but at least I had tried hard and worked hard and the only thing I longed for at that moment was rest. Soon after I fell into a deep sleep. I woke once, somewhere near midnight, with a raging thirst and called rather idiotically to Jeeves to make tea. The faithful Jeeves would undoubtedly have responded, but he was snoring many yards away and as my voice was quite inaudible above the rushing water I could just as well try to rouse him from the grave.

The next time I woke, Jeeves was indeed beside me with a mug of tea. It was 6:30. The fever had left me but I was desperately weak. I swallowed the tea with another mouthful of Paludrine tablets and for the first time for nearly five weeks surrendered to the luxury, on first waking, of rolling over once more and returning to sleep. I was dimly aware of Pasang squatting beside my head a deeply anxious expression on his face. The thought occurred to me that if I became truly incapacitated and incapable of giving orders, leadership of our little party would naturally devolve on Pasang. Jeeves was the perfect servant, but he was not a man for making big decisions or exacting obedience unsupported. Pasang was a natural leader and there was little doubt that whatever he decided would be unquestioned. I wondered vaguely what he would do. We could stay where we were, sending runners off to Katmandu for help. We could abandon some of the loads—a big decision in itself for we were so streamlined it would be difficult to know what to leave behind—and some of the coolies could carry me. Pasang could try and recruit additional porters from some neighboring village. Personally I was past caring; for the first time I began to understand the resignation with which the native inhabitants of remote places accept sickness and death. When one is beyond reach of medical aid one's sole hope rests in miracles and miracles are not of frequent enough occurrence to warrant much faith being placed in them. I woke again at 10 A.M. to find the sun beating hotly on the tent. Pasang was still beside me; Jeeves was brewing more tea and the coolies were idling in the shade beside their laden carrying baskets. For the first time since I had fallen ill I felt a dim spark of vitality deep down inside me. In a few minutes I was arguing to myself that if I could manage only one march nearer home before collapsing, I should be two days nearer help; if I could manage two marches I should be four days nearer, and so on. Finally I sat up. The blinding headache at once returned and I felt wretchedly giddy but there was no going back to bed now. Pasang hauled me to my feet and snapped the coolies into activity. The tent was down in a trice, the air mattress deflated, the sleeping bag rolled and stowed and the march began.

It so happens that the climb up through the pine trees from the foot of this gorge is one of the fiercest of the whole journey. I had not the strength or the courage to look upward. When I thought of the robust strength I had enjoyed only twenty-four hours before and compared it with my present pitiful condition I could have wept. I was now not only feebleness itself but a miserable hypochondriac in the bargain, for I suddenly became convinced I must be overstraining my heart. Up that slope I made only 20 yards at a time, heaving myself upwards on my stick, before slumping down with shaking knees on some rock or log. Of much of that day's march I remember nothing at all except that on some of the steeper cliff paths either Pasang or Jeeves steadied me in case I fell off, and that once, in the afternoon, Diamonds carried me over the stepping stones across one of the rivers in case I fell in.

We camped that night in a shallow valley where the crops had just been taken from some terraced fields. I had not been able to eat anything all day but now Jeeves produced a rich chicken soup and I felt some appetite return. A thunderstorm which had been lurking round the mountains all afternoon broke over us as the sun set, but as I was already warm and dry within the tent I paid little heed to it. Fever was on me once again but no longer of the frightening strength of the previous night. My confidence was growing that I should reach Katmandu after all, at least there was still strength enough in me for one more day's march even if my condition did not improve—and I now began to feel that it might. I slept well. When I woke next morning to receive Jeeves' mug of tea my head was clearer. It was still an effort to get out of the bag but when I had done so I felt strong enough to walk down to the nearby river to wash and shave—I hold to a belief that when one is dispirited a needed shave is a great early morning morale booster. The storm had moistened the grass by the riverbank and when I arrived at the water I found a number of leeches had fastened themselves to my bare ankles. These were the first I had encountered on the trek, although I had been anticipating them for some days, and once more I pitied the expedition members when they came to return during the monsoon, for the handful that had singled me out could by then have swelled to many hundreds of thousands. When I returned to the camp I noticed something unusual was afoot and in some respects it proved to be the worst thing that could have happened. Beside the fire stood Sanju, the expedition's star Sherpa runner with a ragged and rather goitrous companion. Sanju, a magnificent athlete, had last passed me just below Namche Bazar when he was going up. While I had plugged on as best I could towards Katmandu, Sanju had gone on up to at least as far as Thyangboche, where he had received messages from both Colonel Hunt and James Morris.

Then he had turned round and here he was overtaking me when I was still three or four days from home. In this book I have been able to include my own experiences round Everest and what little I learned about the expedition there, in their logical place in preceding chapters. For newspaper purposes I had still to reach Katmandu before I could cable any dispatches date-lined "Everest," to London. By pitting my own legs against a good Sherpa I had lamely allowed myself to be "scooped," for in his wallet Sanju carried news of what had happened after I had left the Khumbu glacier and Thyangboche monastery. And it was important; had I known it, Sanju was bringing tidings of the forcing of the Icefall by Hillary, Band and Westmacott. I have now the deepest respect for Sanju. As it turned out I was to reach Katmandu in thirteen days—in spite of illness, a day less than I had needed for the journey out—and until then a record march for any European. Normally Sanju took eight days over the same distance, but I believe on one memorable occasion, when the bakshish must have been phenomenal, he actually accomplished it in six and a half days. If ever there is an Olympic Games endurance test over mountain country I should back Sanju to win it with all the money I have. He is a fine figure of a man with copper bronze skin and long black hair and is now in middle age. He is tall for a Sherpa, with deep chest, slender arms and magnificently developed legs. I also understand he is a man of resource. Once when called upon to carry a message up the Icefall to Camp IV in the Western Cwm he found the immense ice blocks had shifted overnight and obliterated the marked trail. Sanju found a detour of his own which from then on was known as "Sanju's route." With him Sanju was bringing a gaily striped piece of Sherpa cloth woven from yak's wool for sale in Katmandu bazaar. This I obtained—as a consolation prize—for 10 rupees.

When we left camp that morning Sanju and his companion

were still cooking their substantial breakfast—their one indulgence—but within two hours they had once more caught up with us. At this point Pasang suggested he should go on ahead with the two Sherpas and carry a message into Katmandu. As I now felt well enough—or rather, less ill—I at once agreed and wrote out a message to Saksena to have a Jeep waiting at Banepa on the morning of the third day. This I gave to Pasang with exact instructions how to reach Saksena at the Himalaya Hotel and bade him farewell with my blessing. Pasang and the two Sherpas reached Katmandu at lunchtime on the second day and Pasang's first action was to hunt out Saksena.

We ourselves made a prodigious march. I now kept going on will power alone. I was still certain I was going to collapse but I was obsessed with the idea that when I did so it should be in good hands. On that first day I had no other goal than to walk into Katmandu, up the steps of the hospital, into one of the wards, fling myself down on one of the beds and collapse there. Towards evening Jeeves, Diamonds and myself arrived at Dolalghat. We crossed the two rivers and on the farthest bank Diamonds and Jeeves suggested in chorus we should camp there. I was determined to keep going. Diamonds pointed out that the next reasonable camping ground was at Hukse another good two hours' going up hill. If we camped in between, said Diamonds, coolie fashion, we should be overwhelmed in the night by "bad men." "Then Hukse be it," I said rather appalled at my own temerity. Diamonds demurred—it was far too far to ask of any coolie at that hour. At that I promised a staggering bonus for everybody and stumbled off up the trail alone. For some time it appeared that even Jeeves forbore to follow, but after half an hour when I stopped to look round there was the familiar brown balaclava bobbing philosophically up the track beneath me. Farther behind was the indomitable Diamonds, with

Spades and the Joker close on his heels. Night fell long before we reached Hukse. In the evening light the occupants of the occasional shaggily thatched cottages looked at me oddly as I shuffled along—a solitary European in a land where few are ever seen, coming from nowhere and obviously not going much farther. It was another dreadful drag up the last slope to Hukse. This pleasant little village, almost of Tudor aspect, has bad memories for me whichever way I approached it. At last I reached the saddle whereon the village is built and slumped down beneath the pipal tree where I had spent my first night on the road to Everest. Once more I was too ill and weary to think and Jeeves when he arrived, his face a ghastly mask of dust and fatigue in the light of the lamp, looked in scarcely better condition. One by one the coolies trailed in with the Sirdar, for once in his life, helping the Old Man with his load. At that I felt thoroughly ashamed of myself and prouder than ever of my splendid team. My last thought as I lay in my tent before sleeping was that, by another long march, we should reach Banepa by the next night. With a Jeepable road connecting the two, Banepa was just as good a place to be sick in as Katmandu.

The next morning Diamonds, once more restored in strength and good humor, indicated in his queer pantomime and with his favorite "Shih, shih, shih, eee—eee—eee," denoting a winding and ascending road, announced that we should be in Banepa by midday. This I could hardly believe when I remembered the tortures of our first day's march, but so it proved. What had seemed a stupendous performance five weeks ago was now, in the reverse direction and going mostly uphill, and even in my weakened condition, a comfortable morning's march. True the sun beat down fiercer than ever as we crossed the stretch of paddy fields and true the last climb was a telling one by any standards, but at 11:30 A.M. Jeeves and I stood at the top of the pass leading into the Great Nepal

Valley. Here I turned for a last look back over the way we had come. Off to the north the serene snow slopes of the high Himalaya were shrouded in cloud banks, but due east one could see for 50 miles or more across the turmoil of wooded mountainsides and purple-shadowed gorges. I looked back with the eyes of a man who is certain, at the time, that he will never pass that way again. Now I am already not so sure, for if the chance offered I am fairly certain I should seize it.

On the pass Jeeves and I exchanged the time of day with a party of polite and pleasant baboos, returning from a visit to a none-too-distant relation. The news that we had come from Namche Bazar they received with astonishment mounting to incredulity. Again I heard the remark I had first heard in the Nepal Foreign Office: "But that journey is a penance." Jeeves and I fairly pounded down the long slope into the valley towards Banepa. As Diamonds had predicted, we arrived in the town not long after midday. At once we were surrounded by the same familiar crowd of grubby children. In elation we scattered the last of our Bus cigarettes among the horde and diving for the nearest booth bought some good Virginies of a popular brand. We now had all the time necessary to reach Katmandu itself before nightfall—at least so we thought. In practice it proved by no means easy.

By now the entire town appeared to be assembling in full force to greet us and propelled backwards by the multitude we sought refuge in the tobacconist's booth. Here, amid all the clamor and excitement, it was next to impossible to get any coherent answers to questions about transport, until once more we were rescued by a local schoolmaster. To my entreaties to furnish us with at least enough breathing space to sustain life, he merely shrugged his shoulders and grinned, as much as to say: "This is Banepa; there is nothing you can do about it," but he did, however, provide us with the information that a bus was due at five that afternoon—that is, it should be due, it had broken down two days before and had not been seen since. This appeared to satisfy Jeeves who with oriental patience was quite prepared to settle down for an indefinite wait, but it did not suit me. There were no private cars available in Banepa; the butcher, the baker or the candlestick maker had a bicycle if it could be found. As the telephone had broken down it was suggested a messenger should be sent off to Bhatgaon on the bicycle to summon a taxi. I suggested that I borrow the bicycle, do the trip myself and return with the machine in the back of a Jeep. Neither suggestion was unanimously approved. Negotiations broke down when the bicycle was produced and it was found that the front wheel was buckled nearly square and the back wheel was minus a tire. Although Jeeves still had pathetic faith in the bus, it seemed to me there was nothing to do but walk if we wished to be in Katmandu that night. As soon as the decision was made Jeeves agreed without demur. It was stiflingly hot in the midday sun and both of us were hungry and thirsty. We stopped at a coolies' tea-house on the outskirts of the town and shared a mess of golden raspberries, which we ate from a broad, flat leaf and drank innumerable cups of tea. Coolies' tea bears only a remote resemblance to the genuine beverage. It is the color of gray milk and when I flicked what I took to be a single large leaf from the surface of my fourth cup, to the ground, I was astonished to see it shake itself and walk away.

It was a long drag up the road to the next village but the way was lined with masses of wild roses and we had no lack of company. Traveler after traveler fell into step with us until we were quite a procession. Either they lent importance to our progress or we to theirs. I never discovered. The next village provided some scalding hot milk, for which no payment was asked or expected. The day had now grown intolerably sultry and we had barely come in sight of Bhatgaon about 3 miles away when another terrific thunderstorm burst over us. Gusts of wind of gale force drove bitterly chill sheets of rain over us and without more ado the procession broke ranks and stormed for shelter into a tiny cottage, somewhat to the distress of the startled occupants who included a young mother with a baby at the breast. For a full forty minutes the wind and rain lashed the hut while all of us, with the addition of ever more stray refugees, huddled inside, a steaming and none too sweetly scented mass of humanity. With the first signs of cessation of the storm I was anxious to be away, for more reasons than one, but we had hardly gone another mile before the storm returned with redoubled fury. This time we were caught squarely and soaked to the skin within seconds before we could find shelter. This we did under the verandah of a long low building which stood with its back to the storm, but was open to all other points of the compass. Evening was now fast approaching, the storm showed no signs of ceasing, indeed the sky was solid black above us, and the temperature had dropped abysmally so that clad only in shirt and drill trousers, neither of which could possibly be wetter, my teeth began to chatter so that I could hardly hold a cigarette to my lips. As neither Jeeves nor I had spare clothing with us it would have been madness to spend the night where we were, so finally we chose the scarcely lesser evil of trudging on through the storm into Bhatgaon. The ditches by the roadside had deposited a thin film of mud over the cobbles so that we slipped and skidded as if on a skating rink, sometimes regaining our balance and sometimes falling full length. Half drowned and plastered with mud from head to foot we must have looked two of the most unwholesome objects ever to pass through the second town of the valley. Here, however, Jeeves the never failing, discovered an ancient hire car—an open tourer—upon the backseat of which we lowered ourselves rather gingerly. To have gone back to Banepa in this rackety vehicle would have been a sheer impossibility. At the best of times the road is only barely more than Jeepable, and I doubt that once in open country we should have made more than a hundred yards or so without sliding into the ditch. I therefore abandoned the coolies, not such an unkind decision as it may seem, for I was fairly certain that they would not have come beyond Banepa where they would be warm, dry and well housed (I was right), and had I brought them in that night I should have deprived them of the chance of earning an additional day's wage, for which no coolie will thank you. As it was, on the comparatively good road to Katmandu, our smooth-tired conveyance went down most of the hills broadside, a maneuver which our hardy driver corrected by taking his hands off the wheel and leaning over the back of his seat to laugh at us. The gods of the valley protected us, however, and in tolerably good order we eventually passed through the arch leading to Joodha Street and ground to a stop outside the Himalaya Hotel. Here Mrs. Saksena received us with some astonishment and anxiety. Pasang had arrived that noon and had explained my condition to Sax. He, being the good fellow he is, as soon as the storm broke, had set off with Pasang in a jeep for Banepa laden with comforts (including a bottle of Scotch) with the intention of trekking on until he found me. Somewhere we must have passed each other along the road. There was no point in chasing him and I knew with absolute certainty that he would not get far beyond Bhatgaon before being forced to turn back. This reassured Mrs. Saksena who had lost no time in brewing piping hot tea for us and as soon as we had swallowed it I gathered up a massive bundle of mail to be off to the Nepal Hotel, leaving a message for Sax to join me there. I dropped Jeeves on the way telling him to get out of his clothes as quickly as he could. Probably nothing had bound the pair of us closer together than the tribulations of this past day. We clasped hands, agreed to meet the next day, and he in parting smiled his shy, companionable smile. It was the last time I ever did see him smile.

The Nepal Hotel in rather changed circumstances, was hardly the haven of comfort and rest I had been anticipating. The owner had left for India and the manager, being no longer under supervision, had taken what might be termed "local leave." The running of the establishment had therefore devolved upon the junior domestic staff. As no one had paid the electricity bill, lighting of the cavernous saloons and chambers was by three dim hurricane lanterns and a half dozen guttering candles, all of which were constantly being removed and taken elsewhere according to the needs of the distraught guests. Only the bar could be said to be in full operation for here, the skeleton staff had soon discovered, tips were more easily come by than elsewhere in the institution. To my surprise and pleasure a dim shape at the far end of the counter gradually materialized into the form and presence of Colin Reid of *The Daily Telegraph*. Reid and I had been given almost parallel assignments by our respective papers for some years past, and we had traveled widely together in India, the Middle East and Africa. While no correspondent should relish the appearance of a rival on a hitherto exclusive scene, this time I was more than thankful to have Colin's company. We had had unexpected meetings in many odd places before but none so strange as this. Colin was taking a stiffener before going out to dine with David Haye-Neave, but we had time to add "a couple or three"—myself standing in a rapidly spreading pool of water—to celebrate a reunion for which Colin blamed me and the copy I had been sending. He was, he said, merely the forerunner of a strong force of correspondents who at that moment were queuing up for visas in New Delhi. Colin having been seen on his road, I groped my way to a bedroom and after bellowing myself hoarse for a servant, managed to retrieve the suitcase of clothing which I had left in the storeroom before setting out for Everest. Hopes of a hot bath had to be abandoned when I learned that the hot water system had broken down. As something had to be done to remedy my filthy condition I took a cold bath. This may seem drastic treatment for a sick man—and I do not recommend it—but I can only add that from that evening the fever left me and never returned.

I had just returned to the bar, clean and in dry clothes, when Sax entered with Pasang. As I had thought, they had been forced to turn back soon after passing Bhatgaon. Talking over the news, we sat down to a dinner of rissoles—the first of an army of rissoles which were to be devoured two by two, morning noon and night for the next five weeks.

From Sax I heard of the forcing of Icefall which, in the strictly "news" sense, already outdated the information I had worked so hard to get. As the evening drew on, and Sax's bottle of Scotch diminished, we were joined by the returning Colin and it was past midnight when we finally broke up. We then discovered, belatedly, that there was no accommodation available for Pasang, so for want of a better remedy I popped him into the spare bed next to my own. Luxury for Pasang was complete next day when the manager—on one of his rare appearances—arrived in the room bringing early morning tea for us both.

The coolies had now to be thought of, and as the rain had ceased during the night and the roads were rapidly drying, I sent Pasang off with two Jeeps to collect them. They were duly rounded up between Bhatgaon and Banepa (where they had weathered the storm in comfort) and delivered to me at noon. For the last time I lined them up—swashbuckling Sirdar, stalwart Diamonds, squat Spades, bellicose Clubs, artful Joker and kindly Old Man still racked by his appalling cough. They grinned sheepishly while I counted out their wages—adding a substantial bakshish—and distributed the dispensable equipment, reserving the tent and ground sheet for Jeeves. On such expeditions gear no longer required on return, is invariably regarded as porters' "perqs," for it has little secondhand value and does not merit the freight charges of moving it far. Finally we shook hands all round.

There remained Jeeves to be dealt with. He had not appeared that morning which struck me as odd. When at last he did arrive, one glance at his crushed woebegone figure and tragically tear-filled eyes, told me at once that something was very wrong indeed. My own mail had brought me the pleasantest news I remember. There was a bunch of letters from home telling me that my wife and family were all safe and well, a bundle of cuttings, congratulatory messages and "fan" mail from the office—everything in fact that makes a newspaperman's life sweet. Poor Jeeves, loyal, devoted, unselfish, Jeeves, who asked nothing for himself and whose one anxiety was the comfort of others, had returned home to find that his only child had died, during his absence, of smallpox.

At the news my vanity was instantly humbled, the hopes and fears of men who hire themselves for timeless journeys, where there is no possibility of interception or recall, were brought home to me and I grieved with Jeeves as if his child had been one of my own.

CHAPTER XI

CLIMAX

IT MAY SEEM ABSURD that my own little effort should end at the very moment that the expedition was limbering up for the colossal exertion of placing two men on the summit of Everest. As it turned out—although I was not to know it—my timing could scarcely have been better. I had been traveling when there was a dearth of news about the expedition itself—it was the comparatively low-level acclimatization period—thus it did not appear impertinent for me to send dispatches about my own experiences. I had arrived at the head of the Khumbu glacier—the limit to which any independent reporter could be expected to go—at the very moment when the expedition was about to pass out of sight up into the Western Cwn. Once up in the Cwm the Icefall leading down to the glacier was quite as effective in precluding observation as a raised drawbridge would be in excluding "gate-crashers." From the Cwm onwards the story belonged to Colonel Hunt—who had been sending back a series of businesslike reports to *The Times,* and later to James Morris. All that the "outsider" at the foot of the Icefall could expect would be secondhand stories derived from returning Sherpas, and anyone who has tried to interrogate a Sherpa, (even if he is prepared to talk), will know what that means. My own fault lay in not getting myself organized more quickly and starting earlier—but as far as newspapermen went I was the pioneer. It was left to me to do the trail breaking and prove that it would, in fact, be possible for one of us to reach Everest. By the time I returned to Katmandu the chance for firsthand stories was gone.

Nevertheless I soon discovered on arrival that two representatives of rival organizations were preparing one-man expeditions to follow in my footsteps. They were Colin Reid's Indian colleague Mr. B. D. Mathur, and Peter Jackson of Reuther's Agency. I wished them well. Peter Jackson achieved a good independent account of the actual ascent but too long after the event to have any hope of beating *The Times* (by the time it appeared I was back home in Cyprus). Mathur managed a dispatch from "Thyangboche glacier," a remarkable feat which would have startled the monks of that happy establishment for there is not a glacier within miles of the place. Jackson had his box of silver taken off him by a rascally porter at Namche Bazar (I still find this an extraordinary thing to have happened and I refuse to allow the defection of one man to affect my faith in the coolie population as a whole). Mathur finished up by being kidnaped on the outskirts of Katmandu on his return.

My own immediate task was to get back down to Calcutta again as soon as possible with my films. I was also pretty well convinced that the time had come to afford myself a complete medical checkup. What with fever, drugs, loss of appetite and overexertion I was 18 pounds below normal weight.

The next morning, that of May, 1, there was some confusion at the airfield. Weather reports were bad, the planes were late in arriving, and Ravi Randawa who was again in charge, informed me that to save time he would take the aircraft down to Patna, return to Katmandu and then fly straight on to Calcutta. There was, he said, no point in going down to Patna by the first flight, for I would only find myself back in Katmandu three hours later. What actually happened was that, as soon as Ravi left, clouds closed down on the valley and there was no second flight that day. This was bitter news for me, for I had hoped to place my films on the Comet which was due to leave Calcutta for London on the following day, Saturday May 2. The delay was to have some effect on my fortune, however, for the Comet proved to be the ill-starred one which struck a northwester gale shortly after leaving Calcutta and crashed with loss of all lives. There had been no planes from Katmandu on that Saturday and in the evening I had the honor to be invited to a cocktail party given by the Indian Ambassador, Mr. B. K. Gokhale at which His Majesty King Tribhuvan and his two Queens were present. Also present were Ambassador Summerhayes and Colonel Proud, who had been following my syndicated articles in *The Statesman* and who so far relented in their attitude towards me to pronounce them "very readable." I also had the immense pleasure of meeting General Kaiser then filling the position of Chief Counselor to His Majesty. I had heard much of General Kaiser, both of his learning—his library of Central Asian literature is reputed to be one of the finest in the world—and of his prowess as a hunter. General Kaiser has been responsible for the arrangements of all the big "shoots" which have entertained Nepal's most distinguished visitors in modern times, his first responsibility in this respect being the immense battue of 1911 which so remarkably enabled the late King George V to display his skill as a shot. In that same year General Kaiser had presented to the London Zoo a representative collection of the animals of Nepal which included such rarities as a specimen of the Tibetan deer (of the Wapiti class) which had never even been seen, much less shot, by any white man until the Younghusband expedition to Lhasor, and a pair of singlehorned sheep.

General Kaiser was fully as entertaining as I had expected and our conversation was made the easier by his complete command of English which he had perfected during his years as Nepalese Ambassador in England.

Sunday bore all the promise of another cloudy day but towards noon the skies cleared and with relief I saw the passenger plane appear above the mountain gap leading to Patna and wing its way towards the airfield. Ravi was again at the controls and this time we made an incident free flight down to Calcutta. Ravi and I were now good friends and during the next ten days he, his American wife and myself had many enjoyable meals and meetings.

Coming straight from the clean, keen air of the snows, Calcutta, now nearer to the annual monsoon than ever, was worse than the "hot" chamber of a Turkish bath. In the first day or two perspiration poured off me, I found it almost as difficult to breathe as on the Khumbu glacier, and reaction had set in to such an extent that I felt even the climbing of a short staircase to be an effort.

I lost no time in seeking out the best doctor in Calcutta but I had been exposed to so many infections and diseases that no snap verdict as to my condition could be given. I submitted to a number of rather repellent tests and was told to return in a week to hear the results. In the meantime I was to do nothing but eat, drink and sleep—the sort of prescription I find no difficulty in following. I did, however, vary the routine by a visit to the Calcutta Zoo and later to the Zoological Survey of India where I picked the brains of Dr. B. Biswas, Head of the Mammals Section of the India Museum, regarding the Abominable Snowman. I also visited the Calcutta Meteorological Station which had now begun special weather broadcasts for the Everest expedition. These broadcasts were largely the work of Dr. Mazumdar who gave me interesting information about weather in the high mountains and also showed me some weather reports from Everest, which had been compiled by George Band, but which, having come a good deal of the way by runner, were no longer topical enough to be of interest to me, although they remained most valuable for the record. If I understood Dr. Mazumdar correctly the northwester season which brings snow in the mountains and heavy rain in Calcutta—and which precedes the monsoon—had been an abnormal one. The storms had started very late indeed—which explained the unusual heat spell which we had earlier experienced—and this usually meant they would continue late. This *could* mean that the lull between the northwesters and the arrival of the monsoon on Everest—the vital lull without which any successful climb would be impossible—*could* be very short or might never occur at all. But, and this was great news, if the northwesters were late, so quite obviously was the monsoon. It was now about May 7 and in any normal year the presence of the monsoon would, at this time, have been firmly established, probably somewhere at the approaches to the Bay of Bengal. In this year, if it was anywhere (and this was by no means a certain "plot") it was still some hundreds of miles south of Ceylon. It was therefore most unlikely that the monsoon could possibly reach Everest for another three, or even four weeks. Thus the creation of the lull must depend on cessation of the northwesters. About this Dr. Mazumdar could offer no predictions; he repeated the warning that I had heard before, namely, that mountains of Himalayan height have a habit of making their own weather.

During this week of enforced idleness I also spent some time rummaging in the library of the Himalayan Club by courtesy of the librarian, Mr. V. S. Risoe who also was kind enough to invite me to lunch. May 15, the day on which it had been forecast Colonel Hunt would launch his "assault" on the summit, was now approaching and I was asked to write a "curtain raiser." There has been a good deal of misunderstanding as to what actually constitutes an "assault." It would have been clearer to indicate that May 15, thereabouts, would see the mounting of the first assault phase which would see a large number of men endeavoring to establish a series of camps from the Western Cwm, up the Lhotse Face, across onto the South Col, and finally to complete their work by pitching a single tent on the southeast ridge within 1000 feet of the summit. This tent would be used by the team of two chosen to make the last dash for the top. During the mounting of the assault all men would be working at over 23,000 feet, that is to say at heights where deterioration of physique due to altitude, rapidly exceeds man's capacity to acclimatize. Any amount of build up work could be carried on below the 23,000 foot level, but above it dwindling strength and stamina would sooner or later bring an end to operations. One or two setbacks could be tolerated, but a long drawn out delay during the critical phase must inevitably spell failure. The difficulties of flogging a route up to the South Col, and keeping it open, retarded the timetable by five or six days, a delay which caused some of my colleagues in Katmandu to jump to the conclusion that the entire attempt had failed.

My "curtain raiser" was published in *The Daily Mail* on Tuesday, May 12, and ran:

"The end of this week may bring zero hour for the final assault parties of the British expedition which hopes to climb Everest.

"All that we now require is a favorable lull between the northwest gales, which render the upper slopes of the mountain unendurably cold, and the onset of the southeast monsoon which will clothe the whole mountain in a blanket of soft snow, and makes safe climbing impossible.

"According to past observations, such a lull should occur about the fifteenth of this month. All such calculations could be upset, as so often before, by the early arrival of the monsoon. But down in this city (Calcutta) where we are in the best position to judge, as we lie on the direct path of the monsoon as it sweeps from the Bay of Bengal towards the Himalayas, although it has been unusually hot for the season there is no sign that the monsoon will be unduly premature.

"So far Colonel Hunt seems to have enjoyed abnormally favorable conditions. According to reports, he forced the 2000 foot Icefall which ascends from the Khumbu glacier to the corridor of the Western Cwm as long ago as April 20 (actually it was not until April 25 that the final immense crevasse at the top of the fall was bridged by an expanding aluminum ladder). The Western Cwm, in its turn, leads gently up to the base of the so-called South Col, which connects the peak of Lhotse with the southern flank of Everest.

"Colonel Hunt's program, as he outlined it to me many weeks ago in Katmandu, was to spend about three weeks 'lifting' supplies from the foot of the Icefall to an advance base camp at the head of the Western Cwm and thence to an 'assault camp' on the South Col, which is 25,800 feet high.

"The ascent from the head of the Western Cwm to the South Col is technically very difficult and also hazardous, as it involves a traverse on the face of Lhotse. To avoid this danger, Colonel Hunt will employ, for the first time on Everest, what is known as an 'avalanche gun' (in reality a standard British 2-inch mortar) with which to bombard the Lhotse Face, which is continually swept by avalanches." This was an error on my part. The mortar was never used on the mountain for the simple reason that its range was not great enough, which meant that anyone firing it at its intended target would have buried himself in his own self-created avalanche. Some rounds were discharged on the triumphant return march as a feu de joie to amuse the Sherpas.

"After the avalanches have descended (sic) fixed lines will be positioned across the face to assist porters to carry loads to the South Col camp.

"This camp will not be permanently manned until the assault proper, commences. Once it is established and provisioned the British and the porters will retire to a more tenable level to await the final assault signal." I was proved wrong here by the remarkable tenacity displayed by George Lowe, Wilfred Noyce and certain Sherpas. "At present the South Col is still being swept by blood-freezing winds. It is also at such a high altitude that no man could hope to survive there for more than a few days.

"The main hope for Colonel Hunt's expedition seems to rest on its superb equipment and the great reservoir of experience of past expeditions upon which he can now draw. The question as to who will form the ultimate assault party must naturally be uppermost in the minds of all the expedition members, but in my experience it is the least mentioned among the men themselves.

"Naturally, everyone would like to be chosen, but everyone realizes that the final choice must rest with Colonel Hunt himself. Because we lost nearly a decade of climbing experience through the war years (a handicap which one cannot help remarking did not affect the Swiss, and to a lesser extent the French), we have no automatic choices to match, say, the Smythe-Shipton-Tilman combination of the thirties, or the Norton-Mallory-Somervell combination of the twenties.

"I think it is fair to say we have a technically competent team of mountaineers who have yet to prove their mettle at spectacular heights. We may have one shining star in G. C. Band, bespectacled science student now an undergraduate at Cambridge University. Colonel Hunt generously refers to Band as 'the most brilliant climber in Britain today,' but it would be unfair to expect too much of Band on this trip. It is considered that the best age for an Everest climber is between twenty-five and thirty-five, and it may well be that Band, now twenty-three and on his first Himalayan excursion, is being nursed for an all-out effort in a later year." I was not too wrong here. Band lost his chance for the top by utterly exhausting himself in the appalling task of flogging a route up the Lhotse Face which would enable the team to go through.

"We should not be too hopeful of success, although success would be delicious in this particular year, after three decades of primarily British endeavor.

"Writing in the *Himalayan Journal*, of 1952, W. H. Murray, who was a member of the 1951 reconnaissance expedition, assesses the chances this way:

> No expedition, however strong and energetic, can hope to achieve the summit unless it be aided by three major strokes of good fortune *which must all concur:* freedom from high wind near the top; no deep powder snow on the slopes below or above the South Col; and the right man high at the right time.

"Good fortune of that very special kind has graced none of the previous expeditions.

"To this appreciation it is only fair to add that some of the most brilliant climbers in the present party may have already exhausted themselves in pathfinding for the expedition through such appalling obstacles as the 2000 foot Icefall." Here I had Hillary rather than Band in mind.

"Colonel Hunt's final choice, if it proves unexpected, will be based on that sort of factor."

On Monday, April 11, I was given a clean bill of health, nothing could be found the matter with me. True, I was still losing weight and I was still afflicted by appalling lassitude, but neither condition was likely to be remedied by a prolonged stay in Calcutta at that season. Accordingly I booked a passage back to Katmandu where I arrived three days later—there having been two blank flying days owing to clouds over the valley.

Things had changed considerably in the short time I had been away. The Nepal Hotel was flying additional distress signals in the shape of the undergarments of the domestic staff which were now spread out to dry on the front lawn. As I drove up the cook and various friends were bathing themselves in the central ornamental fountain.

Electric light in the hotel was still cut off; the manager's appearances had become more fleeting than ever. The bar was almost drained of liquor and was therefore only opened when time could be found between the prodigious siestas of the barman. As usual, in the sultry pre-monsoon period, the insect population increased enormously. Mosquitoes abounded, and two spiders of the size and weight of tarantulas were dispatched—one in my bedroom and one in the bar. This second intruder was brought to a halt as it was perambulating over the stone floor by Colin Reid, who deftly soused it with neat whisky. This caused it to spin happily in small circles in the process of doing which it deposited a large sac of eggs. Long afterwards—the time it now generally took to summon a servant—the whole mess was swept away with a dustpan and brush.

It was now that a number of mysterious Indians began to descend on Katmandu and were soon disclosed as radio operators. It had occurred to a number of newspapers—not all of them Indian—that if they could send a radio-transmitter forward to the foot of Everest and station a receiving set in Katmandu, there might be every chance of "scooping" the result of the climb. Those of us who had not thought of this plan, heard with considerable relief that the Nepalese government had rigidly refused to permit the import of any transmitters for the very good reason that the consequences would be quite unforeseeable were a number of "pirate" stations suddenly to start operations within a few miles of the Communist held northern frontier. But the radio operators in Katmandu soon found another profitable field of work. That was to monitor all outgoing telegraphy between Nepal and India. One senior news agency even went to the extent of establishing a twenty-four hour monitoring service so that the messages sent by any of us became known to them long before they reached our own offices. They could, in fact, "scoop" us by picking up the telephone and giving our news verbally to New Delhi before our cables had been cleared through Patna, the next telegraph office down the line. This was of no particular concern to me for by now I had little enough to hide. The monitoring was done quite openly, whatever regulations it might be breaching, and once I had an amusing "complaint": "could I not stick to the point—namely the actual climbing of Everest—and not waste people's time with thousands of words on such digressions as 'the excellence of Sherpas' and 'Abominable Snowmen' ? "

The monitoring was a most serious matter for *The Times,*" for it meant that the copyright on anything cabled by Colonel Hunt, James Morris, or Arthur Hutchinson (now established in Katmandu) could no longer be considered secure. This led finally to the use of code names (which I am assured were quite easily broken) and finally to the dispatching of the more important messages to Calcutta, by courier. Before this happened, whole sentences were quite blatantly "lifted" out of *The Times'* copy long before it reached London, and other sentences were imperfectly disguised. For instance, when on one occasion Colonel Hunt wrote of his plan to launch a "double barreled" attack on the mountain, this appeared as a "two-pronged" attack, which is hardly the same thing, one meaning "two in quick succession" and the other "two simultaneously."

We now had news that three correspondents of senior British newspapers—*The Observer, The Daily Express* and *The Daily Herald,* were being held up, visa-less, in New Delhi, on the advice of the British Ambassador, Mr. Summerhayes, who considered that "there are correspondents enough in Nepal" (in fact there were five of us British, including two of *The Times*). It would have been far better policy to advise the entry of all who cared to come, for those of us who were still trying to do an honest job of work were fighting an obviously hopeless battle.

In those anxious days of waiting for news I found that I, myself, was being regarded as something of a mystery figure. No one to whom I spoke cared to believe that I had taken the trouble to walk up to Everest and back merely to look at the mountain. I was credited with the creation of all sorts of elaborate chains and networks for getting information. For instance, there is, at Okhladunga, a few days off the direct Everest route, an emergency government radio station which was reputedly not working at the time because it had run out of gasoline needed for the engine which drives the generators. The small tin of kerosene which my coolies had carried for my hurricane lamps soon became exaggerated into several jerricans of gasoline which we had carried up to Okhladunga to get the radio station working, presumably for my own personal use. I took no trouble to squash these rumors, or indeed to emphasize that I had nothing up my sleeve—which was the truth—for I felt that as long as attention was directed at me, it would not be diverted to more profitable lines of inquiry.

The craving for news, any news, by any means, soon reached such a pitch that it became obvious that Sherpa runners were being tampered with. Messages sent by Colonel Hunt would arrive with Peter Jackson's runner, or Peter Jackson's messages would arrive by Colin Reid's runner (from Mathur) and on one memorable occasion an expedition mailbag arrived at the embassy with an entirely new type of padlock to which none had a key. It could only be assumed that somewhere along the route the original padlock had been ripped off, the contents of the bag examined, and a new padlock substituted. Exactly who was responsible for these activities I never found out, nor would I care to hazard a guess. Suffice it to say that the embassy regarded the development with aloof distaste and no doubt became more determined than ever that the prized news of the final result of the climb should go to *The Times*, and to no other newspaper. I may however add that during this interim period Colin Reid and myself interviewed the Ambassador together and received the assurance that after a "reasonable interval" had elapsed after he himself received the news and had dispatched it to London over the embassy radio—thus insuring that Her Majesty the Queen should receive it first—he would inform us both and permit us to send short messages to our respective newspapers over his own radio. I took this to be a promise and placed my whole faith in it. Colin Reid assures me that he subsequently saw the Ambassador alone and reached an agreement defining the "reasonable interval" as "two hours," but in fairness I must say that this definition was never made personally to me. To suggest that the Nepalese government condoned the irregular Press practices would be quite unfair. Rather naturally without Press experience, they may well have imagined that such conduct was common the world over—to which, having twenty-two years of working journalism behind me, I can only add a pious "God forbid!"

Those of us who had no Sherpas of our own to bring us messages, contented ourselves with trying to interrogate other people's Sherpas. This I consider legitimate, for a runner is paid for carrying a message and not necessarily for keeping his mouth shut, but it was a thankless, not to say hopeless task. I was at some advantage for I knew most of the regular runners personally, having met them at some time or other along the route. But this advantage availed little or nothing. To Sherpas—providing there is plenty of beer about—the world is always a rosy place peopled by wonderful fellows who are always doing wonderful things. While they have a pretty shrewd business idea of weights and distances, they have little or no conception of times, dates, places and heights when translated into Western terms. Hunt they could identify as the "Colonel Sahib" and Major Wylie as the fluent Gurkhali speaker (who probably also has more than a working knowledge of Khaskra, the Sherpa language). The rest of the expedition seemed to appear as alike to the runners—who only saw them fleetingly between long journeys—as a dozen Chinamen must appear alike to an inexperienced Westerner. By no means all the men interrogated were runners from Everest. Frequently the alarm would be sounded in the Nepal Hotel that a new runner had arrived and a hue and cry would start through the bazaar, and sometimes last for hours, before the object of the search was finally tracked down and discovered to be some grimy, bewildered Tibetan who might well never have heard of the mountain.

Looking back, I am astonished how accurate most of the qualified rumors we sent back at this stage proved to be. Two of them caused us all to be laughed at, yet were later shown to have quite enough truth in them to justify reporting. The first concerned an impending Russian attempt on the mountain; in fact, as I have already written, there is now every reason to believe this attempt had actually occurred. The second concerned the presence of a mysterious, unidentified aircraft round the mountain. This seemed much too good to be true, yet I was later assured by expedition members that this aircraft *did* appear. It arrived during the acclimatization period at Thyangboche monastery and was seen by all members. Tom Stobart, the expedition's film cameraman has now given me authority to quote him personally as having seen it, and also that it was carrying no distinguishable markings.

In the main, however, for some days from May15 onwards all we in Katmandu could do was to report weather conditions. In theory we were in a good position to do this, Everest being within sight from the roof of the hotel, but at that season the heat haze rising from India obscured the mountain in the mornings and the succession of northwesters bringing low clouds and thunderstorms hid it in the afternoons. There was no means of telling which particular storm was likely to pass round the Everest region, or to what height the mountain was likely to be affected. Occasional exceptions were firsthand reports brought in by Himalayan Airways pilots than whom there are no greater experts on Himalayan weather. Of some assistance to us were the special Everest weather forecasts compiled in Calcutta and broadcast daily for the benefit of the climbers. But it was admitted that these could only be intelligent guesswork (from a point some hundreds of miles farther away than we were) and the fact that they were also being broadcast in London rendered it redundant for us to add more than an embellishment or two. The only genuine minor weather sensation during that waiting period was a mild earthquake shock, which we could only earnestly hope had not set the Icefall in motion (it did not).

Before attempting to describe the further progress of events, I feel compelled to restate my opinion that both the expedition and the British Embassy failed to appreciate the political implications inherent in the 1953 climb which were already strongly developed. This was not just another British expedition supported by "hired men." Articulate Asia—and that includes the fanatical student bodies—long frustrated by lack of material achievement and some natural jealousy of the long-dominant European had found an outstanding, indeed unique, champion, in Tenzing who with Lambert in the previous year had climbed higher than any Briton. For India, his further exploits had become a matter of supreme national interest. On leaving Darjeeling to join the present expedition he had been given a rapturous ceremonial send-off and had been presented with an Indian flag which he was charged with carrying to the summit. It was therefore a matter of intense chagrin to the Indian newspaper correspondents in Katmandu that they should be starved completely of news of their hero and that the only authentic account of his doings should appear in a single London newspaper and at that, an expensive one with comparatively small circulation. To them it was additionally galling that in these accounts Tenzing should not be singled out for special mention but, after the British fashion, his contribution should be regarded merely as part of the achievement of the team as a whole. The Indians were not interested in the team; for them the "angle" on the Everest story was Tenzing. Was Tenzing getting a square deal? The Indians could not be sure about it. I have heard this matter thrashed out for hours on end down in the Rangana Café in Joodha Street. Forecasts on the result of the climb varied from Tenzing reaching the top alone to the British deliberately preventing him from attempting the summit in case he showed up their own inability. All this, of course, was heaven-sent propaganda material for Communists (if

Communists recognize a heaven) and among the students at the neighboring close-packed tables there must often have been a Red agent or two.

I had previously had a most illuminating talk on Communism in Nepal with Mr. M. P. Koirala who had only recently relinquished the office of Prime Minister and was shortly to be reappointed to it. He made no secret of the fact there was a good deal of active Communism in the country, and the political situation existing there very easily lends to exploitation by unscrupulous agents. Most of the agents—they are located mostly in the Terai—are Indians who are attempting to stir up the intense nationalism of the Nepalese in order to embarrass their own (the Indian) government. Communist activity of this nature also leaves the present Nepalese government in none too happy a position, for while it yields to no section of the community in patriotism, it sees, very wisely, that during this early stage of its life it must lean very heavily on the guidance and assistance which only India can provide.

Apart from this aspect, there is evidence that a certain amount of Communist influence has filtered over the Tibetan frontier into some of the remoter northern valleys.

Great Britain is also open to attack by Nepalese Reds by reason of the fact that the bulk of troops recruited to the British Brigade of Gurkhas are now engaged in fighting the Communists in Malaya. Reports of casualties have been deliberately and wildly exaggerated in bazaar rumors in Katmandu (up to last summer there had, in fact, been scarcely more than 100 casualties) and a "bring the boys home" campaign had been started on the old familiar Communist pattern. In view of this complex situation I feel the British Ambassador in Katmandu could have done worse than request the High Commissioner in New Delhi for the services of a sympathetic Public Relations Officer throughout the duration of the expedition.

The two weeks which followed the fifteenth of May (the day Colonel Hunt had announced he would commence his first assault phase) were an anxious, indeed nerve-wrecking time for everyone. The weather did little to help us. One day might be clear and brilliantly sunny, luring the unwary amongst us into reporting that the famous lull had arrived; the next three days would bring northwesters possibly even fiercer and more unrelenting than ever. If news from Everest were to come by runner, we had at least a clear week to wait in which to learn whether, in fact, the assault phase had actually commenced. Time was difficult to kill. Colin Reid and myself, generally accompanied by Sax and Balram Tandon, visited and admired some of the more exotic temples—with no designs, I hasten to add, on the green eyes of any little yellow gods. On one of our walks we also discovered, to my surprise, for I had no idea it was there, a small Christian cemetery, which proves that when Milton Hayes recited: "There's a green eyed yellow idol to the north of Katmandu, There's a little cross of stone beneath the town," he knew more about the country than most of his hearers probably gave him credit for.

In this period I was also challenged to a round of golf by David Haye-Neave—Press versus the Diplomatic Corps. I have played in this perennial fixture in many parts of the world, but never in such fantastic circumstances. Haye-Neave, a former winner of the Silver Boomerang of the Royal and Ancient Club, was a worthy opponent—and a sure-footed climbing partner with a good head for heights. I may say that any one of the Katmandu golf course holes, if it could be exported bodily, would enliven any course in the world, and would be considered a sporting addition—although it might be necessary for older members to "rope up" to descend into some of the deeper hazards. Eighteen such holes in succession—most of them with "carries" of up to 200 yards over chasms up to 200 feet deep—is work for strong men like Haye-Neave and myself. After a few hundred strokes apiece, and a display of no mean mountaineering skill on some of the steeper "pitches" we halved our match. He was to beat me later, but at least I escaped from our series without a broken leg. Certain features of the course naturally known to Haye-Neave, but unfamiliar to me, acted in his favor. There were no flags on the greens, this office being performed by a small boy with an umbrella who ran on ahead and stuck it in each hole as we came to it. Large monkeys abounded on some of the fairways who raced for your ball and barracked derisively if you got there first. In the nesting season, I am told, large birds flap down from the surrounding trees, seize the balls, fly with them up to their nests and then spend the next week or two endeavoring to hatch them out. I was once taken to task by a critic for using the word "fantastic" in describing something which did not justify it. I hope I may be excused on this occasion. Fantastic the Katmandu golf course certainly is; but for those who play for pleasure it is also utterly enjoyable and I hope nothing is ever done to improve matters.

The week end of May 24 brought a spate of runners from Everest—although none, of course, for me. The only authentic message was that addressed to Arthur Hutchinson of *The Times* and all eyes were turned enviously in his direction and the monitors sharpened their pencils in anticipation. To Hutch's annoyance, and our amusement, his message had been opened and read by the Ambassador before it reached him, as were all his subsequent messages, which tended to prove that not all the current irregularities were being committed by Press circles.

By that Sunday it was known—although not yet to me—that the gist of the message was the fact that Band and Westmacott had had to be withdrawn from the assault owing to exhaustion and altitude sickness. Colin Reid heard this news and (a fate which threatened all of us) was unfortunately betrayed into reporting the failure of the first assault (before it had been made) by Band and Westmacott (who never made it). This report, plus photographs of the luckless climbers was printed with considerable prominence (*The Daily Telegraph* May 25) and caused some of us to receive heartbroken cables from London regretting that we had missed the "news."

In expedition terms, withdrawal of Band and Westmacott meant a setback and consequent delay in breaking the trail up the Lhotse Face to the South Col, whence the two assaults proper were to be made. The delay—which lengthened to five or six days when conditions on the Face were found to be unexpectedly difficult—could however be tolerated, and need not mean disaster and defeat, as long as the monsoon remained at a safe distance. There was still no indication that the monsoon was firmly established even to the south of the Bay of Bengal which should mean there was still a good two weeks' climbing weather in hand—more than sufficient for the task. In Katmandu, in that second critical week, however, suspicions that all was not going well on the mountain grew so rapidly that by Wednesday, May 27, defeat was being openly talked about. Twelve days had elapsed since the opening of the final assault phase, surely—many of us felt—the effort must now be over and, if it were over, and had been successful, surely we must have heard of it by this time?

The next "alarm" which occurred on Thursday, May 28, had an element of humor about it. Towards evening, Alec MacMillan, who I have introduced earlier in this book as arriving in Katmandu to supervise the building of the new British Embassy, was turning the dials of his radio set when he picked up a faint voice saying ". . . Namche Bazar. The first and second assaults have failed. It is hoped to start a third attempt before dawn." The voice then faded. A few of us, including Arthur Hutchinson, Colin Reid and myself, happened to be at the embassy at the time and MacMillan lost time in informing us. There was not then the slightest indication who the voice belonged to or whether it was actually speaking from Namche Bazar. A quick inquiry at the embassy elicited the information that no official news whatsoever had been received through its prearranged channels with the expedition. But it was impossible to ignore the "voice" completely. All of us, including Hutchinson, felt compelled to report its message qualifying it as strongly as we could with such phrases as "entirely unconfirmed reports etc." The message caused the wildest excitement among the Indian correspondents. Someone had obviously scored a world "scoop." The question was: whose "scoop" was it? Claims of ownership came thick and fast. On the following day May 29, (which was actually to see the triumphant ascent), Peter Jackson's Reuter colleagues in Katmandu did him the dubious service of reporting:

> It became known today that the terse radio message picked up on Thursday at Katmandu came from Reuter's correspondent Peter Jackson who is at the British base camp on the Khumbu glacier. From the base camp it is believed he sent a runner to Namche Bazar where it was transmitted by radio. The message came faintly over the 170 intervening miles.
>
> Listeners heard only fragments but made out that the double assault had failed and that the expedition was leaving the mountain on June 7.

For fear of spoiling a good story I add with some hesitation that it was subsequently discovered that the radio link between Namche Bazar and Katmandu is by Morse-buzzer and not by radio-telephone.

The true explanation of the "voice" was discovered on the following day. It was none other than an Indian correspondent speaking over the Indian Embassy radio link with India. By purest chance MacMillan, seated a few hundred yards away, had tuned in momentarily to correct wave length and intercepted the fateful message. But the word "defeat" was now running round the world and Colonel Hunt later commented wryly that the expedition heard of their "failure" over the radio at the very moment the assault parties were setting out for their attempts.

It has been well said: "immortal deeds are absolute and stand from their outset in a realm apart." The story of the victorious ascent of Everest belongs properly to the gallant and devoted company who achieved it. It is not for me to do more than sketch in the details.

Ten days were required—double the estimated time—to master the precipitous and glaciated Lhotse Face and reach the South Col. Time and again on this appallingly difficult 4000 feet stretch the agonizing work of whole days of flogging out a track which could be used by laden Sherpas was blotted out by fresh snowfalls. It was not until May 21 that Wilfred Noyce and one Sherpa, Annullu, completed the final traverse from Camp VII and gained the indescribably bleak plateau of the Col whereon fluttered the skeleton remains of a single Swiss tent. The way was open. On the following day Hillary and Tenzing—prematurely committed as previous expeditions had been forced prematurely to commit their best climbers when unexpectedly severe obstacles had been encountered, and knowing they might be jeopardizing their own chances of reaching the summit—spearheaded a long straggling line of Sherpas under the charge of Major Wylie in the first successful "lift" to the Col. Here Camp VIII, the key to the final assault proper was established and adequately stocked.

The South Col (26,000 feet) is itself as high as Annapurna. On this expedition no less than nine climbers reached the Col plus nineteen Sherpas, each carrying between thirty and forty pounds. Six of the Sherpas made the journey twice. But the

South Col is not Everest. What the emotions of the exhausted climbers can have been when they looked upward from the South Col and saw what appeared to be an entirely new mountain towering above them and fraught with technical difficulties can only be guessed. Yet this was the task which had now to be tackled. It was work which fell heaviest on the "Europeans" for three of the five Sherpas chosen to go higher than the South Col succumbed to altitude sickness and had to be sent back before their work had begun. Thus the support groups which were to back up the two assault teams—the first consisting of Charles Evans and Tom Bourdillon and the second of Hillary and Tenzing—were reduced to three "Europeans" and two Sherpas, instead of eight men in all. The supporting "porters" were Colonel Hunt himself, Alfred Gregory, Hillary's fellow New Zealander George Lowe, and the Sherpas Da Namgyal and Ang Nima. We are told that the "Europeans" carried loads of between fifty and sixty pounds, a tremendous feat at heights over 27,000 feet, and the Sherpas about forty pounds each, a fact which should dispel a popular belief that high altitude climbing is an unencumbered pleasure for "Europeans," only made possible by the lifting capacity of their sweated native "hired men."

On May 27 Evans and Bourdillon, using closed-circuit oxygen apparatus set off from the Col for their great climb to the South Summit. Beyond the South Summit is a farther 500 foot ridge leading to the true summit. This is invisible from below. The instructions given to Evans and Bourdillon were to attain the South Summit and from it to make as careful an examination as possible of the hitherto unknown final ridge—intelligence which could be used later by Hillary and Tenzing. They were not to go beyond the South Summit unless exceptional conditions warranted the move. This task they brilliantly completed, returning to the South Col that evening at 6:30 having climbed far higher than man had ever climbed before. In the earlier hours of the day Hunt accompanied by the faithful Da Namgyal, carrying between them the tent, food and fuel later to be used at the last assault camp by Hillary and Tenzing, had plodded painfully upwards—their oxygen sets working imperfectly—to a height of 27,350 feet where they were compelled to dump their loads. They arrived back at the Col, utterly spent at 1:30 P.M. The next day, May 27, the storms were back over Everest in all their relentless fury. Climbing was out of the question and the climbers huddled in their straining tents on the Col must have wondered if once again weather, grimmest and most unpredictable of the Everest defenses, would intervene to preserve the sanctity of the summit. But the next morning the gales had blown themselves out, the sun shone in clear skies, and Hillary and Tenzing set forth in good heart to accept the last great challenge. With them went Lowe, Gregory and Ang Nima. They reached Hunt's dump and added the two loads to their already overburdened shoulders. They toiled on upwards for 600 feet and here, upon an awkward double step of rock just under the 28,000 foot mark, they pitched the tiny tent where Hillary and Tenzing must wait out the night. Back down to the Col went the "porters," their reward the knowledge that they had helped establish the highest "camp" ever known.

At 11:30 on the morning of Friday, May 29, Edmund Hillary and Tenzing Norkey attained that knob of ice and snow which is the summit of Everest, 2 feet, if we are to believe the surveyors, above the 29,000 foot mark. This was no more than another "little patch of ground that hath in it no profit but the name"—but what a name! It now represented the apex of the pyramid of experience, endurance, and sacrifice which it had taken hundreds upon hundreds of men over thirty years to build. For the first time in history the entire world lay beneath the feet of two mere mortals. After

Tenzing had held aloft the Union Jack and the flags of India, Nepal and the United Nations—flown from his ice ax—and Hillary had photographed him, the Sherpa knelt down and making a small hole in the snow had placed there a handful of sweets, a biscuit or two and a piece of mint cake, all he had to offer to the gods of the mountain. Beside the Buddhist, tall, gaunt, tough Hillary had knelt down and making an adjacent hole had laid there a crucifix which Colonel Hunt had entrusted to him two days previously on the South Col—a fact which was not known even to some members of the expedition until many months afterwards.

Behind Hillary and Tenzing lay five and a half hours of desperate effort. The ascent to the South Summit had been bad enough, for the steps cut in the ice by Evans and Bourdillon had been obliterated by the subsequent gale. Here they took it in turns to lead and cut the steps. The final ridge Hillary later described as "of high Alpine standard," but this particular ridge was between 28,000 and 29,000 feet high, and to conserve oxygen they had been forced to reduce the flow rate of the open-circuit equipment. There were also technical difficulties which entailed the taking of risks which in other circumstances would not be considered acceptable. But of all conceivable special circumstances where a man may permit himself to take an additional risk clearly the last 500 feet of Everest, on a fine day, is one.

Throughout the last forty minutes Hillary was in the lead and, if it must be known, it was Hillary who reached the top first. To all mountaineers this fact is not of the slightest importance. A "rope" of two is a "rope" of two and if the rope itself had united Hillary and Tenzing in death as it undoubtedly would have done at that height had either put a foot wrong, surely it cannot be allowed to divide them in victory?

The remainder of the story descends to the murkier level of Katmandu. News of the successful ascent of Everest and the safe return of the victors, arrived in the capital at 6:30 P.M. on the evening of June 1—the eve of the Coronation of Her Majesty Queen Elizabeth II. The message from Everest arrived over the police radio link from Namche Bazar. As this link is Indian-operated it was delivered, in the normal fashion, first to the Indian Embassy. Here it was scrutinized with no particular interest, for it appeared to contain nothing that was not known already. It was at once sent over to the British Embassy. On receiving the message, I am reliably informed, Mr. Summerhayes broke down and wept for joy. The message ran: "Bad snow; Hillary and Tenzing failed; all well."

Unknown to Colonel Hunt, and unknown to the Indian Ambassador, Mr. Gokhale (who had expressly asked that no such thing should be attempted), a code had been arranged between *The Times* correspondents and the British Ambassador. Decoded, the message ran: "Hillary and Tenzing succeeded twenty-ninth all well."

No reasonable person could possibly censure *The Times* representatives for trying to safeguard their cherished scoop—they had suffered enough in all conscience from their rivals—but the connivance of the British Ambassador was injudicious diplomacy, for it exposed his Indian colleague to charges that he had not taken sufficient precautions to prevent unauthorized persons from sending coded messages over a Security Police radio link—a practice which no country could be expected to tolerate.

The subsequent conduct of the British Ambassador was even stranger. The message had been primarily addressed to Arthur Hutchinson of *The Times* but in jealous determination to keep the glad news from Everest as his own personal exclusive Mr. Summerhayes informed no one in Katmandu, and relayed it through to London on his own responsibility. He then sat out the night. It was a big responsibility to take; for while Mr. Summerhayes was reporting "success" to London, Mr. Gokhale, working from the same original, might with equal confidence have been reporting "failure" to New Delhi. The same desire to "scoop" the world, led Mr. Summerhayes also into the error of not taking immediate steps to inform His Majesty the King of Nepal of the victory. It was, after all, the King of Nepal's mountain, and even if Tenzing's nationality was in dispute—in fact it was thought at the time that he was Nepalese—a large number of other subjects of His Majesty were engaged on the mountain and news of their success and safety was awaited anxiously at Court. But it was to be not before early the next morning, from the other side of the world, namely by radio broadcasts from America, that news of the ascent of Everest (only 200 miles away) became known in Katmandu. We of the less favored Press had gone to bed the previous night with our gloom and anxieties unrelieved. There had been another storm, this time of almost incredible violence, in the evening. Colin Reid had been caught in it during his return to the hotel. His Jeep had stalled, he had been forced to get out and push and he arrived back wetter than I had ever been on my return from the mountain. At nine o'clock the next morning a station wagon arrived from the British Embassy with invitations to Hutchinson, Reid and myself, to use it to bring us at once to the Ambassador. We were still in complete ignorance of the news but as a precaution we took our typewriters with us. As we entered the gates of the "Lines" the Indian correspondents who had long heard the American radio reports were already streaming away, having been officially informed prior to ourselves. Mr. Summerhayes was standing on the porch of the building with Colonel Proud beside him. My own reaction to the news was one of such overwhelming joy coupled with thankfulness and relief that this "story," which had been the toughest I had ever been assigned to, was over, that I was prepared to forgive the jealous intrigue which had robbed the announcement of all topical value. I hurried off to make what I could of one terse sentence. In my dispatch I pointed out that it had been essentially a team victory, and that while there might be regrets that no climber from Great Britain had reached the top, none could grudge the New Zealander Hillary, or Tenzing, their success—they had been consistently fine performers both in this and previous expeditions. I also pointed out that, owing to delays, if the attempt on May 29 had failed the whole expedition would probably have had to be abandoned, for the monsoon was now firmly established in the Bay of Bengal and would probably have precluded any third attempt being made with reasonable prospects of a safe retreat down the Icefall. By the time I had filed this message thousands of words had already been filed by the Indians and thousands upon thousands more continued to pour in on top of it. As this was Coronation Day and the newspaper of the morrow was bound to be filled with Coronation news, I forbore to send any more speculation and packed up for the day. There was as yet no indication whatsoever as to what had happened on Everest. The messages sent by my Indian colleagues largely consisted of eulogies on the exploits of Tenzing. It was not long, a matter of an hour or two, before the word was spread around that Tenzing had reached the summit first. None cared to dispute this rumor, and as soon as the first message announcing the "fact" had been sent to India, all other Indian correspondents, for fear of being left behind, followed suit. From this beginning the story started that not only had Tenzing reached the top first—he had hauled the exhausted Hillary up behind him on the rope. It was some such story as this that the Communists had been waiting for, and they made full use of it.

In case it be thought that I am airing a personal grievance regarding the transmission of the Everest message, let me say that I made no comment upon it at all at the time. Other newspapers were not so lenient.

On June 5, Colin Reid writing in *The Daily Telegraph* stated:

> The determination of Mr. Summerhayes to be the exclusive source of the news, while Colonel Hunt was under private contract to *The Times* in London, has resulted in a situation in which the Ambassador, as well as his First Secretary Colonel Proud, have been the jealous agents of a single newspaper throughout the period of the expedition.
>
> The British Ambassador specifically promised all British correspondents here that he would notify them of the news of success or failure on Everest as soon as possible after he had transmitted it to the Foreign Office. The promise of a British Ambassador was trusted. But it was not until the following day that they and the Indian correspondents were summoned to the steps of the British Embassy to learn what most of the world had learned from the American radio the previous day. *The Times* correspondent, also in ignorance, was among those present.

The cry was taken by Alastair Forbes, one of London's pithiest political commentators writing in *The Sunday Dispatch:*

> It was unfortunate in the first place that the Foreign Service should have been acting in this instance for *The Times* newspaper, a team-up the existence of which in other fields Foreign Secretaries have always sought to deny to suspicious foreigners.
>
> So busy was Her Majesty's Ambassador in seeking to get a scoop for Printing House Square (*The Times* London office) that he succeeded in gratuitously offending the King of Nepal to whose government he was accredited. No man should serve

two masters, particularly in diplomacy. Mr. Summerhayes seems to have shown incompetence and tactlessness unusual even in a British Ambassador.

On June 20, Mr. Rawle Knox of *The Observer*, who had at last succeeded in reaching Katmandu when all was over bar the shouting—the shouting however was at its height—wrote: "The gaunt, austere figure of the Ambassador attempting sometimes by rather unorthodox methods to keep the story as his own personal exclusive has gloriously added to the confusion."

Three days previously, on June 17, the matter had been raised in the House of Commons. Mr. Fitzroy Maclean (Conservative, Lancaster) asked the Secretary of State for Foreign Affairs under what circumstances the news of the successful ascent of Mount Everest was withheld from the King of Nepal by the British Embassy in Katmandu until after he had already learned of it from other sources.

Mr. Anthony Nutting, Under-Secretary, Foreign Office (Conservative, Melton) answered: "Her Majesty's Ambassador informed the King of Nepal of the ascent of Everest at the first opportunity. The King's Senior Counselor has confirmed to Her Majesty's Ambassador that the King did not hear of the ascent from any other source before the news was conveyed to him by the Ambassador early on June 2."

Mr. Garner Evans (National Liberal, Denbigh) then asked the Secretary of State for Foreign Affairs what arrangements were made by Her Majesty's Embassy in Katmandu for the transmission of messages from the Everest expedition to *The Times*.

Mr. Nutting (in a written reply):

Her Majesty's Ambassador was instructed to accept any reasonably short message about the final ascent of Everest from any correspondent without discrimination. The first news received at Her Majesty's Embassy was contained in a message which Her Majesty's Ambassador was requested to pass to *The Times* and to the Himalayan Committee. This was done.

Two messages were also passed by Her Majesty's Ambassador for *The Daily Telegraph*. They were transmitted immediately upon their receipt by Her Majesty's Ambassador in Katmandu. If other correspondents had asked for similar facilities they would have been granted.

While I am pleased that Mr. Summerhayes' actions should be considered defensible I cannot help feeling that the defense was of the smoke-screen variety. The fact cannot be altered that the British Ambassador was himself in possession of the result of the climb fully fifteen hours before he considered it necessary or expedient to inform His Majesty. Only *The Times* benefited from embassy transmission facilities on June 1. Facilities were made available to other newspapers only on June 2, by which time they were valueless, for the Ambassador had himself already insured that the entire world's press should be "scooped" by one whole day.

To return to the events of June 2. That evening a truce was called in the trying disputes of the day as we assembled beneath the fairy lights hung from trees in the grounds of the British Embassy, to celebrate the Coronation and toast Her Majesty Queen Elizabeth II in champagne. The party was honored by the presence of King Tribhuvana and his Queens and included a large concourse of Nepal notables, and members of the diplomatic corps and others of the foreign colony in Katmandu. Earlier in the day an apology had been sent by the British to the Indian Embassy regretting that the "gentlemen's agreement" regarding the use of code had been breached in the Everest message, and this had been handsomely accepted. True as the guests split into groups one could hear certain expressions of bewilderment and coolness, chiefly centering round the nationality of Tenzing, but the evening was brought to a triumphant and spectacular end by an improvised fireworks display staged by the Nepalese Army who had sprung to the aid of the embassy when it was learned that the fireworks ordered from England had been delayed in transit. For those who like their fireworks loud and strong with pleasurable uncertainty about the ultimate outcome, the substitute display left nothing to be desired. For the next two or three days work for newspapermen was virtually impossible, for telegraphic traffic was inundated to an unprecedented degree by hundreds upon hundreds of incoming congratulatory cables. With these cables came scores of offers from newspapers, periodicals and publishers to individual expedition members for books, pictures and articles. None of these offers could be accepted—at any rate for the time being—owing to the contract with *The Times*. News from Everest was still being smuggled through Katmandu to London and, locally, in the absence of any firsthand account, the legend that Tenzing reached the summit first grew ever stronger. It was now generally accepted that Tenzing had reached the top six minutes before Hillary and that he had hauled Hillary up the last 15 feet. Crudely drawn placards—the work of Communist agitators—showing Tenzing engaged in this feat, now began to make their appearance in various parts of the city. When later Colonel Hunt—while again emphasizing most strongly that the victory was that of a team, and while maintaining that all true mountaineers would regard Hillary and Tenzing as having reached the summit together—let it be known that it was, in fact, Hillary who was leading at the climactic moment, he was frankly disbelieved, and the words were at once spread around that the British had obviously "bought" Tenzing's silence.

But the dispute over the ascent of Everest was soon completely submerged by the dispute as to whether Tenzing was Indian or Nepalese. The basic facts were that Tenzing had been born of Tibetan parents in Nepal and had been living in Darjeeling, India, for the past twenty years. Tenzing, who has no papers to prove any of these facts, later tactfully referred to himself as having "been born from the womb of Nepal and reared in the lap of India," but Tenzing had still to be heard and during his continued absence his Indian and Nepalese admirers were soon in open conflict. This was happily a dispute which in no way concerned the British. The Indians, by reason of the fact that they possessed by far the more efficient propaganda machine, both in weight of newspapers and power of radio broadcasting, got off to a good start. Extremist Nationalist factions among the Nepalese—who in no way had the support of their government—soon became aware of this and made up in vehemence what they had previously lacked in speed. These factions had an advantage in that they were on the spot. They received every encouragement from Communist elements. Onus for declaring Tenzing to be an Indian was laid—not entirely incorrectly—at the door of the Indian correspondents in Katmandu and for some days many of them had an uncomfortable time of it, for there were dark threats as to what might happen if they continued in promulgating their heresy.

I had now decided that my own work in Katmandu was finished—a rather premature decision but I had still not recovered my health—and I booked a passage for Calcutta and home for Monday, June 8. On the Saturday before my departure General Kaiser, the King's Chief Counselor, summoned me to his palace to say farewell. The General's genuine joy over the Everest news was a pleasure to witness and he told me happily of the plans that the Council of State had made the previous day for a state reception of the climbers. The General remained quite unruffled by the dispute over the nationality of Tenzing, and with typical wisdom he emphasized that this was a matter which only Tenzing himself could decide. He added that in any case Tenzing would be admitted to the first-class Order of the Star of Nepal. To this might be added a money purse should he opt for India and a grant of a house and land should he opt for Nepal.

We had just heard the news that the Queen had conferred Knighthoods on both Colonel Hunt and Edmund Hillary, and that the nature of a special award for Tenzing would be announced at a later date. General Kaiser was anxious to learn what this special award might be in order that an equivalent Nepalese distinction might be conferred on Hillary and Hunt. We then said, "good-by."

To a suggestion made in the House of Commons on June 17 that there was "general disappointment" that Tenzing was not subsequently offered a Knighthood, and to general criticism outside the House that he was "fobbed off" with a George Medal, one can only say that it cannot be generally realized what a unique distinction the award of a George Medal is in the circumstances. To the best of my knowledge this is the first time that the Medal has been awarded for an outstanding performance by a professional sportsman. Had a Knighthood been conferred on Tenzing it could only have been embarrassing, if not offensive, to the Government of India which, on principle, has long since rejected such honors.

I left Katmandu, as I had planned, on June 8, and for the rest of the story I am indebted to Narendra Saksena.

On Saturday, June 13, Saksena drove out to Banepa with the intention of spending the night there and walking on the following day to meet the expedition. To his astonishment Colonel Hunt arrived in the town at 7:30 that evening accompanied by Gregory and Bourdillon. They had compressed three normal days' stages into one day and with no porters and carrying very little themselves had taken only eight days from Namche Bazar—knocking five days off my time and very nearly equaling the almost incredible performance of Sherpa runners like Sanju. Saksena at once loaded the party into his Land Rover and drove back to Katmandu, where, after stopping for glasses of tea at Bhatgaon, they arrived that night. The British Ambassador, who was in the process of planning a reception party, was once more taken by surprise, this time quite understandably. Colonel Hunt had, however, been determined to "get back to civilization" as quickly as possible, and he was anxious to meet his wife who was due at the airport the following day.

The news which Colonel Hunt received in Katmandu—the then popularly accepted version of the climb—apparently shocked him, for on Monday, June 15, at a Press conference at the embassy, he spoke out more strongly than he had ever done previously, or has done since. He explained that Tenzing was not the equal of a first-class Alpine Guide. He added: "The conquest of Everest could not have been possible without the climbing experience of the past expeditions and the wonderful teamwork of our expedition." He emphasized that Tenzing's role was secondary throughout the final assault, when Hillary was seen to be leading, cutting footholds in the ice face with Tenzing below. "At no single stage did Tenzing guide the party," said Colonel Hunt. "Throughout the final two and a half hours' climb to the top Hillary led the whole way, with Tenzing doing the rope work as No. 2. He was a full member of the climbing team, but it is wrong to think that only Tenzing made the conquest of Everest possible." The next event of importance was the arrival at Katmandu of Tenzing's wife and two daughters, who, after being greeted at the airfield by Mrs. Hunt, were driven to a state guest house where they were installed in considerable luxury and afforded the services of their own A.D.C., a change of fortune which must have happily surprised Tenzing if he still harbored memories of the stone floor of the stable which had been his own habitation during his own last visit to the capital.

Meanwhile, the main party of the expedition was approaching Katmandu at a more leisurely pace. There had been time for experiments, and in the Dudh Kosi gorge Hillary and his fellow New Zealander Lowe, tiring of the interminable ascents and descents round outcrops, lashed two air-mattresses together and endeavored to shoot the rapids. After a hundred yards the crazy raft overturned but both men reached the bank safely amidst considerable applause from the less adventurous members of the party. There was now some monsoon rain and a fair number of leeches, but the evenings passed pleasantly enough in debates as to which particular climb in North Wales could be undertaken to delight Tenzing if, and when, he could be persuaded to join the party in England. This must have seemed rather like a busman's holiday to Tenzing—and rather an arduous one, for he is essentially a snow and ice climber.

By June 17 the returning climbers had approached near enough to Katmandu to warrant advance "reception committees" of both Indians and Nepalese being sent out to meet them. Neither party was in any sense official—the Indians consisted of a number of newspapermen and photographers anxious to interview Tenzing, and the Nepalese of students and extremists who were determined that none should see Tenzing except themselves. The two parties clashed on the track between Hukse and Dolalghat. The advantage was entirely with the Nepalese, some of whom were on pony-back and most of whom were carrying kukris. After some voluble argument in which Harish Srivastava seems to have played a leading part, the Indians were routed and forced to retreat on Banepa where the government, unaware of what was happening farther up the line, was preparing its official reception.

Left in possession of the field, the unofficial Nepalese advanced on Dolalghat where they fell in with the expedition. The encounter was a bewildering one for Tenzing, for his signature—which he can barely write—was suddenly required for all manner of documents relating to nationality, priority on Everest and other matters, none of which he could read. It was also an unpleasant meeting for Colin Reid's colleague B. D. Mathur, who being the only Indian with the party was now blamed—quite erroneously—for being the author of the reports that Hillary had reached the summit first and that Tenzing was an Indian.

Everyone now headed for Hukse where Colonel and Mrs. Hunt had traveled out to meet them.

On the morning of Saturday, June 20, the main party arrived at Banepa where an immense and colorful crowd filled the streets rapidly rousing itself to a pitch of semihysteria. Banners waved overhead, triumphal arches spanned the way and beneath them leaders of rival political factions marched up and down shouting their own particular slogans. Garlands were heaped round the necks of the embarrassed heroes who also found themselves daubed from head to foot with handfuls of ceremonial vermilion kum kum powder. Fervent speech followed fervent speech, from which it was plain to hear that Tenzing remained the national hero of Everest, Hunt and Hillary filled secondary roles and the rest of the expedition was considered as nowhere. A particular commotion in the crowd signaled the kidnaping of the luckless Mathur who was only rescued late that night upon the personal intervention of the Prime Minister, and not until after he had been paraded through the streets of Katmandu, the target of much misguided abuse.

It was not until later that afternoon that the climbers arrived on the outskirts of Katmandu. Here an open landau drawn by four horses carrying liveried postilions and escorted by colorfully dressed Nepalese girls on horseback was waiting behind the Army Guards Band in their scarlet and maroon uniforms. Tenzing was accorded the place of honor on the hood of this vehicle, Hunt and Hillary remained half buried beneath the masses of flowers and the bodies of Mrs. Tenzing and her two daughters and those of several of the more prominent members of the reception committee. As the procession set off on its ceremonial five mile drive through the city accompanied by earslitting acclamations, the heads of Hunt and Hillary could occasionally be seen coming up for air and, more often than not, to receive another handful of kum kum powder full in the face. Somewhere in the rear wheezed a battered sedan carrying the remaining expedition members, some of them crammed inside and others, for lack of space, clinging to the roof.

At length the cortege drew up outside the Royal Palace and with no pause for washing or brushing up the victorious climbers were led to the Royal Durbar Hall where His Majesty was waiting to receive them. In contrast to the immaculate and glittering uniforms of the Court, the "Everesters," with matted beards, dust-grimed, sweat-soaked and smeared all over with red dye, looked like nothing so much as a collection of "guys" who had been collecting for a November 5 bonfire. Hunt was still in shorts, Hillary in skiing trousers and windproof, and Dr. Griffith Pugh, who had been conducting a physiological experiment on himself by wearing pajamas throughout the return march from the mountain, was still in those pajamas, conjuring up the vision of a nightmare situation which most of us are thankful we have only experienced in our more bizarre dreams. With due solemnity Tenzing was invested by His Majesty with the Order of the Star of Nepal First Class, and both Hunt and Hillary with the red sash of the Order of the Gurkha Right Hand. And here, at the height of the first of countless celebrations which were to accompany the expedition across half the world I propose to leave the members, only adding that Tenzing subsequently did much to allay the current controversies firstly by his tactful reference to his nationality, secondly by a public statement that he reached the top of Everest "simultaneously" with Hillary, and thirdly by agreeing to travel with other members to England, thus preserving the unity of the party which at one time had seemed threatened with disruption.

Some months later I was asked to review Sir John Hunt's own account of the mighty drama of Everest. In common with other critics I felt that Sir John had too speedily forsaken the "whys" for the "hows." It is, of course, acknowledged that the relationship between a man and the mountain he sets out to climb is a very personal one, but the only clue we are given to Sir John's own mountaineering philosophy is the fact that, in the British edition, he caused the proposed title of his book *The Conquest of Everest,* to be changed to *The Ascent of Everest.* One takes it that in doing so he wished to pay tribute to an old, formidable and respected enemy whose ultimate defeat he could only accept with chivalrous regret. He apparently shares the sentiment which Sir Francis Younghusband expressed many years ago (*Everest the Challenge:* Nelson): "The climber who first 'conquers' Everest will probably be humbler than any other of those who have seen her, for he better than anyone else will know what effort and sacrifice conquest of the mountain means."

Not all Britons are as articulate in emotional matters as was Sir Francis, and I therefore close this book with a quotation from the writing of Maurice Herzog, the gallant Frenchman who accepted permanent mutilation as the price for "conquering" Annapurna. Herzog explains his mountain philosophy thus (*Annapurna:* E. P. Dutton & Co., Inc.): "Men of adventure in other fields have had a logical end in mind: Marco

Polo, Magellan, Lindbergh, the men of Kon-Tiki, had a specific purpose, a justification. But the conquest of a mountain, even Everest, means nothing—except the satisfaction for the mountaineer of succeeding, of discovering something new and especially in the end of discovering himself. In making the ascent he fulfills himself and frees himself. It can be called 'free adventure,' an adventure that is pure and without special goal other than the compulsion to know all, to have touched everything."

BIBLIOGRAPHY

HERZOG, MAURICE. *Annapurna.* New York and London: E. P. Dutton & Co., Inc. and Jonathan Cape, Ltd.

IRVING, R. G. *The Romance of Mountaineering.* New York and London: E. P. Dutton & Co., Inc. and J. M. Dent & Sons, Ltd.

LANDON, PERCEVAL. *Nepal.* (Vols. I and II) London: Constable & Co., Ltd.

MURRAY, W. H. *The Story of Everest.* New York and London: E. P. Dutton & Co., Inc. and J. M. Dent & Sons, Ltd.

ROERICH, NICHOLS. *Altai Himalaya.* London: Jarrolds Publishers, Ltd.

SHIPTON, ERIC. *Upon That Mountain.* London: Hodder & Stoughton, Ltd.

———. *The Mount Everest Reconnaissance 1951.* New York and London: E. P. Dutton & Co., Inc. and Hodder & Stoughton, Ltd.

THE SWISS FOUNDATION FOR ALPINE RESEARCH. *The Mountain World, 1953.* London: George Allen and Unwin, Ltd.

TILMAN, H. W. *China to Chitral.* Cambridge: Cambridge University Press.

———. *Mount Everest: 1938.* Cambridge: Cambridge University Press.

———. *Nepal Himalaya.* Cambridge: Cambridge University Press.

TOMBAZI, A. N. *Account of a Photographic Expedition to the Southern Slopes of Kangchenjunga.*

WADDEL, COL. L. A. *Among the Himalayas.* London: Constable & Co., Ltd.

YOUNGHUSBAND, SIR FRANCIS. *Everest: The Challenge.* London: Thomas Nelson & Sons, Ltd.